HEAD to HEAD
ARSENAL

Peter Waring

breedon books
PUBLISHING

First published in Great Britain in 2004 by
The Breedon Books Publishing Company Limited
Breedon House, 3 The Parker Centre,
Derby, DE21 4SZ.

The publisher would like to thank Joe Cohen at Arsenal FC for his assistance in the production of this book.

This publication is not endorsed by Arsenal Football Club.

ISBN 1 85983 413 8

Printed and bound by Cromwell Press Ltd,
Trowbridge, Wiltshire.

Introduction

This book contains the results of all matches played by Arsenal in the following competitions:

- Premiership and Football League
- FA Cup
- League Cup
- Football League play-offs and test matches
- European Cup, Cup-Winners Cup and UEFA Cup

Some clubs have changed their names over the course of their history. Where this has happened, the results are nonetheless included under the club's current name, unless there have been no matches since the name change. Some of the more significant name changes are as follows:

- Arsenal (known as Royal Arsenal until 1893, then Woolwich Arsenal until 1914)
- Birmingham (known as Small Heath until 1905)
- Gateshead (known as South Shields until 1930)
- Leyton Orient (known as Clapton Orient until 1946, and Orient between 1967 and 1987)
- Manchester City (known as Ardwick until 1894)
- Manchester United (known as Newton Heath until 1902)

Furthermore, some clubs have merged, notably in Burton, Rotherham and Walsall, though these are explained under the relevant entries where applicable.

Notes on cups

FA Cup ties have always been straight knockout affairs, except in 1945-46, when all ties up to and including the quarter-finals were played over two legs. Between 1970 and 1974, the losing semi-finalists participated in third place play-offs. Penalty shoot-outs were introduced in 1991 to replace multiple replays.

League cup ties have been decided over one leg, with the following exceptions (played over two legs):

- First round ties (1975-76 to 2000-01)
- Second round ties (1979-80 to 2000-01)
- Semi-finals (every season)

To give you some idea of exactly what stage of the competition each FA Cup tie was played, the following is a list of each season's round of 16 (ie. the round immediately preceding the quarter-finals):

1873-74 to 1875-76	Round 2
1876-77 to 1878-79	Round 3
1879-80 to 1883-84	Round 4
1884-85 to 1887-88	Round 5
1889-90 to 1904-05	Round 2
1905-06 to 1924-25	Round 3
1925-26 to present	Round 5

In the league cup, Round 4 has been the round of 16 every season.

An asterisk after a cup result denotes extra-time was played.

Two final points

The letters appearing after some final league positions denote the following:

- P club was promoted
- R club was relegated
- F club failed to retain league membership for the following season

In the lists entitled 'Played for both clubs', an entry reading, for example, Liverpool 1980-83 would indicate that the player first appeared in a league match for Liverpool in the 1980-81 season, and last appeared in the 1982-83 season. Only league matches are taken into consideration on these lists.

v. Ashford United

FA Cup		Date	Result	Home Arsenal	Home Ashford	Division Arsenal	Division Ashford
1893-94	1st Qual	14 October	Won	**12**	**0**	Div 2	Non L

Summary	P	W	D	L	F	A
Arsenal's cup record:	1	1	0	0	12	0
TOTAL:	**1**	**1**	**0**	**0**	**12**	**0**

FACT FILE

- **This is Arsenal's biggest ever win in the FA Cup.**

Arsenal's top scorers vs Ashford

Arthur Elliott, Jimmy Henderson 3

Charles Booth, Billy Heath 2

Arsenal hat-tricks vs Ashford

14 Oct 1893 Arthur Elliott (cup)

14 Oct 1893 Jimmy Henderson (cup)

v. Aston Villa

		Home					Away			Final Positions	
Season	*League*	*Date*	*Result*	Arsenal	Villa	*Date*	*Result*	Arsenal	Villa	Arsenal	Villa
1904-05	Division 1	8 October	Won	**1**	**0**	26 December	Lost	**1**	**3**	10th	4th
1905-06	Division 1	13 April	Won	**2**	**1**	27 December	Lost	**1**	**2**	12th	8th
1906-07	Division 1	1 April	Won	**3**	**1**	29 September	Drew	**2**	**2**	7th	5th
1907-08	Division 1	8 February	Lost	**0**	**1**	12 October	Won	**1**	**0**	14th=	2nd
1908-09	Division 1	7 November	Lost	**0**	**1**	13 March	Lost	**1**	**2**	6th	7th
1909-10	Division 1	11 April	Won	**1**	**0**	1 September	Lost	**1**	**5**	18th	1st
1910-11	Division 1	15 March	Drew	**1**	**1**	17 September	Lost	**0**	**3**	10th	2nd
1911-12	Division 1	6 January	Drew	**2**	**2**	9 September	Lost	**1**	**4**	10th	6th
1912-13	Division 1	16 September	Lost	**0**	**3**	24 March	Lost	**1**	**4**	20thR	2nd
1919-20	Division 1	24 January	Lost	**0**	**1**	11 February	Lost	**1**	**2**	10th	9th
1920-21	Division 1	4 September	Lost	**0**	**1**	28 August	Lost	**0**	**5**	9th	10th
1921-22	Division 1	25 March	Won	**2**	**0**	18 March	Lost	**0**	**2**	17th	5th
1922-23	Division 1	31 March	Won	**2**	**0**	7 April	Drew	**1**	**1**	11th	6th
1923-24	Division 1	16 February	Lost	**0**	**1**	12 March	Lost	**1**	**2**	19th	6th
1924-25	Division 1	18 October	Drew	**1**	**1**	1 April	Lost	**0**	**4**	20th	15th
1925-26	Division 1	5 April	Won	**2**	**0**	2 April	Lost	**0**	**3**	2nd	6th
1926-27	Division 1	15 April	Won	**2**	**1**	18 April	Won	**3**	**2**	11th	10th
1927-28	Division 1	21 January	Lost	**0**	**3**	10 September	Drew	**2**	**2**	10th	8th
1928-29	Division 1	24 November	Lost	**2**	**5**	6 April	Lost	**2**	**4**	9th	3rd
1929-30	Division 1	3 May	Lost	**2**	**4**	25 September	Lost	**2**	**5**	14th	4th
1930-31	Division 1	8 November	Won	**5**	**2**	14 March	Lost	**1**	**5**	1st	2nd
1931-32	Division 1	31 October	Drew	**1**	**1**	25 April	Drew	**1**	**1**	2nd	5th
1932-33	Division 1	1 April	Won	**5**	**0**	19 November	Lost	**3**	**5**	1st	2nd
1933-34	Division 1	10 March	Won	**3**	**2**	28 October	Won	**3**	**2**	1st	13th
1934-35	Division 1	17 November	Lost	**1**	**2**	30 March	Won	**3**	**1**	1st	13th
1935-36	Division 1	18 April	Won	**1**	**0**	14 December	Won	**7**	**1**	6th	21stR
1938-39	Division 1	24 September	Drew	**0**	**0**	28 January	Won	**3**	**1**	5th	12th
1946-47	Division 1	18 January	Lost	**0**	**2**	14 September	Won	**2**	**0**	13th	8th
1947-48	Division 1	11 October	Won	**1**	**0**	28 February	Lost	**2**	**4**	1st	6th
1948-49	Division 1	11 September	Won	**3**	**1**	22 January	Lost	**0**	**1**	5th	10th
1949-50	Division 1	29 March	Lost	**1**	**3**	26 November	Drew	**1**	**1**	6th	12th
1950-51	Division 1	10 March	Won	**2**	**1**	21 October	Drew	**1**	**1**	5th	15th
1951-52	Division 1	5 January	Won	**2**	**1**	8 September	Lost	**0**	**1**	3rd	6th
1952-53	Division 1	20 December	Won	**3**	**1**	23 August	Won	**2**	**1**	1st	11th
1953-54	Division 1	6 April	Drew	**1**	**1**	29 August	Lost	**1**	**2**	12th	13th
1954-55	Division 1	12 March	Won	**2**	**0**	23 October	Lost	**1**	**2**	9th	6th
1955-56	Division 1	1 October	Won	**1**	**0**	11 February	Drew	**1**	**1**	5th	20th
1956-57	Division 1	3 November	Won	**2**	**1**	16 March	Drew	**0**	**0**	5th	10th
1957-58	Division 1	2 October	Won	**4**	**0**	26 December	Lost	**0**	**3**	12th	14th
1958-59	Division 1	13 December	Lost	**1**	**2**	22 October	Won	**2**	**1**	3rd	21stR
1960-61	Division 1	15 October	Won	**2**	**1**	4 March	Drew	**2**	**2**	11th	9th
1961-62	Division 1	31 March	Lost	**4**	**5**	11 November	Lost	**1**	**3**	10th	7th
1962-63	Division 1	4 September	Lost	**1**	**2**	10 September	Lost	**1**	**3**	7th	15th
1963-64	Division 1	10 September	Won	**3**	**0**	19 October	Lost	**1**	**2**	8th	19th

			Home					Away		Final Positions	
Season	League	Date	Result	Arsenal	Villa	Date	Result	Arsenal	Villa	Arsenal	Villa
1964-65	Division 1	29 August	Won	**3**	**1**	19 December	Lost	**1**	**3**	13th	16th
1965-66	Division 1	4 December	Drew	**3**	**3**	30 April	Lost	**0**	**3**	14th	16th
1966-67	Division 1	27 August	Won	**1**	**0**	31 December	Won	**1**	**0**	7th	21stR
1975-76	Division 1	10 January	Drew	**0**	**0**	13 September	Lost	**0**	**2**	17th	16th
1976-77	Division 1	25 April	Won	**3**	**0**	20 October	Lost	**1**	**5**	8th	4th
1977-78	Division 1	4 February	Lost	**0**	**1**	10 September	Lost	**0**	**1**	5th	8th
1978-79	Division 1	7 October	Drew	**1**	**1**	25 April	Lost	**1**	**5**	7th	8th
1979-80	Division 1	9 February	Won	**3**	**1**	22 September	Drew	**0**	**0**	4th	7th
1980-81	Division 1	2 May	Won	**2**	**0**	29 November	Drew	**1**	**1**	3rd	1st
1981-82	Division 1	27 March	Won	**4**	**3**	7 November	Won	**2**	**0**	5th	11th
1982-83	Division 1	7 December	Won	**2**	**1**	14 May	Lost	**1**	**2**	10th	6th
1983-84	Division 1	18 February	Drew	**1**	**1**	29 October	Won	**6**	**2**	6th	10th
1984-85	Division 1	10 November	Drew	**1**	**1**	13 March	Drew	**0**	**0**	7th	10th
1985-86	Division 1	5 October	Won	**3**	**2**	8 March	Won	**4**	**1**	7th	16th
1986-87	Division 1	2 May	Won	**2**	**1**	29 November	Won	**4**	**0**	4th	22ndR
1988-89	Division 1	3 September	Lost	**2**	**3**	31 December	Won	**3**	**0**	1st	17th
1989-90	Division 1	11 April	Lost	**0**	**1**	30 December	Lost	**1**	**2**	4th	2nd
1990-91	Division 1	3 April	Won	**5**	**0**	23 December	Drew	**0**	**0**	1st	17th
1991-92	Division 1	11 January	Drew	**0**	**0**	24 August	Lost	**1**	**3**	4th	7th
1992-93	Prem'ship	12 April	Lost	**0**	**1**	28 December	Lost	**0**	**1**	10th	2nd
1993-94	Prem'ship	6 November	Lost	**1**	**2**	23 April	Won	**2**	**1**	4th	10th
1994-95	Prem'ship	26 December	Drew	**0**	**0**	17 April	Won	**4**	**0**	12th	18th
1995-96	Prem'ship	21 October	Won	**2**	**0**	2 December	Drew	**1**	**1**	5th	4th
1996-97	Prem'ship	28 December	Drew	**2**	**2**	7 September	Drew	**2**	**2**	3rd	5th
1997-98	Prem'ship	26 October	Drew	**0**	**0**	10 May	Lost	**0**	**1**	1st	7th
1998-99	Prem'ship	16 May	Won	**1**	**0**	13 December	Lost	**2**	**3**	2nd	6th
1999-00	Prem'ship	11 September	Won	**3**	**1**	5 March	Drew	**1**	**1**	2nd	6th
2000-01	Prem'ship	14 October	Won	**1**	**0**	18 March	Drew	**0**	**0**	2nd	8th
2001-02	Prem'ship	9 December	Won	**3**	**2**	17 March	Won	**2**	**1**	1st	8th
2002-03	Prem'ship	30 November	Won	**3**	**1**	5 April	Drew	**1**	**1**	2nd	16th
2003-04	Prem'ship	27 August	Won	**2**	**0**	18 January	Won	**2**	**0**	1st	6th

FA Cup										*Division*	
1925-26	Round 5	24 February	Won	**2**	**0**	20 February	Drew	**1**	**1**	Div 1	Div 1
1927-28	Round 5	18 February	Won	**4**	**1**					Div 1	Div 1
1928-29	Q'ter Final					2 March	Lost	**0**	**1**	Div 1	Div 1
1930-31	Round 3	10 January	Drew	**2**	**2**	14 January	Won	**3**	**1**	Div 1	Div 1
1933-34	Q'ter Final	3 March	Lost	**1**	**2**					Div 1	Div 1
1953-54	Round 3	9 January	Won	**5**	**1**					Div 1	Div 1
1955-56	Round 4	28 January	Won	**4**	**1**					Div 1	Div 1
1973-74	Round 4	26 January	Drew	**1**	**1**	30 January	Lost	**0**	**2**	Div 1	Div 2
1982-83	Q'ter Final	12 March	Won	**2**	**0**					Div 1	Div 1

League Cup											
1985-86	Q'ter Final	4 February	Lost	**1**	**2**	22 January	Drew	**1**	**1**	Div 1	Div 1
1993-94	Round 4	30 November	Lost	**0**	**1**					Prem	Prem
1995-96	Semi Final	14 February	Drew	**2**	**2**	21 February	Drew*	**0**	**0**	Prem	Prem

Bill Dodgin of Arsenal heads clear from Dave Walsh of Aston Villa during the FA Cup third-round game at Highbury in January 1954. The Gunners won 5-1 but were then sensationally knocked out by Third Division South club Norwich City in the next round.

Summary	P	W	D	L	F	A
Arsenal's home league record:	75	40	15	20	126	84
Arsenal's away league record:	75	19	18	38	104	143
Arsenal's cup record:	17	6	6	5	29	19
TOTAL:	**167**	**65**	**39**	**63**	**259**	**246**

FACT FILE

- **In 1935, Ted Drake became the only man since the turn of the century to score seven goals in a top flight league match. His seven goals came from just eight shots (the other hit the crossbar).**
- **Arsenal are unbeaten in their last 11 matches against Villa.**
- **Arsenal are unbeaten in their last 11 home matches against Villa, stretching back to 1993.**
- **Between 1909 and 1926, Arsenal earned just two draws and no wins in 13 visits to Villa Park.**
- **Villa have won all three league cup ties between the sides.**

Arsenal's top scorers vs Villa

David Jack 12
Ted Drake 9
Jimmy Brain, Thierry Henry, Jack Lambert, Don Roper, Tony Woodcock 8
Ian Wright 7
Cliff Bastin, Reg Lewis, Alan Skirton 6

Arsenal hat-tricks vs Villa

14 Dec 1935 Ted Drake (7)
10 Sep 1963 Joe Baker
29 Oct 1983 Tony Woodcock (5)

Played for both clubs

Charlie Hare	Aston Villa 1891-95	Arsenal 1894-96
Robert Gordon	Aston Villa 1894-95	Arsenal 1895-96
Frank Lloyd	Arsenal 1899-1900	Aston Villa 1900-02
Bobby Templeton	Aston Villa 1898-1903	Arsenal 1904-06
Peter Kyle	Arsenal 1906-08	Aston Villa 1907-09
Andy Ducat	Arsenal 1904-12	Aston Villa 1912-21
Dick Roose	Aston Villa 1911-12	Arsenal 1911-12
Chris Buckley	Aston Villa 1906-13	Arsenal 1914-21
Andrew Young	Aston Villa 1919-22	Arsenal 1921-27
George Graham	Aston Villa 1962-64	Arsenal 1966-73
John MacLeod	Arsenal 1961-65	Aston Villa 1964-68
Jimmy Rimmer	Arsenal 1973-77	Aston Villa 1977-83
Alex Cropley	Arsenal 1974-77	Aston Villa 1976-80
Martin Keown	Arsenal 1985-86/1992-2004	Aston Villa 1986-89
Kevin Richardson	Arsenal 1987-90	Aston Villa 1991-95
David Platt	Aston Villa 1987-91	Arsenal 1995-98
Paul Merson	Arsenal 1986-97	Aston Villa 1998-2002

v. Barnsley

Season	League	Home Date	Home Result	Home Arsenal	Home Barnsley	Away Date	Away Result	Away Arsenal	Away Barnsley	Final Positions Arsenal	Final Positions Barnsley
1898-99	Division 2	22 April	Won	**3**	**0**	24 December	Lost	**1**	**2**	7th	11th
1899-00	Division 2	28 April	Won	**5**	**1**	23 April	Lost	**2**	**3**	8th	16th
1900-01	Division 2	22 September	Lost	**1**	**2**	19 January	Lost	**0**	**3**	7th	15th
1901-02	Division 2	2 September	Won	**2**	**1**	28 December	Lost	**0**	**2**	4th	11th
1902-03	Division 2	17 January	Won	**4**	**0**	20 September	Drew	**1**	**1**	3rd	8th
1903-04	Division 2	27 February	Won	**3**	**0**	31 October	Lost	**1**	**2**	2ndP	8th
1913-14	Division 2	24 January	Won	**1**	**0**	27 September	Lost	**0**	**1**	3rd	5th
1914-15	Division 2	5 April	Won	**1**	**0**	1 January	Lost	**0**	**1**	5thP	3rd
1997-98	Prem'ship	4 October	Won	**5**	**0**	25 April	Won	**2**	**0**	1st	19thR

FA Cup

Season	Round	Home Date	Home Result	Arsenal	Barnsley	Away Date	Away Result	Arsenal	Barnsley	Division Arsenal	Division Barnsley
1906-07	Q'ter Final					9 March	Won	**2**	**1**	Div 1	Div 2
1935-36	Q'ter Final	29 February	Won	**4**	**1**					Div 1	Div 2
1951-52	Round 4	2 February	Won	**4**	**0**					Div 1	Div 2
1986-87	Round 5	21 February	Won	**2**	**0**					Div 1	Div 2

League Cup

Season	Round	Home Date	Home Result	Arsenal	Barnsley	Away Date	Away Result	Arsenal	Barnsley	Division Arsenal	Division Barnsley
1971-72	Round 2	8 September	Won	**1**	**0**					Div 1	Div 3
1995-96	Round 3					24 October	Won	**3**	**0**	Prem	Div 1

Summary	*P*	*W*	*D*	*L*	*F*	*A*
Arsenal's home league record:	9	8	0	1	25	4
Arsenal's away league record:	9	1	1	7	7	15
Arsenal's cup record:	6	6	0	0	16	2
TOTAL:	**24**	**15**	**1**	**8**	**48**	**21**

FACT FILE

- **Arsenal have won their last 10 home matches, a run going back to 1901.**
- **Barnsley have scored just once in their last nine away matches.**
- **Arsenal have won their last eight matches against Barnsley.**
- **Arsenal had to wait 99 years for their first league win in Barnsley.**
- **Fifteen of the 18 league games have resulted in home wins.**
- **Arsenal have won all six cup matches between the sides.**

Arsenal's top scorers vs Barnsley

Dennis Bergkamp 4

Reg Lewis, Frank Lloyd, Tommy Shanks 3

Arsenal hat-tricks vs Barnsley

2 Feb 1952 Reg Lewis (cup)

Reg Lewis was to score a hat-trick against Barnsley in the Cup match in 1952; he is in this team picture taken the year before of Arsenal's playing and coaching staff on the eve of the 1950-51 season, with the FA Cup won against Liverpool the previous April. Back row (left to right): J. Chenhall, R. Barr, D. Tilley, D. Oakes, C. Holton, R. Marden, T. Vallance. Third row: E. Stanley, D. Rossiter, W. Healey, D. Bowen, L. Davies, G. Dunkley, P. Hancock, C. Grimshaw, L. Wills, J. Gray, H. Dove, F. Grosvenor. Second row: A. James, G. Male, K. Atkinson, R. Daniel, A. Shaw, E. Platt, L. Compton, G. Swindin, A. Forbes, J. Kelsey, A. Fields, J. Wade, J. Holland, E. Collett, D. Cripps. Seated: H. Owen, J. Crayston, I. McPherson, L. Scott, D. Roper, R. Lewis, J. Mercer, T. Whittaker, W. Barnes, L. Smith, P. Goring, D. Lishman, N. Smith, W. Milne, J. Shaw. On ground: A. Milton, M. Ryan, J. Logie, F. Cox, R. Poulton, D. Bennett. Several former Arsenal stars, such as Alex James, George Male and Joe Shaw, were still on the backroom staff.

Played for both clubs

Arthur Worrall	Arsenal 1893-94	Barnsley 1898-99
Andrew Swann	Barnsley 1900-01	Arsenal 1901-02
Frank Heppinstall	Barnsley 1904-05	Arsenal 1909-11
Jackie Mordue	Barnsley 1906-07	Arsenal 1906-08
Len Thompson	Barnsley 1919-20	Arsenal 1927-32
Pat Howard	Barnsley 1965-72	Arsenal 1976-66
Siggi Jonsson	Barnsley 1985-86	Arsenal 1989-91
Viv Anderson	Arsenal 1984-87	Barnsley 1993-94
Kevin Richardson	Arsenal 1987-90	Barnsley 1998-2000
Isaiah Rankin	Arsenal 1997-98	Barnsley 2000-03

Barnsley goalkeeper Tom Ellis punches clear from an Arsenal attack at Highbury in February 1936. The Gunners, who were wearing unfamiliar hooped shirts as both teams had to change, won this FA Cup quarter-final match 4-1.

v. Bedford Town

			Home					Away		Division	
FA Cup		*Date*	*Result*	Arsenal	Bedford	*Date*	*Result*	Arsenal	Bedford	Arsenal	Bedford
1955-56	Round 3	7 January	Drew	**2**	**2**	12 January	Won*	**2**	**1**	Div 1	Non L

Summary	P	W	D	L	F	A
Arsenal's cup record:	2	1	1	0	4	3
TOTAL	**2**	**1**	**1**	**0**	**4**	**3**

Arsenal's top scorers vs Bedford

Vic Groves, Derek Tapscott 2

Vic Groves was still with the club when this team picture was taken, several years after scoring two vital goals against non-league Bedford in 1956, after being held at Highbury 2-2. Here are Arsenal on the eve of the 1962-63 season. Back row (left to right): Ted Magill, Eddie Clamp, Vic Groves, Jack Kelsey, Billy McCulloch, John Snedden, Laurie Brown and Terry Neill. Middle row: Bertie Mee (physiotherapist), John Barnwell, Geoff Strong, George Eastham, Billy Wight (manager), John McLeod, John Petts, Alan Skirton and Dave Bacuzzi. On ground: Joe Baker, Arfon Griffiths and Gerry Ward.

v. Birmingham City

		Home				Away				Final Positions	
Season	League	Date	Result	Arsenal	Birm'ham	Date	Result	Arsenal	Birm'ham	Arsenal	Birm'ham
1893-94	Division 2	31 March	Lost	1	4	21 October	Lost	1	4	9th	2ndP
1896-97	Division 2	29 March	Lost	2	3	14 November	Lost	2	5	10th	4th
1897-98	Division 2	5 March	Won	4	2	23 April	Lost	1	2	5th	6th
1898-99	Division 2	5 November	Won	2	0	4 March	Lost	1	4	7th	8th
1899-00	Division 2	25 November	Won	3	0	31 March	Lost	1	3	8th	3rd
1900-01	Division 2	22 April	Won	1	0	20 October	Lost	1	2	7th	2ndP
1902-03	Division 2	4 April	Won	6	1	6 December	Lost	0	2	3rd	2ndP
1904-05	Division 1	1 April	Drew	1	1	3 December	Lost	1	2	10th	7th
1905-06	Division 1	3 March	Won	5	0	28 October	Lost	1	2	12th	7th
1906-07	Division 1	13 April	Won	2	1	8 December	Lost	1	5	7th	9th
1907-08	Division 1	14 December	Drew	1	1	11 April	Won	2	1	14th=	20thR
1913-14	Division 2	22 November	Won	1	0	28 March	Lost	0	2	3rd	14th
1914-15	Division 2	13 March	Won	1	0	7 November	Lost	0	3	5thP	6th
1921-22	Division 1	12 November	Won	5	2	5 November	Won	1	0	17th	18th
1922-23	Division 1	9 December	Won	1	0	2 December	Lost	2	3	11th	17th
1923-24	Division 1	29 September	Drew	0	0	22 September	Won	2	0	19th	14th
1924-25	Division 1	26 December	Lost	0	1	25 December	Lost	1	2	20th	8th
1925-26	Division 1	1 May	Won	3	0	19 December	Lost	0	1	2nd	14th
1926-27	Division 1	30 April	Won	3	0	11 December	Drew	0	0	11th	17th
1927-28	Division 1	31 March	Drew	2	2	19 November	Drew	1	1	10th	11th
1928-29	Division 1	15 September	Drew	0	0	13 March	Drew	1	1	9th	15th
1929-30	Division 1	15 March	Won	1	0	9 November	Won	3	2	14th	11th
1930-31	Division 1	31 January	Drew	1	1	27 September	Won	4	2	1st	19th
1931-32	Division 1	16 January	Won	3	0	5 September	Drew	2	2	2nd	9th
1932-33	Division 1	31 December	Won	3	0	27 August	Won	1	0	1st	13th
1933-34	Division 1	26 August	Drew	1	1	30 December	Drew	0	0	1st	20th
1934-35	Division 1	29 September	Won	5	1	9 February	Lost	0	3	1st	19th
1935-36	Division 1	4 January	Drew	1	1	7 September	Drew	1	1	6th	12th
1936-37	Division 1	20 March	Drew	1	1	14 November	Won	3	1	3rd	11th
1937-38	Division 1	16 April	Drew	0	0	4 December	Won	2	1	1st	18th
1938-39	Division 1	3 December	Won	3	1	8 April	Won	2	1	5th	21stR
1948-49	Division 1	6 November	Won	2	0	2 April	Drew	1	1	5th	17th
1949-50	Division 1	24 September	Won	4	2	4 February	Lost	1	2	6th	22ndR
1955-56	Division 1	14 April	Won	1	0	3 December	Lost	0	4	5th	6th
1956-57	Division 1	22 December	Won	4	0	25 August	Lost	2	4	5th	12th=
1957-58	Division 1	19 October	Lost	1	3	1 March	Lost	1	4	12th	13th
1958-59	Division 1	4 May	Won	2	1	14 April	Lost	1	4	3rd	9th
1959-60	Division 1	31 October	Won	3	0	16 April	Lost	0	3	13th	19th
1960-61	Division 1	6 September	Won	2	0	14 September	Lost	0	2	11th	19th
1961-62	Division 1	23 September	Drew	1	1	10 February	Lost	0	1	10th	17th
1962-63	Division 1	21 August	Won	2	0	29 August	Drew	2	2	7th	20th
1963-64	Division 1	5 November	Won	4	1	28 December	Won	4	1	8th	20th
1964-65	Division 1	6 April	Won	3	0	7 November	Won	3	2	13th	22ndR
1972-73	Division 1	26 September	Won	2	0	23 December	Drew	1	1	2nd	10th

				Home				Away		Final Positions	
Season	League	Date	Result	Arsenal	Birm'ham	Date	Result	Arsenal	Birm'ham	Arsenal	Birm'ham
1973-74	Division 1	6 October	Won	1	0	23 February	Lost	1	3	10th	19th
1974-75	Division 1	15 March	Drew	1	1	28 September	Lost	1	3	16th	17th
1975-76	Division 1	21 February	Won	1	0	15 November	Lost	1	3	17th	19th
1976-77	Division 1	6 November	Won	4	0	18 January	Drew	3	3	8th	13th
1977-78	Division 1	29 October	Drew	1	1	21 March	Drew	1	1	5th	11th
1978-79	Division 1	30 December	Won	3	1	5 May	Drew	0	0	7th	21stR
1980-81	Division 1	31 March	Won	2	1	7 October	Lost	1	3	3rd	13th
1981-82	Division 1	22 September	Won	1	0	4 May	Won	1	0	5th	16th
1982-83	Division 1	30 October	Drew	0	0	15 March	Lost	1	2	10th	17th
1983-84	Division 1	27 December	Drew	1	1	23 April	Drew	1	1	6th	20thR
1985-86	Division 1	30 November	Drew	0	0	3 May	Won	1	0	7th	21stR
2002-03	Prem'ship	18 August	Won	2	0	12 January	Won	4	0	2nd	13th
2003-04	Prem'ship	1 May	Drew	0	0	22 November	Won	3	0	1st	10th

FA Cup

										Division	
1891-92	Round 1					16 January	Lost	1	5	Non L	Non L
1929-30	Round 4	25 January	Drew	2	2	29 January	Won	1	0	Div 1	Div 1
1955-56	Q'ter Final	3 March	Lost	1	3					Div 1	Div 1
1966-67	Round 5					11 March	Lost	0	1	Div 1	Div 2
1967-68	Round 5	9 March	Drew	1	1	12 March	Lost	1	2	Div 1	Div 2

League Cup

1997-98	Round 3	14 October	Won*	4	1					Prem	Div 1

Summary	P	W	D	L	F	A
Arsenal's home league record:	57	36	17	4	111	37
Arsenal's away league record:	57	15	13	29	73	108
Arsenal's cup record:	8	2	2	4	11	15
TOTAL	**122**	**53**	**32**	**37**	**195**	**160**

FACT FILE

- **Birmingham last won at Highbury in 1957; they have visited 23 times since and scored just eight goals.**
- **Arsenal have lost just two of their last 54 home league matches.**
- **Arsenal lost their first 11 away matches.**
- **Arsenal lost eight away matches in a row between 1950 and 1962.**
- **Arsenal have won just once in seven FA Cup matches.**
- **Birmingham have not scored in the sides' last six league meetings.**

Arsenal's top scorers vs Birmingham

Ted Drake 9
Joe Baker 7
Cliff Bastin, Tim Coleman, David Jack,
Jack Lambert 5
Joe Hulme, Malcolm Macdonald 4

Arsenal hat-tricks vs Birmingham

5 Mar 1898 Davy Hannah
27 Sep 1930 Jack Lambert
29 Sep 1934 Ted Drake (4)
5 Nov 1963 Joe Baker
18 Jan 1977 Malcolm Macdonald

Played for both clubs

Caesar Jenkyns	Birmingham City 1892-95	Arsenal 1895-96
Charlie Hare	Arsenal 1894-96	Birmingham City 1896-98
Jack Aston	Arsenal 1899-1900	Birmingham City 1899-1902
Harry King	Birmingham City 1907-10	Arsenal 1914-15
Archie Roe	Birmingham City 1919-20	Arsenal 1922-23
Len Thompson	Birmingham City 1921-23	Arsenal 1927-32
Billy Blyth	Arsenal 1914-29	Birmingham City 1929-31
Jimmy Bloomfield	Arsenal 1954-61	Birmingham City 1960-64
George Johnston	Arsenal 1967-69	Birmingham City 1969-70
John Roberts	Arsenal 1969-73	Birmingham City 1972-76
Pat Howard	Arsenal 1976-77	Birmingham City 1977-79
Paul Gorman	Arsenal 1981-84	Birmingham City 1984-85
David Madden	Arsenal 1983-84	Birmingham City 1989-90
Chris Whyte	Arsenal 1981-86	Birmingham City 1993-96
David Seaman	Birmingham City 1984-86	Arsenal 1990-2003
Alan Miller	Birmingham City 1991-92	Arsenal 1992-94
Anders Limpar	Arsenal 1990-94	Birmingham City 1996-1997
Isaiah Rankin	Arsenal 1997-98	Birmingham City 1999-2000
Christopher Wreh	Arsenal 1997-99	Birmingham City 1999-2000
Matthew Upson	Arsenal 1997-2002	Birmingham City 2002-04

Billy Blyth spent 15 years at Highbury after World War One and transferred to Birmingham City in 1929.

What a signing David Seaman was for Arsenal, an ex-Birmingham City goalkeeper who announced his retirement in 2004 after leaving for Manchester City.

v. Blackburn Rovers

		Home					Away			Final Positions	
Season	League	Date	Result	Arsenal	Blackburn	Date	Result	Arsenal	Blackburn	Arsenal	Blackburn
1904-05	Division 1	11 February	Won	**2**	**0**	15 October	Drew	**1**	**1**	10th	13th
1905-06	Division 1	17 February	Won	**3**	**2**	14 October	Lost	**0**	**2**	12th	9th
1906-07	Division 1	30 March	Won	**2**	**0**	24 November	Won	**3**	**2**	7th	12th
1907-08	Division 1	30 November	Won	**2**	**0**	28 March	Drew	**1**	**1**	14th=	14th=
1908-09	Division 1	5 December	Lost	**0**	**1**	10 April	Won	**3**	**1**	6th	4th
1909-10	Division 1	12 February	Lost	**0**	**1**	2 October	Lost	**0**	**7**	18th	3rd
1910-11	Division 1	15 October	Won	**4**	**1**	18 February	Lost	**0**	**1**	10th	12th
1911-12	Division 1	22 April	Won	**5**	**1**	25 November	Lost	**0**	**4**	10th	1st
1912-13	Division 1	30 November	Lost	**0**	**1**	5 April	Drew	**1**	**1**	20thR	5th
1919-20	Division 1	4 October	Lost	**0**	**1**	27 September	Drew	**2**	**2**	10th	20th
1920-21	Division 1	13 November	Won	**2**	**0**	6 November	Drew	**2**	**2**	9th	11th
1921-22	Division 1	10 December	Drew	**1**	**1**	3 December	Won	**1**	**0**	17th	15th
1922-23	Division 1	2 April	Drew	**1**	**1**	1 January	Won	**5**	**0**	11th	14th
1923-24	Division 1	1 December	Drew	**2**	**2**	8 December	Lost	**0**	**2**	19th	8th
1924-25	Division 1	4 October	Won	**1**	**0**	7 February	Lost	**0**	**1**	20th	16th
1925-26	Division 1	3 April	Won	**4**	**2**	21 November	Won	**3**	**2**	2nd	12th
1926-27	Division 1	6 November	Drew	**2**	**2**	28 April	Won	**2**	**1**	11th	18th
1927-28	Division 1	17 March	Won	**3**	**2**	5 November	Lost	**1**	**4**	10th	12th
1928-29	Division 1	29 March	Won	**1**	**0**	25 December	Lost	**2**	**5**	9th	7th
1929-30	Division 1	29 March	Won	**4**	**0**	23 November	Drew	**1**	**1**	14th	6th
1930-31	Division 1	10 September	Won	**3**	**2**	15 September	Drew	**2**	**2**	1st	10th
1931-32	Division 1	7 May	Won	**4**	**0**	31 August	Drew	**1**	**1**	2nd	16th
1932-33	Division 1	25 February	Won	**8**	**0**	15 October	Won	**3**	**2**	1st	15th
1933-34	Division 1	21 February	Won	**2**	**1**	7 October	Drew	**2**	**2**	1st	8th
1934-35	Division 1	5 September	Won	**4**	**0**	17 September	Lost	**0**	**2**	1st	15th
1935-36	Division 1	5 October	Won	**5**	**1**	8 February	Won	**1**	**0**	6th	22ndR
1939-40	Division 1	30 August	Won	**1**	**0**						
1946-47	Division 1	4 September	Lost	**1**	**3**	17 September	Won	**2**	**1**	13th	17th
1947-48	Division 1	3 April	Won	**2**	**0**	15 November	Won	**1**	**0**	1st	21stR
1958-59	Division 1	14 March	Drew	**1**	**1**	25 October	Lost	**2**	**4**	3rd	10th
1959-60	Division 1	6 February	Won	**5**	**2**	19 September	Drew	**1**	**1**	13th	17th
1960-61	Division 1	11 March	Drew	**0**	**0**	22 October	Won	**4**	**2**	11th	8th
1961-62	Division 1	3 March	Drew	**0**	**0**	14 October	Drew	**0**	**0**	10th	16th
1962-63	Division 1	23 March	Won	**3**	**1**	3 November	Drew	**5**	**5**	7th	11th
1963-64	Division 1	11 April	Drew	**0**	**0**	30 November	Lost	**1**	**4**	8th	7th
1964-65	Division 1	8 September	Drew	**1**	**1**	16 September	Won	**2**	**1**	13th	10th
1965-66	Division 1	23 October	Drew	**2**	**2**	15 January	Lost	**1**	**2**	14th	22ndR
1992-93	Prem'ship	12 September	Lost	**0**	**1**	18 August	Lost	**0**	**1**	10th	4th
1993-94	Prem'ship	25 February	Won	**1**	**0**	1 September	Drew	**1**	**1**	4th	2nd
1994-95	Prem'ship	31 August	Drew	**0**	**0**	8 March	Lost	**1**	**3**	12th	1st
1995-96	Prem'ship	26 November	Drew	**0**	**0**	27 April	Drew	**1**	**1**	5th	7th
1996-97	Prem'ship	19 April	Drew	**1**	**1**	12 October	Won	**2**	**0**	3rd	13th
1997-98	Prem'ship	13 December	Lost	**1**	**3**	13 April	Won	**4**	**1**	1st	6th
1998-99	Prem'ship	6 April	Won	**1**	**0**	25 October	Won	**2**	**1**	2nd	19thR

				Home				Away		Final Positions	
Season	*League*	*Date*	*Result*	Arsenal	Blackburn	*Date*	*Result*	Arsenal	Blackburn	Arsenal	Blackburn
2001-02	Prem'ship	20 October	Drew	**3**	**3**	30 January	Won	**3**	**2**	1st	10th
2002-03	Prem'ship	26 October	Lost	**1**	**2**	15 March	Lost	**0**	**2**	2nd	6th
2003-04	Prem'ship	14 December	Won	**1**	**0**	13 March	Won	**2**	**0**	1st	15th

FA Cup										*Division*	
1900-01	Round 1	9 February	Won	**2**	**0**					Div 2	Div 1
1925-26	Round 4	30 January	Won	**3**	**1**					Div 1	Div 1
1927-28	Semi Final	24 March		Filbert Street			Lost	**0**	**1**	Div 1	Div 1
1965-66	Round 3					22 January	Lost	**0**	**3**	Div 1	Div 1
2000-01	Q'ter Final	10 March	Won	**3**	**0**					Prem	Div 1

League Cup											
1967-68	Round 4	1 November	Won	**2**	**1**					Div 1	Div 2
2001-02	Q'ter Final					11 December	Lost	**0**	**4**	Prem	Prem

Summary	P	W	D	L	F	A
Arsenal's home league record:	47	25	14	8	90	42
Arsenal's away league record:	46	17	14	15	72	81
Arsenal's cup record:	7	4	0	3	10	10
TOTAL	**100**	**46**	**28**	**26**	**172**	**133**

FACT FILE

- **Blackburn won once in 29 visits to Highbury between 1920 and 1967. This included a run of 10 Arsenal wins in succession (1928-39).**
- **Arsenal have never gone more than six away matches without a win.**
- **Blackburn's league double over Arsenal in 2002-03 is the only double by anyone against Arsenal for the last four seasons.**
- **Arsenal are the only team in the series to win four away league matches ina row (1996-2002).**
- **The win at Ewood Park in October 1996 was the first under the management of Arsene Wenger, only the second manager in English history to win the double twice.**

Arsenal's top scorers vs Blackburn

Cliff Bastin 10

Joe Baker, Dennis Bergkamp, Jimmy Brain, Joe Hulme 6

Ray Bowden, Charlie Buchan, Jack Lambert 5

Arsenal hat-tricks vs Blackburn

22 Apr 1912 John Grant

1 Jan 1923 Bobby Turnbull (4)

25 Feb 1933 Ernie Coleman

5 Oct 1935 Ray Bowden

6 Feb 1960 Mel Charles

Ted Drake in a heading duel with a Blackburn defender and Alex James just behind them. Arsenal won this game 5-1 in October 1935.

Played for both clubs

Jim Stuart	Blackburn Rovers 1894-97	Arsenal 1897-98
Jock Russell	Arsenal 1896-97	Blackburn Rovers 1901-02
Tommy Briercliffe	Blackburn Rovers 1897-1900	Arsenal 1901-05
Jimmy Ashcroft	Arsenal 1900-08	Blackburn Rovers 1908-13
Billy Garbutt	Arsenal 1905-08	Blackburn Rovers 1908-12
Joe Hulme	Blackburn Rovers 1923-26	Arsenal 1925-38
Jackie Milne	Blackburn Rovers 1933-35	Arsenal 1935-38
George Marks	Arsenal 1938-40	Blackburn Rovers 1946-48
Joe Haverty	Arsenal 1954-61	Blackburn Rovers 1961-63
John Radford	Arsenal 1963-77	Blackburn Rovers 1977-79
Frank Stapleton	Arsenal 1974-81	Blackburn Rovers 1989-91
Andy Cole	Arsenal 1990-91	Blackburn Rovers 2001-04
Alan Miller	Arsenal 1992-94	Blackburn Rovers 2000-01
Kaba Diawara	Arsenal 1998-99	Blackburn Rovers 2000-01

Charlie Buchan puts the Blackburn Rovers goalkeeper under pressure during the 1928 FA Cup semi-final at Filbert Street. The Gunners lost 1-0, their hopes of a second successive Wembley appearance ended.

v. Blackpool

Season	League	Home Date	Result	Arsenal	Blackpool	Away Date	Result	Arsenal	Blackpool	Final Positions Arsenal	Blackpool
1896-97	Division 2	19 December	Won	4	2	4 January	Drew	1	1	10th	8th
1897-98	Division 2	27 November	Won	2	1	1 January	Drew	3	3	5th	11th
1898-99	Division 2	18 March	Won	6	0	22 March	Drew	1	1	7th	16thF
1900-01	Division 2	8 April	Won	3	1	6 October	Drew	1	1	7th	12th
1901-02	Division 2	25 December	Drew	0	0	1 March	Won	3	1	4th	13th
1902-03	Division 2	8 November	Won	2	1	7 March	Drew	0	0	3rd	14th
1903-04	Division 2	5 September	Won	3	0	2 January	Drew	2	2	2ndP	15th
1913-14	Division 2	28 February	Won	2	1	25 October	Drew	1	1	3rd	16th
1914-15	Division 2	17 October	Won	2	0	20 February	Won	2	0	5thP	10th
1930-31	Division 1	27 December	Won	7	1	30 August	Won	4	1	1st	20th
1931-32	Division 1	20 February	Won	2	0	10 October	Won	5	1	2nd	20th
1932-33	Division 1	11 February	Drew	1	1	1 October	Won	2	1	1st	22ndR
1937-38	Division 1	27 December	Won	2	1	25 December	Lost	1	2	1st	12th
1938-39	Division 1	10 April	Won	2	1	7 April	Lost	0	1	5th	15th
1946-47	Division 1	8 February	Drew	1	1	5 October	Lost	1	2	13th	5th
1947-48	Division 1	8 November	Won	2	1	27 March	Lost	0	3	1st	9th
1948-49	Division 1	18 April	Won	2	0	15 April	Drew	1	1	5th	16th
1949-50	Division 1	22 October	Won	1	0	8 April	Lost	1	2	6th	7th
1950-51	Division 1	9 December	Drew	4	4	2 May	Won	1	0	5th	3rd
1951-52	Division 1	14 April	Won	4	1	11 April	Drew	0	0	3rd	9th
1952-53	Division 1	4 October	Won	3	1	21 February	Lost	2	3	1st	7th
1953-54	Division 1	28 December	Drew	1	1	26 December	Drew	2	2	12th	6th
1954-55	Division 1	9 April	Won	3	0	4 December	Drew	2	2	9th	19th
1955-56	Division 1	17 December	Won	4	1	20 August	Lost	1	3	5th	2nd
1956-57	Division 1	19 April	Drew	1	1	22 April	Won	4	2	5th	4th
1957-58	Division 1	11 January	Lost	2	3	7 September	Lost	0	1	12th	7th
1958-59	Division 1	29 November	Lost	1	4	18 April	Won	2	1	3rd	8th
1959-60	Division 1	26 September	Won	2	1	13 February	Lost	1	2	13th	11th
1960-61	Division 1	8 April	Won	1	0	19 November	Drew	1	1	11th	20th
1961-62	Division 1	7 October	Won	3	0	24 February	Won	1	0	10th	13th
1962-63	Division 1	8 December	Won	2	0	27 April	Lost	2	3	7th	13th
1963-64	Division 1	23 November	Won	5	3	4 April	Won	1	0	8th	18th
1964-65	Division 1	19 April	Won	3	1	16 April	Drew	1	1	13th	17th
1965-66	Division 1	5 March	Drew	0	0	16 October	Lost	3	5	14th	13th
1966-67	Division 1	17 September	Drew	1	1	21 January	Won	3	0	7th	22ndR
1970-71	Division 1	20 March	Won	1	0	7 November	Won	1	0	1st	22ndR

FA Cup		Home Date	Result	Arsenal	Blackpool	Away Date	Result	Arsenal	Blackpool	Division Arsenal	Blackpool
1952-53	Q'ter Final	28 February	Lost	1	2					Div 1	Div 1
1969-70	Round 3	3 January	Drew	1	1	15 January	Lost	2	3	Div 1	Div 2
1999-00	Round 3	13 December	Won	3	1					Prem	Div 2

League Cup		Date	Result	Home Arsenal	Home Blackpool	Date	Result	Away Arsenal	Away Blackpool	Division Arsenal	Division Blackpool
1968-69	Q'ter Final	29 October	Won	**5**	**1**					Div 1	Div 2
1976-77	Round 3	28 September	Drew	**0**	**0**	21 September	Drew	**1**	**1**	Div 1	Div 2
		5 October	Won	**2**	**0**	2nd replay					

Summary	P	W	D	L	F	A
Arsenal's home league record:	36	26	8	2	85	34
Arsenal's away league record:	36	12	13	11	57	50
Arsenal's cup record:	8	3	3	2	15	9
TOTAL	**80**	**41**	**24**	**15**	**157**	**93**

FACT FILE

- **Incredibly, Arsenal were unbeaten in their first 24 matches in this series, a run that ended on Christmas Day 1937.**
- **Arsenal were unbeaten in their first 25 home league matches.**
- **Blackpool have only won two league matches at Highbury, both in 1958.**
- **The FA Cup match in December 1999 was Arsenal's first before Christmas for 96 years.**
- **Between 1937 and 1950, Blackpool were unbeaten in six home games.**

Arsenal's top scorers vs Blackpool

Cliff Bastin 9
Doug Lishman, Don Roper 8
David Herd, David Jack, Derek Tapscott 6
John Radford 5
George Armstrong, Ernest Cottrell,
Adam Haywood, Jon Sammels, Geoff Strong 4

Arsenal hat-tricks vs Blackpool

18 Mar 1899 Ernest Cottrell
27 Dec 1930 Jimmy Brain
27 Dec 1930 David Jack
10 Oct 1931 Cliff Bastin

Played for both clubs

Adam Haywood	Arsenal 1895-99	Blackpool 1907-08
Tom Pratt	Arsenal 1903-04	Blackpool 1904-05
Fred Pagnam	Blackpool 1912-13	Arsenal 1919-21
Bert White	Arsenal 1919-23	Blackpool 1922-25
Alexander McKenzie	Arsenal 1920-23	Blackpool 1923-24
Frank Hill	Arsenal 1932-36	Blackpool 1936-38
Alan Ball	Blackpool 1962-66/80-81	Arsenal 1971-77
Alan Skirton	Arsenal 1960-67	Blackpool 1966-69
George Wood	Blackpool 1971-77/89-90	Arsenal 1980-83
Kevin Richardson	Arsenal 1987-90	Blackpool 1999-2000
Vince Bartram	Blackpool 1989-90	Arsenal 1994-95

v. Bolton Wanderers

		Home					Away			Final Positions	
Season	League	Date	Result	Arsenal	Bolton W	Date	Result	Arsenal	Bolton W	Arsenal	Bolton W
1899-00	Division 2	24 February	Lost	0	1	21 October	Lost	0	1	8th	2ndP
1903-04	Division 2	26 March	Won	3	0	28 November	Lost	1	2	2ndP	7th
1905-06	Division 1	30 September	Drew	0	0	1 January	Lost	1	6	12th	6th
1906-07	Division 1	3 November	Drew	2	2	27 March	Lost	0	3	7th	6th
1907-08	Division 1	4 April	Drew	1	1	7 December	Lost	1	3	14th=	19thR
1909-10	Division 1	29 January	Won	2	0	18 September	Lost	0	3	18th	20thR
1911-12	Division 1	10 February	Won	3	0	7 October	Drew	2	2	10th	4th
1912-13	Division 1	14 September	Lost	1	2	4 January	Lost	1	5	20thR	8th
1919-20	Division 1	8 November	Drew	2	2	15 November	Drew	2	2	10th	6th
1920-21	Division 1	9 October	Drew	0	0	16 October	Drew	1	1	9th	3rd
1921-22	Division 1	12 December	Drew	1	1	19 November	Lost	0	1	17th	6th
1922-23	Division 1	26 December	Won	5	0	25 December	Lost	1	4	11th	13th
1923-24	Division 1	27 October	Drew	0	0	20 October	Won	2	1	19th	4th
1924-25	Division 1	7 March	Won	1	0	1 November	Lost	1	4	20th	3rd
1925-26	Division 1	10 October	Lost	2	3	28 April	Drew	1	1	2nd	8th
1926-27	Division 1	1 September	Won	2	1	6 September	Drew	2	2	11th	4th
1927-28	Division 1	29 October	Lost	1	2	10 March	Drew	1	1	10th	7th
1928-29	Division 1	1 September	Won	2	0	5 January	Won	2	1	9th	14th
1929-30	Division 1	28 September	Lost	1	2	1 February	Drew	0	0	14th	15th
1930-31	Division 1	2 May	Won	5	0	1 September	Won	4	1	1st	14th
1931-32	Division 1	17 October	Drew	1	1	2 March	Lost	0	1	2nd	17th
1932-33	Division 1	17 September	Won	3	2	1 February	Won	4	0	1st	21stR
1935-36	Division 1	1 April	Drew	1	1	29 April	Lost	1	2	6th	13th
1936-37	Division 1	1 May	Drew	0	0	1 January	Won	5	0	3rd	20th
1937-38	Division 1	7 May	Won	5	0	15 September	Lost	0	1	1st	7th
1938-39	Division 1	4 March	Won	3	1	29 October	Drew	1	1	5th	8th
1946-47	Division 1	30 November	Drew	2	2	5 April	Won	3	1	13th	18th
1947-48	Division 1	10 September	Won	2	0	1 January	Won	1	0	1st	17th
1948-49	Division 1	26 February	Won	5	0	2 October	Lost	0	1	5th	14th
1949-50	Division 1	21 January	Drew	1	1	17 September	Drew	2	2	6th	16th
1950-51	Division 1	21 April	Drew	1	1	2 December	Lost	0	3	5th	8th
1951-52	Division 1	24 November	Won	4	2	12 April	Lost	1	2	3rd	5th
1952-53	Division 1	15 April	Won	4	1	25 December	Won	6	4	1st	14th
1953-54	Division 1	14 November	Won	4	3	3 April	Lost	1	3	12th	5th
1954-55	Division 1	26 March	Won	3	0	6 November	Drew	2	2	9th	18th
1955-56	Division 1	31 December	Won	3	1	3 September	Lost	1	4	5th	8th
1956-57	Division 1	17 November	Won	3	0	30 March	Lost	1	2	5th	9th
1957-58	Division 1	18 February	Lost	1	2	5 October	Won	1	0	12th	15th
1958-59	Division 1	9 September	Won	6	1	17 September	Lost	1	2	3rd	4th
1959-60	Division 1	15 September	Won	2	1	9 September	Won	1	0	13th	6th
1960-61	Division 1	10 December	Won	5	1	1 April	Drew	1	1	11th	18th
1961-62	Division 1	13 January	Lost	1	2	2 September	Lost	1	2	10th	11th
1962-63	Division 1	16 February	Won	3	2	29 September	Lost	0	3	7th	18th
1963-64	Division 1	7 September	Won	4	3	11 January	Drew	1	1	8th	21stR

				Home				Away		Final Positions	
Season	League	Date	Result	Arsenal	Bolton W	Date	Result	Arsenal	Bolton W	Arsenal	Bolton W
1978-79	Division 1	16 September	Won	**1**	**0**	26 March	Lost	**2**	**4**	7th	17th
1979-80	Division 1	23 February	Won	**2**	**0**	13 October	Drew	**0**	**0**	4th	22ndR
1995-96	Prem'ship	5 May	Won	**2**	**1**	30 October	Lost	**0**	**1**	5th	20thR
1997-98	Prem'ship	13 September	Won	**4**	**1**	31 March	Won	**1**	**0**	1st	18thR
2001-02	Prem'ship	22 September	Drew	**1**	**1**	29 April	Won	**2**	**0**	1st	16th
2002-03	Prem'ship	21 September	Won	**2**	**1**	26 April	Drew	**2**	**2**	2nd	17th
2003-04	Prem'ship	20 March	Won	**2**	**1**	20 December	Drew	**1**	**1**	1st	8th

FA Cup										Division	
1894-95	Round 1					2 February	Lost	**0**	**1**	Div 2	Div 1
1911-12	Round 1					13 January	Lost	**0**	**1**	Div 1	Div 1
1937-38	Round 3	8 January	Won	**3**	**1**					Div 1	Div 1
1966-67	Round 4	22 February	Won	**3**	**0**	18 February	Drew	**0**	**0**	Div 1	Div 2
1979-80	Round 5	19 February	Won	**3**	**0**	5 February	Drew	**1**	**1**	Div 1	Div 1
1982-83	Round 3	8 January	Won	**2**	**1**					Div 1	Div 2
1993-94	Round 4	9 February	Lost*	**1**	**3**	31 January	Drew	**2**	**2**	Prem	Div 1

Summary	P	W	D	L	F	A
Arsenal's home league record:	51	30	14	7	115	50
Arsenal's away league record:	51	12	15	24	66	90
Arsenal's cup record:	10	4	3	3	15	10
TOTAL	**112**	**46**	**32**	**34**	**196**	**150**

FACT FILE

- **Bolton's last league win at Highbury was in 1962; they have visited nine times since.**
- **Arsenal were unbeaten in 19 home games between 1931 and 1956.**
- **Arsenal did not win in Bolton until their 15th attempt.**
- **In 1998, Arsenal won in Bolton for the first time since 1959.**
- **In 1997, Ian Wright became Arsenal's all-time leading scorer with a hat-trick against Bolton.**

Arsenal's top scorers vs Bolton

Doug Lishman 10
Joe Hulme 7
Cliff Bastin, Ted Drake, Cliff Holton, Reg Lewis 6
Jack Lambert, Derek Tapscott, Bobby Turnbull 5

Arsenal hat-tricks vs Bolton

26 Dec 1922 Bobby Turnbull (4)
1 Sep 1930 Jack Lambert
1 Feb 1933 Ernie Coleman
1 Jan 1937 Ted Drake (4)
24 Nov 1951 Doug Lishman
14 Nov 1953 Cliff Holton
22 Feb 1967 John Radford (cup)
13 Sep 1997 Ian Wright

Played for both clubs

Tommy Hynds	Bolton Wanderers 1898-99	Arsenal 1906-07
Billy Bannister	Bolton Wanderers 1901-03	Arsenal 1902-04
John Elvey	Bolton Wanderers 1920-22	Arsenal 1922-23
David Jack	Bolton Wanderers 1920-29	Arsenal 1928-34
George Hunt	Arsenal 1937-38	Bolton Wanderers 1937-47
Brian Kidd	Arsenal 1974-76	Bolton Wanderers 1980-82
Isaiah Rankin	Arsenal 1997-98	Bolton Wanderers 2000-01

Cliff Bastin was a regular scorer against Bolton Wanderers. Here he is featured with the Arsenal 1936 Cup winners. Back row (left to right): Wilf Copping, George Male, Jack Crayston, Alex Wilson, Herbert Roberts, Ted Drake, Eddie Hapgood. Front row: George Allison (manager), Joe Hulme, Ray Bowden, Alex James, Cliff Bastin, Tom Whittaker.

David Jack, a player for both Bolton and Arsenal.

v. AFC Bournemouth

League Cup		Date	Result	Home Arsenal	Home B'mouth	Division Arsenal	Division B'mouth
1987-88	Round 3	27 October	Won	**3**	**0**	Div 1	Div 2

Summary	P	W	D	L	F	A
Arsenal's cup record:	1	1	0	0	3	0
TOTAL	**1**	**1**	**0**	**0**	**3**	**0**

FACT FILE

- **Kevin Richardson, Alan Smith and Michael Thomas scored the goals.**

Played for both clubs

Arthur Roe	Arsenal 1924-25	Bournemouth 1925-27
Jock Robson	Arsenal 1922-26	Bournemouth 1926-28
Andrew Young	Arsenal 1921-27	Bournemouth 1927-28
Reg Trim	Bournemouth 1930-33	Arsenal 1934-35
Brian Chambers	Arsenal 1973-74	Bournemouth 1979-81
Charlie George	Arsenal 1969-75	Bournemouth 1981-82
Eddie Kelly	Arsenal 1969-76	Bournemouth 1981-82
David Madden	Bournemouth 1982-83	Arsenal 1983-84
Vince Bartram	Bournemouth 1991-92	Arsenal 1994-95

West Ham's Billy Jennings gets in a header at Highbury in October 1974. Eddie Kelly, Terry Mancini and John Radford are the Arsenal players. The Gunners won 3-0. Kelly played one season for Bournemouth.

v. Bradford City

		Home					Away				Final Positions	
Season	*League*	*Date*	*Result*	Arsenal	Bradford C	*Date*	*Result*	Arsenal	Bradford C	Arsenal	Bradford C
1903-04	Division 2	25 December	Won	**4**	**1**	19 April	Won	**3**	**0**	2ndP	10th
1908-09	Division 1	17 April	Won	**1**	**0**	12 December	Lost	**1**	**4**	6th	18th
1909-10	Division 1	6 November	Lost	**0**	**1**	19 March	Won	**1**	**0**	18th	7th
1910-11	Division 1	11 February	Drew	**0**	**0**	8 October	Lost	**0**	**3**	10th	5th
1911-12	Division 1	14 October	Won	**2**	**0**	17 February	Drew	**1**	**1**	10th	11th
1912-13	Division 1	1 March	Drew	**1**	**1**	26 October	Lost	**1**	**3**	20thR	13th
1919-20	Division 1	25 October	Lost	**1**	**2**	1 November	Drew	**1**	**1**	10th	15th
1920-21	Division 1	1 January	Lost	**1**	**2**	18 December	Lost	**1**	**3**	9th	15th
1921-22	Division 1	6 May	Won	**1**	**0**	29 April	Won	**2**	**0**	17th	21stR
1999-00	Prem'ship	25 August	Won	**2**	**0**	5 February	Lost	**1**	**2**	2nd	17th
2000-01	Prem'ship	30 January	Won	**2**	**0**	9 September	Drew	**1**	**1**	2nd	20thR

FA Cup										*Division*	
1913-14	Round 1					10 January	Lost	**0**	**2**	Div 2	Div 1
1961-62	Round 3	6 January	Won	**3**	**0**					Div 1	Div 4
1972-73	Round 4	3 February	Won	**2**	**0**					Div 1	Div 4

Summary	P	W	D	L	F	A
Arsenal's home league record:	11	6	2	3	15	7
Arsenal's away league record:	11	3	3	5	13	18
Arsenal's cup record:	3	2	0	1	5	2
TOTAL	**25**	**11**	**5**	**9**	**33**	**27**

Woolwich Arsenal, 1908-09. Back row (left to right): John Dick, David Greenaway, Roddie McEachrane, Billy Curle. Middle row: Archie Gray, Hugh McDonald, Joe Shaw, Andy Ducat, Archie Cross, Sam Raybould, Percy Sands. Front row: Charlie Lewis, Charlie Satterthwaite, Harry Lee, David Neave.

FACT FILE

- **Arsenal have won their last five home matches, without conceding a single goal. Bradford's last win (and goal) at Highbury was in 1921.**
- **Arsenal have only won one of their last nine away matches.**
- **The longest unbeaten run by either side is eight matches (Bradford, 1913-21).**

Arsenal's top scorers vs Bradford

Tim Coleman 3

Billy Blyth, Mel Charles, Alec Graham, Bert White 2

Played for both clubs

Thomas Drain	Bradford City 1903-05	Arsenal 1909-10
Jimmy Blair	Arsenal 1905-07	Bradford City 1910-12
Archie Devine	Bradford City 1910-13	Arsenal 1912-14
Harold Walden	Bradford City 1911-20	Arsenal 1920-21
Harold Peel	Arsenal 1926-30	Bradford City 1929-36
George Swindin	Bradford City 1934-36	Arsenal 1936-54
Ernie Tuckett	Arsenal 1935-36	Bradford City 1936-38
Laurie Scott	Bradford City 1935-37	Arsenal 1946-52
Eddie Carr	Arsenal 1937-39	Bradford City 1949-53
Frank Stapleton	Arsenal 1974-81	Bradford City 1991-94
John Hawley	Arsenal 1981-83	Bradford City 1983-85
Isaiah Rankin	Arsenal 1997-98	Bradford City 1998-2001

Later to join Bradford City, Frank Stapleton gets in a shot as Ipswich's Kevin Beattie launches a tackle.

v. Bradford Park Avenue

Season	League	Date	Result	Home Arsenal	Home Bradford PA	Date	Result	Away Arsenal	Away Bradford PA	Final Positions Arsenal	Final Positions Bradford PA
1913-14	Division 2	26 December	Won	**2**	**0**	25 December	Won	**3**	**2**	3rd	2ndP
1919-20	Division 1	1 May	Won	**3**	**0**	28 April	Drew	**0**	**0**	10th	11th
1920-21	Division 1	9 April	Won	**2**	**1**	16 April	Won	**1**	**0**	9th	22ndR

FA Cup										*Division*	
1921-22	Round 2					28 January	Won	**3**	**2**	Div 1	Div 2
1947-48	Round 3	10 January	Lost	**0**	**1**					Div 1	Div 2

Summary	P	W	D	L	F	A
Arsenal's home league record:	3	3	0	0	7	1
Arsenal's away league record:	3	2	1	0	4	2
Arsenal's cup record:	2	1	0	1	3	3
TOTAL	**8**	**6**	**1**	**1**	**14**	**6**

FACT FILE

- **Arsenal were unbeaten in their first seven matches.**
- **Arsenal kept four clean sheets in six league matches.**

Arsenal's top scorers vs Park Avenue

Stephen Stonley 3

Joe Toner, Bert White 2

Arsenal hat-tricks vs Park Avenue

25 Dec 1913 Stephen Stonley

Played for both clubs

Hugh McDonald	Arsenal 1905-10/12-13	Bradford Park Avenue 1911-13
George Jobey	Arsenal 1913-14	Bradford Park Avenue 1914-15
Harold Peel	Bradford Park Avenue 1920-27	Arsenal 1926-30
Jack Moody	Arsenal 1926-28	Bradford Park Avenue 1929-30
Jack Crayston	Bradford Park Avenue 1930-34	Arsenal 1934-40
Laurie Brown	Arsenal 1961-64	Bradford Park Avenue 1968-70

In his first season for Arsenal, after transferring from Park Avenue, Jack Crayston picked up a championship medal. The picture shows Arsenal in 1934-35. Back row (left to right,: Ray Bowden, Frank Hill, Leslie Compton, Frank Moss, Tom Whittaker (trainer), Norman Sidey, Ted Drake, Jack Crayston. Front row: Joe Hulme, Pat Beasley, Cliff Bastin, George Allison (manager), Eddie Hapgood, Peter Dougall, Wilf Copping.

v. Brentford

		Home					Away			Final Positions	
Season	League	Date	Result	Arsenal	Brentford	Date	Result	Arsenal	Brentford	Arsenal	Brentford
1935-36	Division 1	4 April	Drew	**1**	**1**	2 November	Lost	**1**	**2**	6th	5th
1936-37	Division 1	9 September	Drew	**1**	**1**	3 September	Lost	**0**	**2**	3rd	6th
1937-38	Division 1	15 April	Lost	**0**	**2**	18 April	Lost	**0**	**3**	1st	6th
1938-39	Division 1	6 May	Won	**2**	**0**	8 September	Lost	**0**	**1**	5th	18th
1946-47	Division 1	12 October	Drew	**2**	**2**	26 May	Won	**1**	**0**	13th	21stR

FA Cup										*Division*
1902-03	Intermed'te	17 December	Won	**5**	**0**	13 December	Drew	**1**	**1**	Div 2 Non L

Summary	P	W	D	L	F	A
Arsenal's home league record:	5	1	3	1	6	6
Arsenal's away league record:	5	1	0	4	2	8
Arsenal's cup record:	2	1	1	0	6	1
TOTAL	**12**	**3**	**4**	**5**	**14**	**15**

FACT FILE

- **Of all the teams that have played Arsenal more than once, Brentford have the best record.**
- **Brentford were unbeaten in seven games between 1935 and 1938.**

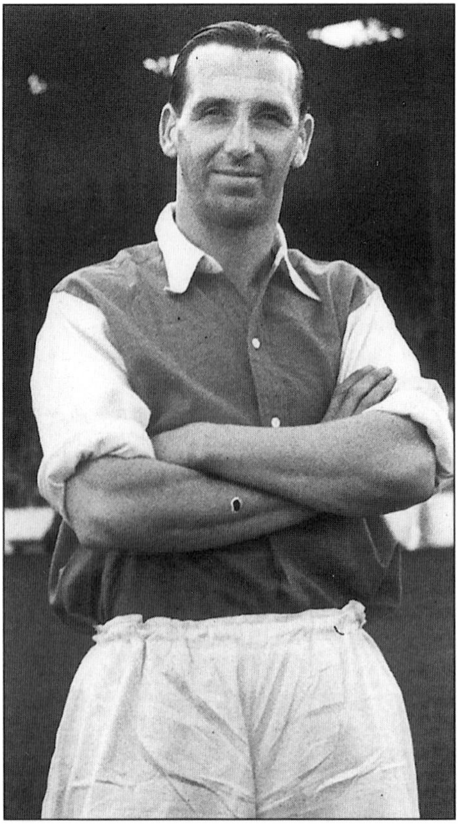

Thirty-four-year-old Tommy Lawton was in the twilight of his career when he joined Arsenal in September 1953, from Brentford for £10,000. He scored 13 goals in his 35 league games for the Gunners.

Arsenal's top scorers vs Brentford

Tim Coleman, Ted Drake, Bill Gooing 2

Played for both clubs

Harry King	Arsenal 1914-15	Brentford 1920-21
Alex Graham	Arsenal 1912-24	Brentford 1924-26
Bert Lawson	Arsenal 1925-26	Brentford 1926-32
Archie Clark	Brentford 1926-27	Arsenal 1927-28
James Shaw	Arsenal 1926-28	Brentford 1930-31
Dave Nelson	Arsenal 1936-47	Brentford 1947-50
Alan Smith	Arsenal 1946-47	Brentford 1946-49
Archie Macaulay	Brentford 1946-47	Arsenal 1947-50
Kevin O'Flanagan	Arsenal 1946-47	Brentford 1949-50
Arthur Shaw	Brentford 1946-47	Arsenal 1949-55
Ian McPherson	Arsenal 1946-51	Brentford 1953-54
James Robertson	Arsenal 1951-52	Brentford 1953-56
Tommy Lawton	Brentford 1951-54	Arsenal 1953-56
Brian Tawse	Arsenal 1964-65	Brentford 1969-71
Jimmy Bloomfield	Brentford 1952-54/64-66	Arsenal 1954-61
Tony Burns	Arsenal 1964-66	Brentford 1976-77
Tommy Baldwin	Arsenal 1964-67	Brentford 1977-78
Gordon Neilson	Arsenal 1965-67	Brentford 1968-72
David Jenkins	Arsenal 1967-69	Brentford 1972-73
David Court	Arsenal 1962-70	Brentford 1972-73
Wilf Rostron	Arsenal 1974-77	Brentford 1990-93
Paul Merson	Brentford 1986-87	Arsenal 1986-97
Graham Rix	Arsenal 1976-88	Brentford 1987-88
Paul Davis	Arsenal 1979-95	Brentford 1995-96
Scott Marshall	Arsenal 1992-98	Brentford 1999-2003

Graham Rix leaves Leicester City's Peter Walsh in his wake at Highbury in October 1980, when Frank Stapleton scored the only goal of the game. Rix played in over 450 first-team games for Arsenal. He moved to Brentford for one season in 1987.

v. Brighton & Hove Albion

		Home					Away			Final Positions	
Season	*League*	*Date*	*Result*	Arsenal	B&HA	*Date*	*Result*	Arsenal	B&HA	Arsenal	B&HA
1979-80	Division 1	3 November	Won	**3**	**0**	18 August	Won	**4**	**0**	4th	16th
1980-81	Division 1	1 November	Won	**2**	**0**	4 April	Won	**1**	**0**	3rd	19th
1981-82	Division 1	26 January	Drew	**0**	**0**	10 April	Lost	**1**	**2**	5th	13th
1982-83	Division 1	5 February	Won	**3**	**1**	7 September	Lost	**0**	**1**	10th	22ndR

FA Cup										*Division*	
1934-35	Round 2					12 January	Won	**2**	**0**	Div 1	Div 3S
1979-80	Round 4	26 January	Won	**2**	**0**					Div 1	Div 1
1987-88	Round 4					30 January	Won	**2**	**1**	Div 1	Div 3

League Cup											
1979-80	Round 4	13 November	Won	**4**	**0**	30 October	Drew	**0**	**0**	Div 1	Div 1

Summary	P	W	D	L	F	A
Arsenal's home league record:	4	3	1	0	8	1
Arsenal's away league record:	4	2	0	2	6	3
Arsenal's cup record:	5	4	1	0	10	1
TOTAL	**13**	**9**	**2**	**2**	**24**	**5**

FACT FILE

- **Brighton have never won at Highbury in six attempts. Indeed they have only ever scored one goal there.**
- **Brighton have scored five goals in 13 matches.**
- **Arsenal were undefeated in their first nine matches with Brighton.**

Ian Wright, Marc Overmars, Martin Keown and Dennis Bergkamp couldn't look happier after the win over Everton which confirmed Arsenal as Premiership champions in 1997-98. Keown transferred to Arsenal from Brighton in 1985.

Arsenal's top scorers vs Brighton

Graham Rix, Frank Stapleton, Alan Sunderland 3

Played for both clubs

Freddie Groves	Arsenal 1912-21	Brighton & Hove Albion 1921-24
Jimmy Hopkins	Arsenal 1920-23	Brighton & Hove Albion 1922-29
Andy Neil	Brighton & Hove Albion 1920-24/25-27	Arsenal 1923-26
Alex Wilson	Arsenal 1933-39	Brighton & Hove Albion 1947-48
Les Jones	Arsenal 1937-40	Brighton & Hove Albion 1948-49
Cyril Hodges	Arsenal 1946-47	Brighton & Hove Albion 1946-47
Mike Tiddy	Arsenal 1955-58	Brighton & Hove Albion 1958-62
Mike Everitt	Arsenal 1959-61	Brighton & Hove Albion 1968-70
Eddie Magill	Arsenal 1959-65	Brighton & Hove Albion 1965-68
Brian Tawse	Arsenal 1964-65	Brighton & Hove Albion 1965-70
Tony Burns	Arsenal 1964-66	Brighton & Hove Albion 1966-69
Sammy Nelson	Arsenal 1969-81	Brighton & Hove Albion 1981-83
Steve Gatting	Arsenal 1978-81	Brighton & Hove Albion 1981-91
Willie Young	Arsenal 1976-82	Brighton & Hove Albion 1983-84
Raphael Meade	Arsenal 1981-85	Brighton & Hove Albion 1991-92/94-95
Martin Keown	Brighton & Hove Albion 1984-86	Arsenal 1985-86/92-2004
Colin Pates	Arsenal 1989-92	Brighton & Hove Albion 1990-91
Paul Dickov	Arsenal 1992-97	Brighton & Hove Albion 1993-94
Graham Barrett	Arsenal 1999-2000	Brighton & Hove Albion 2002-03

Former Spurs and Aberdeen centre-half Willie Young goes up for a high ball against Manchester United's Lou Macari. Young made almost 250 senior appearances for Arsenal between March 1977 and December 1981.

v. Bristol City

Season	League	Home Date	Home Result	Home Arsenal	Home Bristol C	Away Date	Away Result	Away Arsenal	Away Bristol C	Final Positions Arsenal	Final Positions Bristol C
1901-02	Division 2	22 February	Won	**2**	**0**	26 October	Won	**3**	**0**	4th	6th
1902-03	Division 2	11 October	Won	**2**	**1**	4 October	Lost	**0**	**1**	3rd	4th
1903-04	Division 2	14 March	Won	**2**	**0**	26 September	Won	**4**	**0**	2ndP	4th
1906-07	Division 1	16 February	Lost	**1**	**2**	13 October	Won	**3**	**1**	7th	2nd
1907-08	Division 1	7 September	Lost	**0**	**4**	4 January	Won	**2**	**1**	14th=	10th
1908-09	Division 1	23 January	Drew	**1**	**1**	19 September	Lost	**1**	**2**	6th	8th
1909-10	Division 1	20 November	Drew	**2**	**2**	2 April	Won	**1**	**0**	18th	16th
1910-11	Division 1	25 March	Won	**3**	**0**	19 November	Won	**1**	**0**	10th	19thR
1913-14	Division 2	4 April	Drew	**1**	**1**	29 November	Drew	**1**	**1**	3rd	8th
1914-15	Division 2	28 November	Won	**3**	**0**	3 April	Drew	**1**	**1**	5thP	13th
1976-77	Division 1	21 August	Lost	**0**	**1**	22 January	Lost	**0**	**2**	8th	18th
1977-78	Division 1	18 March	Won	**4**	**1**	22 October	Won	**2**	**0**	5th	17th
1978-79	Division 1	10 March	Won	**2**	**0**	28 October	Won	**3**	**1**	7th	13th
1979-80	Division 1	11 March	Drew	**0**	**0**	27 October	Won	**1**	**0**	4th	20thR

FA Cup										*Division*	
1904-05	Round 1	4 February	Drew	**0**	**0**	8 February	Lost	**0**	**1**	Div 1	Div 2
1906-07	Round 2	2 February	Won	**2**	**1**					Div 1	Div 1
1919-20	Round 2					31 January	Lost	**0**	**1**	Div 1	Div 2

Summary	P	W	D	L	F	A
Arsenal's home league record:	14	7	4	3	23	13
Arsenal's away league record:	14	9	2	3	23	10
Arsenal's cup record:	4	1	1	2	2	3
TOTAL	**32**	**17**	**7**	**8**	**48**	**23**

A view from behind the Manor Ground goal as Woolwich Arsenal attack the Bristol City goal in 1907.

FACT FILE

- **Arsenal have lost two of their last 17 league matches.**
- **Bristol City last finished above Arsenal in the league in 1910.**

Arsenal's top scorers vs Bristol City

Bill Gooing 5

Tim Coleman, Frank Stapleton 4

Wally Hardinge 3

Played for both clubs

Paddy O'Brien	Arsenal 1894-97	Bristol City 1901-02
Joe Connor	Bristol City 1901-02	Arsenal 1902-03
Willis Rippon	Bristol City 1907-10	Arsenal 1910-11
Frank Townrow	Arsenal 1922-24	Bristol City 1930-31
Ted Bowen	Arsenal 1926-27	Bristol City 1932-34
Bert Humpish	Arsenal 1929-30	Bristol City 1930-32
Pat Beasley	Arsenal 1931-37	Bristol City 1950-52
George Marks	Arsenal 1938-40	Bristol City 1948-49
Tom Rudkin	Arsenal 1946-47	Bristol City 1949-51
Con Sullivan	Bristol City 1950-53	Arsenal 1953-58
Arthur Milton	Arsenal 1950-55	Bristol City 1954-55
Alan Skirton	Arsenal 1960-67	Bristol City 1968-71
Bobby Gould	Arsenal 1967-70	Bristol City 1972-74
Jimmy Harvey	Arsenal 1977-79	Bristol City 1986-88
Gus Caesar	Arsenal 1985-90	Bristol City 1991-92
Andy Cole	Arsenal 1990-91	Bristol City 1991-93
Neil Heaney	Arsenal 1991-94	Bristol City 1998-99
Alan Miller	Arsenal 1992-94	Bristol City 2000-01
Tommy Black	Arsenal 1999-2000	Bristol City 1999-2000

Action at Highbury in January 1909 where Woolwich Arsenal and Bristol City drew 1-1.

v. Bristol Rovers

		Home					Away			Division	
FA Cup		*Date*	*Result*	Arsenal	Bristol R	*Date*	*Result*	Arsenal	Bristol R	Arsenal	Bristol R
1903-04	Intermed'te	15 December	Drew	**1**	**1**	12 December	Drew	**1**	**1**	Div 2	Non L
		21 December				Tottenham (2nd replay)	Won	**1**	**0**		
1906-07	Round 3	23 February	Won	**1**	**0**					Div 1	Non L
1935-36	Round 3					11 January	Won	**5**	**1**	Div 1	Div 3S
1966-67	Round 3					28 January	Won	**3**	**0**	Div 1	Div 3

League Cup											
1984-85	Round 2	25 September	Won	**4**	**0**	9 October	Drew	**1**	**1**	Div 1	Div 3

Summary	P	W	D	L	F	A
Arsenal's cup record:	8	5	3	0	17	4
TOTAL	**8**	**5**	**3**	**0**	**17**	**4**

FACT FILE

- **No side has played Arsenal as many times without winning at least once.**

Arsenal's top scorers vs Bristol Rovers

Cliff Bastin, Ted Drake, Charlie Nicholas 2

Played for both clubs

Frank Townrow	Arsenal 1922-24	Bristol Rovers 1931-33
Charlie Preedy	Arsenal 1929-33	Bristol Rovers 1933-34
Joe Haverty	Arsenal 1954-61	Bristol Rovers 1964-65
John Petts	Arsenal 1957-62	Bristol Rovers 1965-70
Bobby Gould	Arsenal 1967-70	Bristol Rovers 1977-79
Alan Ball	Arsenal 1971-77	Bristol Rovers 1982-83
David Hillier	Arsenal 1990-97	Bristol Rovers 1998-2002
Graham Barrett	Arsenal 1999-2000	Bristol Rovers 2000-01
Stuart Taylor	Bristol Rovers 1999-2000	Arsenal 2001-03

April 1974 and Alan Ball is the object of close attention from Derby County's Bruce Rioch (who later managed the Gunners). Charlie George, later to join Derby, looks on. The Gunners won this game at Highbury 2-0, with Ball, from the penalty spot, and George the scorers. Ball transferred to Bristol Rovers in 1982.

v. Burnley

		Home				Away				Final Positions	
Season	League	Date	Result	Arsenal	Burnley	Date	Result	Arsenal	Burnley	Arsenal	Burnley
1897-98	Division 2	2 April	Drew	1	1	6 September	Lost	0	5	5th	1stP
1900-01	Division 2	6 April	Won	3	1	1 December	Lost	0	3	7th	3rd
1901-02	Division 2	21 September	Won	4	0	18 January	Drew	0	0	4th	9th
1902-03	Division 2	27 December	Won	5	1	15 November	Won	3	0	3rd	18th
1903-04	Division 2	29 February	Won	4	0	2 April	Lost	0	1	2ndP	5th
1919-20	Division 1	10 April	Won	2	0	3 April	Lost	1	2	10th	2nd
1920-21	Division 1	19 March	Drew	1	1	12 March	Lost	0	1	9th	1st
1921-22	Division 1	21 January	Drew	0	0	20 February	Lost	0	1	17th	3rd
1922-23	Division 1	28 August	Drew	1	1	4 September	Lost	1	4	11th	15th
1923-24	Division 1	5 April	Won	2	0	28 April	Lost	1	4	19th	17th
1924-25	Division 1	18 April	Won	5	0	13 December	Lost	0	1	20th	19th
1925-26	Division 1	3 February	Lost	1	2	19 September	Drew	2	2	2nd	20th
1926-27	Division 1	26 February	Won	6	2	9 October	Lost	0	2	11th	5th
1927-28	Division 1	31 August	Won	4	1	5 September	Won	2	1	10th	19th
1928-29	Division 1	22 December	Won	3	1	4 May	Drew	3	3	9th	19th
1929-30	Division 1	14 September	Won	6	1	18 January	Drew	2	2	14th	21stR
1947-48	Division 1	14 February	Won	3	0	27 September	Won	1	0	1st	3rd
1948-49	Division 1	9 October	Won	3	1	5 March	Drew	1	1	5th	15th
1949-50	Division 1	20 August	Lost	0	1	17 December	Drew	0	0	6th	10th
1950-51	Division 1	16 December	Lost	0	1	19 August	Won	1	0	5th	10th
1951-52	Division 1	13 October	Won	1	0	1 March	Won	1	0	3rd	14th
1952-53	Division 1	1 May	Won	3	2	13 December	Drew	1	1	1st	6th
1953-54	Division 1	17 October	Lost	2	5	6 March	Lost	1	2	12th	7th
1954-55	Division 1	25 September	Won	4	0	12 February	Lost	0	3	9th	10th
1955-56	Division 1	26 November	Lost	0	1	7 April	Won	1	0	5th	7th
1956-57	Division 1	21 August	Won	2	0	28 August	Lost	1	3	5th	7th
1957-58	Division 1	19 April	Drew	0	0	7 December	Lost	1	2	12th	6th
1958-59	Division 1	26 August	Won	3	0	2 September	Lost	1	3	3rd	7th
1959-60	Division 1	12 December	Lost	2	4	19 March	Lost	2	3	13th	1st
1960-61	Division 1	17 December	Lost	2	5	20 August	Lost	2	3	11th	4th
1961-62	Division 1	19 August	Drew	2	2	16 December	Won	2	0	10th	2nd
1962-63	Division 1	11 May	Lost	2	3	1 September	Lost	1	2	7th	3rd
1963-64	Division 1	8 February	Won	3	2	28 September	Won	3	0	8th	9th
1964-65	Division 1	17 October	Won	3	2	27 February	Lost	1	2	13th	12th
1965-66	Division 1	5 February	Drew	1	1	28 August	Drew	2	2	14th	3rd
1966-67	Division 1	3 December	Drew	0	0	29 April	Won	4	1	7th	14th
1967-68	Division 1	27 April	Won	2	0	2 December	Lost	0	1	9th	14th
1968-69	Division 1	15 February	Won	2	0	30 November	Won	1	0	4th	14th
1969-70	Division 1	13 December	Won	3	2	13 September	Won	1	0	12th	14th
1970-71	Division 1	20 April	Won	1	0	12 September	Won	2	1	1st	21stR
1973-74	Division 1	2 February	Drew	1	1	15 December	Lost	1	2	10th	6th
1974-75	Division 1	7 September	Lost	0	1	22 March	Drew	3	3	16th	10th
1975-76	Division 1	20 December	Won	1	0	16 August	Drew	0	0	17th	21stR

FA Cup		Home Date	Home Result	Home Arsenal	Home Burnley	Away Date	Away Result	Away Arsenal	Away Burnley	Division Arsenal	Division Burnley
1895-96	Round 1					2 February	Lost	**1**	**6**	Div 2	Div 1
1897-98	Round 1					29 January	Lost	**1**	**3**	Div 2	Div 2
1936-37	Round 5					20 February	Won	**7**	**1**	Div 1	Div 2
1949-50	Round 5	11 February	Won	**2**	**0**					Div 1	Div 1
1952-53	Round 5					14 February	Won	**2**	**0**	Div 1	Div 1

League Cup											
1967-68	Q'ter Final	5 December	Won	**2**	**1**	29 November	Drew	**3**	**3**	Div 1	Div 1

Summary	P	W	D	L	F	A
Arsenal's home league record:	43	25	9	9	94	46
Arsenal's away league record:	43	12	10	21	50	67
Arsenal's cup record:	7	4	1	2	18	14
TOTAL	**93**	**41**	**20**	**32**	**162**	**127**

FACT FILE

- **Arsenal were undefeated in their first 11 home matches.**
- **Arsenal won once in their first 15 visits to Burnley.**
- **Straight after this run, however, Arsenal went 11 away matches undefeated.**
- **Arsenal were unbeaten in 10 home matches (1964-74).**
- **On 1 May 1953, Arsenal's narrow win gave them the league title, beating Preston on goal average (1.516 to 1.417).**

Lee Dixon, a member of one of the most successful sides in Arsenal's history, enjoyed football in the lower divisions before joining the Gunners from Stoke City in 1986.

Arsenal's top scorers vs Burnley	***Arsenal hat-tricks vs Burnley***
Jimmy Brain 12	27 Dec 1902 Tim Coleman
Reg Lewis, John Radford 5	29 Feb 1904 Tommy Shanks
George Armstrong, Jimmy Bloomfield,	18 Apr 1925 Jimmy Brain
Tommy Briercliffe, Ted Drake, George Graham,	26 Feb 1927 Jimmy Brain (4)
Cliff Holton, David Jack, Doug Lishman,	14 Sep 1929 Jack Lambert
Don Roper, Geoff Strong 4	14 Sep 1929 Jack Lambert

Played for both clubs

William Jeffrey	Burnley 1891-92	Arsenal 1893-94
Henry Boyd	Burnley 1892-93	Arsenal 1894-97
William McNab	Burnley 1892-94	Arsenal 1893-94
Bob Buchanan	Burnley 1892-94	Arsenal 1894-96
Walter Place	Burnley 1893-1900	Arsenal 1900-02
Richard Hannigan	Arsenal 1899-1900	Burnley 1899-1900
Abe Hartley	Arsenal 1899-1900	Burnley 1899-1900
Billy Bannister	Burnley 1899-1902/10-12	Arsenal 1902-04
Will Bradshaw	Arsenal 1902-04	Burnley 1907-08
Jim Bellamy	Arsenal 1904-07	Burnley 1912-14
Bertie Freeman	Arsenal 1905-08	Burnley 1910-21
Peter Dougal	Burnley 1927-28	Arsenal 1933-36
Tommy Lawton	Burnley 1935-37	Arsenal 1953-56
Jim Furnell	Burnley 1959-61	Arsenal 1963-68
Lee Dixon	Burnley 1982-84	Arsenal 1987-2002
Paul Shaw	Burnley 1994-95	Arsenal 1994-97
Ian Wright	Arsenal 1991-98	Burnley 1999-2000

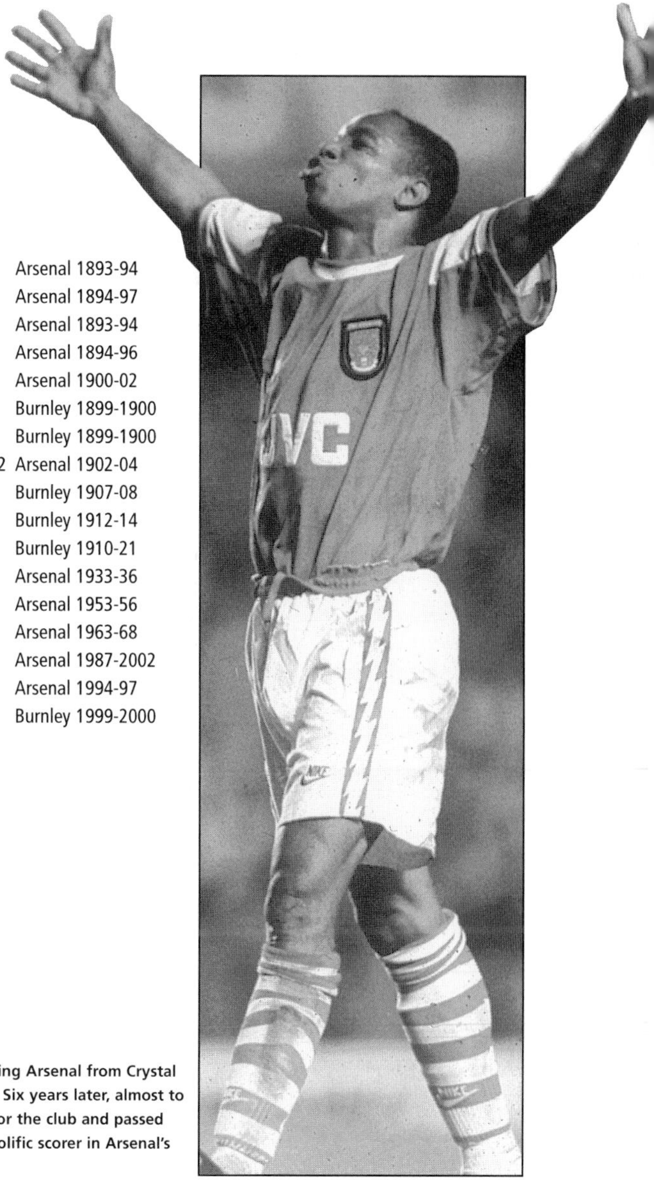

Ian Wright, pictured here shortly after joining Arsenal from Crystal Palace in September 1991 for £2.5 million. Six years later, almost to the day, Wright registered his 179th goal for the club and passed Cliff Bastin's record to become the most prolific scorer in Arsenal's history.

v. Burton Swifts (United)

		Home					Away			Final Positions	
Season	League	Date	Result	Arsenal	Burton	Date	Result	Arsenal	Burton	Arsenal	Burton
1893-94	Division 2	14 April	Lost	0	2	18 November	Lost	2	6	9th	6th
1894-95	Division 2	23 February	Won	3	0	15 September	Lost	0	3	8th	11th
1895-96	Division 2	19 October	Won	5	0	21 December	Lost	2	3	7th	11th
1896-97	Division 2	20 February	Won	3	0	13 March	Won	2	1	10th	14th
1897-98	Division 2	11 April	Won	3	0	15 January	Won	2	1	5th	13th
1898-99	Division 2	22 October	Won	2	1	18 February	Won	2	1	7th	13th
1899-00	Division 2	16 December	Drew	1	1	21 April	Lost	0	2	8th	15th
1900-01	Division 2	12 January	Won	3	1	15 September	Lost	0	1	7th	18th
1901-02	Division 2	21 December	Lost	0	1	19 April	Lost	0	2	4th	10th
1902-03	Division 2	31 January	Won	3	0	25 December	Lost	1	2	3rd	13th
1903-04	Division 2	19 September	Won	8	0	16 January	Lost	1	3	2ndP	14th

Summary	P	W	D	L	F	A
Arsenal's home league record:	11	8	1	2	31	6
Arsenal's away league record:	11	3	0	8	12	25
TOTAL	**22**	**11**	**1**	**10**	**43**	**31**

FACT FILE

- **In 1901, Burton Swifts and Burton Wanderers amalgamated to form Burton United. As Swifts were in the league at the time and Wanderers weren't, I have included the United records with the Swifts records. Burton United were disbanded in 1910.**
- **Arsenal won six matches in a row from 1897 to 1899.**
- **Arsenal lost their last five away games.**

Arsenal's top scorers vs Swifts/United

Tommy Briercliffe 5
Adam Haywood, Peter Mortimer 4
Bob Buchanan, Alex Caie, Tim Coleman, Davy Hannah 3

Arsenal hat-tricks vs United

19 Sep 1903 Tommy Briercliffe

Played for both clubs

Arthur Worrall	Burton Swifts 1892-93	Arsenal 1893-94
Charlie Satterthwaite	Burton Swifts 1897-98	Arsenal 1904-10
Fergus Hunt	Arsenal 1897-1903	Burton United 1905-07
Will Bradshaw	Arsenal 1902-04	Burton United 1905-07

v. Burton Wanderers

		Home					Away			Final Positions	
Season	League	Date	Result	Arsenal	Burton W	Date	Result	Arsenal	Burton W	Arsenal	Burton W
1894-95	Division 2	26 January	Drew	**1**	**1**	20 April	Lost	**1**	**2**	8th	7th
1895-96	Division 2	12 October	Won	**3**	**0**	14 December	Lost	**1**	**4**	7th	4th
1896-97	Division 2	12 October	Won	**3**	**0**	14 September	Won	**3**	**0**	10th	15thF

Summary	P	W	D	L	F	A
Arsenal's home league record:	3	2	1	0	7	1
Arsenal's away league record:	3	1	0	2	5	6
TOTAL	**6**	**3**	**1**	**2**	**12**	**7**

Arsenal's top scorers vs Wanderers

Henry Boyd 4

Played for both clubs

Allen Ward	Burton Wanderers 1894-95	Arsenal 1895-96
Adam Haywood	Burton Wanderers 1894-95	Arsenal 1895-99

Woolwich Arsenal in 1895. Back row, left to right: James Boyle, Joe Powell, Harry Storer, Jock Caldwell, Hollis (trainer.) Middle row: Fred Davis, Caesar Jenkyns, Allen Ward. Front row: Sam Mills, Charlie Hare, Bob Buchanan, Pat O'Brien, Peter Mortimer.

v. Bury

		Home					Away			Final Positions	
Season	League	Date	Result	Arsenal	Bury	Date	Result	Arsenal	Bury	Arsenal	Bury
1894-95	Division 2	22 September	Won	**4**	**2**	2 March	Lost	**0**	**2**	8th	1stP
1904-05	Division 1	28 January	Won	**2**	**1**	1 October	Drew	**1**	**1**	10th	17th
1905-06	Division 1	14 April	Won	**4**	**0**	9 December	Lost	**0**	**2**	12th	17th
1906-07	Division 1	26 December	Won	**3**	**1**	3 September	Lost	**1**	**4**	7th	16th
1907-08	Division 1	5 October	Drew	**0**	**0**	9 September	Lost	**2**	**3**	14th=	7th
1908-09	Division 1	24 October	Won	**4**	**0**	27 February	Drew	**1**	**1**	6th	17th
1909-10	Division 1	9 April	Drew	**0**	**0**	27 November	Won	**2**	**1**	18th	13th
1910-11	Division 1	31 December	Won	**3**	**2**	3 September	Drew	**1**	**1**	10th	18th
1911-12	Division 1	13 April	Won	**1**	**0**	9 December	Lost	**1**	**3**	10th	20thR
1913-14	Division 2	4 October	Lost	**0**	**1**	7 February	Drew	**1**	**1**	3rd	10th
1914-15	Division 2	10 April	Won	**3**	**1**	5 December	Lost	**1**	**3**	5thP	11th
1924-25	Division 1	13 October	Lost	**0**	**1**	2 May	Lost	**0**	**2**	20th	5th
1925-26	Division 1	14 November	Won	**6**	**1**	27 March	Drew	**2**	**2**	2nd	4th
1926-27	Division 1	4 December	Won	**1**	**0**	4 May	Lost	**2**	**3**	11th	19th
1927-28	Division 1	31 December	Won	**3**	**1**	27 August	Lost	**1**	**5**	10th	5th
1928-29	Division 1	30 March	Won	**7**	**1**	17 November	Lost	**0**	**1**	9th	21stR

FA Cup										*Division*	
1952-53	Round 4	31 January	Won	**6**	**2**					Div 1	Div 2
1958-59	Round 3					10 January	Won	**1**	**0**	Div 1	Div 3

Summary	P	W	D	L	F	A
Arsenal's home league record:	16	12	2	2	41	12
Arsenal's away league record:	16	1	5	10	16	35
Arsenal's cup record:	2	2	0	0	7	2
TOTAL	**34**	**15**	**7**	**12**	**64**	**49**

FACT FILE

- **There have been only three away wins in 32 league meetings between the sides.**
- **Arsenal were unbeaten in their first nine home games.**
- **Bury are unbeaten in their last nine home league games.**
- **The only league double by either side was achieved by Bury in 1924-25.**

Arsenal's top scorers vs Bury

Jimmy Brain, Charlie Satterthwaite 6
David Jack, Peter Kyle 4
Andy Ducat, Joe Hulme, Sam Raybould 3

Arsenal hat-tricks vs Bury

24 Oct 1908 Sam Raybould
14 Nov 1925 Jimmy Brain
30 Mar 1929 David Jack (4)

Played for both clubs

Charlie Satterthwaite	Bury 1895-96	Arsenal 1904-10
Jim Smith	Bury 1903-05	Arsenal 1920-21
James Bigden	Arsenal 1904-08	Bury 1908-09
Harold Lee	Arsenal 1907-10	Bury 1909-12
Albert Beney	Arsenal 1908-10	Bury 1910-12
Bert Humpish	Bury 1924-25	Arsenal 1929-30
Peter Dougal	Arsenal 1933-36	Bury 1938-39
Peter Tilley	Arsenal 1953-54	Bury 1953-58
Pat Howard	Arsenal 1976-77	Bury 1979-82
Trevor Ross	Arsenal 1974-78	Bury 1984-87
Lee Dixon	Bury 1985-86	Arsenal 1987-2002

Former Arsenal player Ray Kennedy, now playing for Liverpool, shields the ball from the Gunners' Trevor Ross at Highbury in November 1976. The game ended 1-1. Ross played for three seasons with Bury.

v. Cambridge United

FA Cup		Date	Home Result	Arsenal	Cambridge	Division Arsenal	Cambridge
1990-91	Q'ter Final	9 March	Won	**2**	**1**	Div 1	Div 3

Summary	P	W	D	L	F	A
Arsenal's cup record:	1	1	0	0	2	1
TOTAL	**1**	**1**	**0**	**0**	**2**	**1**

FACT FILE

- **Kevin Campbell and Tony Adams scored to keep Arsenal's hopes of the double alive.**

Played for both clubs

Malcolm Webster	Arsenal 1969-70	Cambridge United 1976-84
Brendan Batson	Arsenal 1971-74	Cambridge United 1973-78
Danny O'Shea	Arsenal 1982-83	Cambridge United 1989-95
Neil Heaney	Cambridge United 1991-92	Arsenal 1991-94

Tony Adams scored the winner in the hard-fought victory over third division Cambridge United.

v. Cardiff City

Season	League	Date	Result	Home Arsenal	Home Cardiff	Date	Result	Away Arsenal	Away Cardiff	Final Positions Arsenal	Final Positions Cardiff
1921-22	Division 1	26 December	Drew	0	0	27 December	Lost	3	4	17th	4th
1922-23	Division 1	16 September	Won	2	1	9 September	Lost	1	4	11th	9th
1923-24	Division 1	19 January	Lost	1	2	26 January	Lost	0	4	19th	2nd
1924-25	Division 1	4 April	Drew	1	1	29 November	Drew	1	1	20th	11th
1925-26	Division 1	17 October	Won	5	0	27 February	Drew	0	0	2nd	16th
1926-27	Division 1	1 January	Won	3	2	27 December	Lost	0	2	11th	14th
1927-28	Division 1	6 April	Won	3	0	9 April	Drew	2	2	10th	6th
1928-29	Division 1	16 March	Won	2	1	3 November	Drew	1	1	9th	22ndR
1952-53	Division 1	7 March	Lost	0	1	22 April	Drew	0	0	1st	12th
1953-54	Division 1	13 February	Drew	1	1	26 September	Won	3	0	12th	10th
1954-55	Division 1	8 April	Won	2	0	11 April	Won	2	1	9th	20th
1955-56	Division 1	23 August	Won	3	1	28 April	Won	2	1	5th	17th
1956-57	Division 1	18 August	Drew	0	0	15 December	Won	3	2	5th	21stR
1960-61	Division 1	11 February	Lost	2	3	24 September	Lost	0	1	11th	15th
1961-62	Division 1	17 March	Drew	1	1	28 October	Drew	1	1	10th	21stR

FA Cup

Season	Round	Date	Result	Home Arsenal	Home Cardiff	Date	Result	Away Arsenal	Away Cardiff	Division Arsenal	Division Cardiff
1923-24	Round 2					2 February	Lost	0	1	Div 1	Div 1
1926-27	Final	23 April		Wembley			Lost	0	1	Div 1	Div 1
1954-55	Round 3	8 January	Won	1	0					Div 1	Div 1
1968-69	Round 3	7 January	Won	2	0	4 January	Drew	0	0	Div 1	Div 2
1979-80	Round 3	8 January	Won	2	1	5 January	Drew	0	0	Div 1	Div 2

League Cup

Season	Round	Date	Result	Home Arsenal	Home Cardiff	Date	Result	Away Arsenal	Away Cardiff	Division Arsenal	Division Cardiff
1982-83	Round 2	5 October	Won	2	1	26 October	Won	3	1	Div 1	Div 3

Summary	P	W	D	L	F	A
Arsenal's home league record:	15	7	5	3	26	14
Arsenal's away league record:	15	4	6	5	19	24
Arsenal's cup record:	9	5	2	2	10	5
TOTAL	**39**	**16**	**13**	**10**	**55**	**43**

One of the most famous goals in FA Cup Final history. Arsenal's Dan Lewis lets a long shot from Hughie Ferguson slip under his body and out of his grasp and Cardiff City are on their way to an historic victory at Wembley in 1927.

FACT FILE

- **Arsenal's first cup final was against Cardiff in 1927. Danny Lewis, a fine goalkeeper for Arsenal, is chiefly remembered for allowing a weak shot to squirm under his body to gift Cardiff the cup. It is the only time the cup has been won by a team from outside England.**
- **All of Arsenal's visits to Cardiff nowadays are to play cup finals and Community Shield matches.**
- **Arsenal failed to win in their first 10 away matches.**
- **Cardiff are undefeated in their last four league matches.**
- **Arsenal are undefeated in their last eight matches overall.**

Arsenal's top scorers vs Cardiff

Jimmy Brain 9
David Herd, Tommy Lawton, Doug Lishman 4
Reginald Boreham, Alan Sunderland, Derek Tapscott 3

Arsenal's hat-tricks vs Cardiff

17 Oct 1925 Jimmy Brain
1 Jan 1927 Jimmy Brain
23 Aug 1955 Tommy Lawton

Played for both clubs

Fred Pagnam	Arsenal 1919-21	Cardiff City 1920-22
Charlie Jones	Cardiff City 1920-21	Arsenal 1928-34
Les Jones	Cardiff City 1929-34	Arsenal 1937-40
Ray Daniel	Arsenal 1948-53	Cardiff City 1957-58
Mike Tiddy	Cardiff City 1950-55	Arsenal 1955-58
Brian Walsh	Arsenal 1953-56	Cardiff City 1955-62
Gordon Nutt	Cardiff City 1954-56	Arsenal 1955-60
Derek Tapscott	Arsenal 1953-58	Cardiff City 1958-65
Mel Charles	Arsenal 1959-62	Cardiff City 1961-65
George Johnston	Cardiff City 1964-67	Arsenal 1967-69
Brian McDermott	Arsenal 1978-84	Cardiff City 1987-89
George Wood	Arsenal 1980-83	Cardiff City 1987-90
Paul Shaw	Arsenal 1994-97	Cardiff City 1995-96
Rhys Weston	Arsenal 1999-2000	Cardiff City 2000-04
Julian Gray	Arsenal 1999-2000	Cardiff City 2003-04

v. Carlisle United

			Home					Away		Final Positions	
Season	League	Date	Result	Arsenal	Carlisle	Date	Result	Arsenal	Carlisle	Arsenal	Carlisle
1974-75	Division 1	11 January	Won	**2**	**1**	7 December	Lost	**1**	**2**	16th	22ndR

FA Cup

										Division	
1950-51	Round 3	6 January	Drew	**0**	**0**	11 January	Won	**4**	**1**	Div 1	Div 3N
1972-73	Round 5					24 February	Won	**2**	**1**	Div 1	Div 2
2000-01	Round 3					6 January	Won	**1**	**0**	Prem	Div 3

League Cup

1976-77	Round 2	31 August	Won	**3**	**2**					Div 1	Div 2

Summary	P	W	D	L	F	A
Arsenal's home league record:	1	1	0	0	2	1
Arsenal's away league record:	1	0	0	1	1	2
Arsenal's cup record:	5	4	1	0	10	4
TOTAL	**7**	**5**	**1**	**1**	**13**	**7**

FACT FILE

- **Arsenal have won the last three meetings.**

Arsenal's top scorers vs Carlisle

Reg Lewis, Trevor Ross 2

Played for both clubs

Bill Henderson	Arsenal 1921-23	Carlisle United 1929-30
Joey Williams	Arsenal 1929-32	Carlisle United 1935-37
Brian Hornsby	Arsenal 1972-76	Carlisle United 1982-84
Paul Gorman	Arsenal 1981-84	Carlisle United 1984-90/91-92
Adrian Clarke	Arsenal 1994-97	Carlisle United 1999-2000
Tommy Black	Arsenal 1999-2000	Carlisle United 1999-2000

v. Charlton Athletic

Season	League	Home Date	Home Result	Home Arsenal	Home Charlton	Away Date	Away Result	Away Arsenal	Away Charlton	Final Positions Arsenal	Final Positions Charlton
1936-37	Division 1	24 February	Drew	**1**	**1**	17 October	Won	**2**	**0**	3rd	2nd
1937-38	Division 1	2 April	Drew	**2**	**2**	20 November	Won	**3**	**0**	1st	4th
1938-39	Division 1	21 January	Won	**2**	**0**	26 December	Lost	**0**	**1**	5th	3rd
1946-47	Division 1	14 December	Won	**1**	**0**	19 April	Drew	**2**	**2**	13th	19th
1947-48	Division 1	3 September	Won	**6**	**0**	27 August	Won	**4**	**2**	1st	13th
1948-49	Division 1	7 May	Won	**2**	**0**	11 December	Lost	**3**	**4**	5th	9th
1949-50	Division 1	19 November	Lost	**2**	**3**	11 March	Drew	**1**	**1**	6th	20th
1950-51	Division 1	24 February	Lost	**2**	**5**	7 October	Won	**3**	**1**	5th	17th
1951-52	Division 1	13 March	Won	**2**	**1**	20 October	Won	**3**	**1**	3rd	10th
1952-53	Division 1	13 September	Lost	**3**	**4**	24 January	Drew	**2**	**2**	1st	5th
1953-54	Division 1	13 March	Drew	**3**	**3**	24 October	Won	**5**	**1**	12th	9th
1954-55	Division 1	11 December	Won	**3**	**1**	5 March	Drew	**1**	**1**	9th	15th
1955-56	Division 1	29 October	Lost	**2**	**4**	10 March	Lost	**0**	**2**	5th	14th
1956-57	Division 1	20 April	Won	**3**	**1**	13 October	Won	**3**	**1**	5th	22ndR
1986-87	Division 1	11 April	Won	**2**	**1**	1 November	Won	**2**	**0**	4th	19th
1987-88	Division 1	27 February	Won	**4**	**0**	3 October	Won	**3**	**0**	6th	17th
1988-89	Division 1	21 March	Drew	**2**	**2**	26 December	Won	**3**	**2**	1st	14th
1989-90	Division 1	23 September	Won	**1**	**0**	27 February	Drew	**0**	**0**	4th	19thR
1998-99	Prem'ship	29 August	Drew	**0**	**0**	28 December	Won	**1**	**0**	2nd	18thR
2000-01	Prem'ship	26 August	Won	**5**	**3**	1 January	Lost	**0**	**1**	2nd	9th
2001-02	Prem'ship	4 November	Lost	**2**	**4**	1 April	Won	**3**	**0**	1st	14th
2002-03	Prem'ship	2 March	Won	**2**	**0**	14 September	Won	**3**	**0**	2nd	12th
2003-04	Prem'ship	28 February	Won	**2**	**1**	26 October	Drew	**1**	**1**	1st	7th

FA Cup

Season	Round	Home Date	Home Result	Arsenal	Charlton	Away Date	Away Result	Arsenal	Charlton	Division Arsenal	Division Charlton
1955-56	Round 5					18 February	Won	**2**	**0**	Div 1	Div 1
1968-69	Round 4	25 January	Won	**2**	**0**					Div 1	Div 2

League Cup

Season	Round	Home Date	Home Result	Arsenal	Charlton	Division Arsenal	Division Charlton
1986-87	Round 4	18 November	Won	**2**	**0**	Div 1	Div 1

Summary	P	W	D	L	F	A
Arsenal's home league record:	23	13	5	5	54	36
Arsenal's away league record:	23	13	6	4	48	23
Arsenal's cup record:	3	3	0	0	6	0
TOTAL	**49**	**29**	**11**	**9**	**108**	**59**

FACT FILE

- **Arsenal were undefeated in 15 matches from 1956 to 2000.**
- **Arsenal lost once in 14 away matches from 1950 to 1998.**
- **Arsenal have never gone more than two matches without a win.**
- **Charlton last finished higher than Arsenal in 1954.**

Arsenal's top scorers vs Charlton

Thierry Henry 9
Reg Lewis, Don Roper 8
Peter Goring 6
Cliff Holton 5
Doug Lishman, Derek Tapscott 4

Arsenal hat-tricks vs Charlton

3 Sep 1947 Reg Lewis (4)
24 Oct 1953 Ben Marden

Played for both clubs

Angus McKinnon	Arsenal 1908-22	Charlton Athletic 1922-23
Arthur Hutchins	Arsenal 1919-23	Charlton Athletic 1923-24
Fred Jones	Arsenal 1923-24	Charlton Athletic 1925-26
Bobby Turnbull	Arsenal 1921-25	Charlton Athletic 1924-25
Reg Tricker	Charlton Athletic 1925-27	Arsenal 1926-29
Charlie Preedy	Charlton Athletic 1923-28	Arsenal 1929-33
Gerry Keizer	Arsenal 1930-31	Charlton Athletic 1931-32
Cliff Holton	Arsenal 1950-59	Charlton Athletic 1965-66
John Snedden	Arsenal 1959-65	Charlton Athletic 1964-66
Tony Burns	Arsenal 1964-66	Charlton Athletic 1968-70
Paul Davies	Arsenal 1971-72	Charlton Athletic 1972-75
Steve Gatting	Arsenal 1978-81	Charlton Athletic 1991-93
Danny O'Shea	Arsenal 1982-83	Charlton Athletic 1983-84
David Madden	Arsenal 1983-84	Charlton Athletic 1984-85
Chris Whyte	Arsenal 1981-86	Charlton Athletic 1995-96
Tommy Caton	Arsenal 1983-86	Charlton Athletic 1988-91
Colin Pates	Charlton Athletic 1988-90	Arsenal 1989-92

Arsenal, the defending league champions, in January 1949. Back row (left to right): Archie Macaulay, Wally Barnes, George Swindin, Billy Milne (trainer), Lionel Smith, Joe Mercer. Front row: Don Roper, Jimmy Logie, Ronnie Rooke, Doug Lishman, Ian McPherson, Leslie Compton.

v. Chatham

FA Cup		Date	Result	Home Arsenal	Home Chatham	Division Arsenal	Division Chatham
1896-97	5th Qual	2 January	Won	**4**	**0**	Div 2	Non L

Summary	P	W	D	L	F	A
Arsenal's cup record:	1	1	0	0	4	0
TOTAL	**1**	**1**	**0**	**0**	**4**	**0**

Arsenal's top scorers vs Chatham

Adam Haywood 2

Harry Storer was the first Arsenal player to gain senior representative honours when he played for the Football League aginst the Scottish League in 1895.

v. Chelsea

		Home					Away			Final Positions	
Season	*League*	*Date*	*Result*	Arsenal	Chelsea	*Date*	*Result*	Arsenal	Chelsea	Arsenal	Chelsea
1907-08	Division 1	7 March	Drew	**0**	**0**	9 November	Lost	**1**	**2**	14th=	13th
1908-09	Division 1	3 April	Drew	**0**	**0**	28 November	Won	**2**	**1**	6th	11th
1909-10	Division 1	25 September	Won	**3**	**2**	28 March	Won	**1**	**0**	18th	19thR
1912-13	Division 1	12 October	Lost	**0**	**1**	15 February	Drew	**1**	**1**	20thR	18th
1919-20	Division 1	6 December	Drew	**1**	**1**	13 December	Lost	**1**	**3**	10th	3rd
1920-21	Division 1	11 December	Drew	**1**	**1**	4 December	Won	**2**	**1**	9th	18th
1921-22	Division 1	14 January	Won	**1**	**0**	31 December	Won	**2**	**0**	17th	9th
1922-23	Division 1	24 February	Won	**3**	**1**	17 February	Drew	**0**	**0**	11th	19th
1923-24	Division 1	29 December	Won	**1**	**0**	5 January	Drew	**0**	**0**	19th	21stR
1930-31	Division 1	4 April	Won	**2**	**1**	29 November	Won	**5**	**1**	1st	12th
1931-32	Division 1	2 April	Drew	**1**	**1**	21 November	Lost	**1**	**2**	2nd	12th
1932-33	Division 1	10 December	Won	**4**	**1**	22 April	Won	**3**	**1**	1st	18th
1933-34	Division 1	16 December	Won	**2**	**1**	28 April	Drew	**2**	**2**	1st	19th
1934-35	Division 1	6 April	Drew	**2**	**2**	24 November	Won	**5**	**2**	1st	12th
1935-36	Division 1	27 April	Drew	**1**	**1**	12 October	Drew	**1**	**1**	6th	8th
1936-37	Division 1	19 December	Won	**4**	**1**	24 April	Lost	**0**	**2**	3rd	13th
1937-38	Division 1	19 February	Won	**2**	**0**	9 October	Drew	**2**	**2**	1st	10th
1938-39	Division 1	18 February	Won	**1**	**0**	15 October	Lost	**2**	**4**	5th	20th
1946-47	Division 1	1 March	Lost	**1**	**2**	26 October	Lost	**1**	**2**	13th	15th
1947-48	Division 1	20 March	Lost	**0**	**2**	1 November	Drew	**0**	**0**	1st	18th
1948-49	Division 1	23 April	Lost	**1**	**2**	30 October	Won	**1**	**0**	5th	13th
1949-50	Division 1	31 August	Lost	**2**	**3**	24 August	Won	**2**	**1**	6th	13th
1950-51	Division 1	23 August	Drew	**0**	**0**	30 August	Won	**1**	**0**	5th	20th
1951-52	Division 1	29 August	Won	**2**	**1**	22 August	Won	**3**	**1**	3rd	19th
1952-53	Division 1	6 April	Won	**2**	**0**	3 April	Drew	**1**	**1**	1st	19th
1953-54	Division 1	8 September	Lost	**1**	**2**	15 September	Won	**2**	**0**	12th	8th
1954-55	Division 1	25 December	Won	**1**	**0**	27 December	Drew	**1**	**1**	9th	1st
1955-56	Division 1	27 August	Drew	**1**	**1**	24 December	Lost	**0**	**2**	5th	16th
1956-57	Division 1	26 December	Won	**2**	**0**	25 December	Drew	**1**	**1**	5th	12th=
1957-58	Division 1	8 March	Won	**5**	**4**	26 October	Drew	**0**	**0**	12th	11th
1958-59	Division 1	11 April	Drew	**1**	**1**	22 November	Won	**3**	**0**	3rd	14th
1959-60	Division 1	9 April	Lost	**1**	**4**	21 November	Won	**3**	**1**	13th	18th
1960-61	Division 1	12 November	Lost	**1**	**4**	15 April	Lost	**1**	**3**	11th	12th
1961-62	Division 1	4 November	Lost	**0**	**3**	24 March	Won	**3**	**2**	10th	22ndR
1963-64	Division 1	14 March	Lost	**2**	**4**	16 November	Lost	**1**	**3**	8th	5th
1964-65	Division 1	26 September	Lost	**1**	**3**	6 February	Lost	**1**	**2**	13th	3rd
1965-66	Division 1	4 September	Lost	**1**	**3**	19 February	Drew	**0**	**0**	14th	5th
1966-67	Division 1	4 February	Won	**2**	**1**	24 September	Lost	**1**	**3**	7th	9th
1967-68	Division 1	30 December	Drew	**1**	**1**	26 December	Lost	**1**	**2**	9th	6th
1968-69	Division 1	23 November	Lost	**0**	**1**	14 April	Lost	**1**	**2**	4th	5th
1969-70	Division 1	17 January	Lost	**0**	**3**	27 September	Lost	**0**	**3**	12th	3rd
1970-71	Division 1	3 April	Won	**2**	**0**	29 August	Lost	**1**	**2**	1st	6th
1971-72	Division 1	14 August	Won	**3**	**0**	16 October	Won	**2**	**1**	5th	7th
1972-73	Division 1	2 September	Drew	**1**	**1**	20 January	Won	**1**	**0**	2nd	12th

		Home						Away			Final Positions	
Season	League	Date	Result	Arsenal	Chelsea	Date	Result	Arsenal	Chelsea		Arsenal	Chelsea
1973-74	Division 1	17 November	Drew	**0**	**0**	13 April	Won	**3**	**1**		10th	17th
1974-75	Division 1	26 December	Lost	**1**	**2**	14 September	Drew	**0**	**0**		16th	21stR
1977-78	Division 1	26 December	Won	**3**	**0**	27 March	Drew	**0**	**0**		5th	16th
1978-79	Division 1	16 April	Won	**5**	**2**	14 May	Drew	**1**	**1**		7th	22ndR
1984-85	Division 1	25 August	Drew	**1**	**1**	19 January	Drew	**1**	**1**		7th	6th
1985-86	Division 1	29 April	Won	**2**	**0**	21 September	Lost	**1**	**2**		7th	6th
1986-87	Division 1	25 October	Won	**3**	**1**	7 March	Lost	**0**	**1**		4th	14th
1987-88	Division 1	3 November	Won	**3**	**1**	2 April	Drew	**1**	**1**		6th	18thR
1989-90	Division 1	17 March	Lost	**0**	**1**	30 September	Drew	**0**	**0**		4th	5th
1990-91	Division 1	15 September	Won	**4**	**1**	2 February	Lost	**1**	**2**		1st	11th
1991-92	Division 1	5 October	Won	**3**	**2**	25 April	Drew	**1**	**1**		4th	14th
1992-93	Prem'ship	3 October	Won	**2**	**1**	1 March	Lost	**0**	**1**		10th	11th
1993-94	Prem'ship	16 April	Won	**1**	**0**	20 November	Won	**2**	**0**		4th	14th
1994-95	Prem'ship	15 October	Won	**3**	**1**	14 May	Lost	**1**	**2**		12th	11th
1995-96	Prem'ship	16 December	Drew	**1**	**1**	30 September	Lost	**0**	**1**		5th	11th
1996-97	Prem'ship	3 September	Drew	**3**	**3**	5 April	Won	**3**	**0**		3rd	6th
1997-98	Prem'ship	8 February	Won	**2**	**0**	21 September	Won	**3**	**2**		1st	4th
1998-99	Prem'ship	31 January	Won	**1**	**0**	9 September	Drew	**0**	**0**		2nd	3rd
1999-00	Prem'ship	6 May	Won	**2**	**1**	23 October	Won	**3**	**2**		2nd	5th
2000-01	Prem'ship	13 January	Drew	**1**	**1**	6 September	Drew	**2**	**2**		2nd	6th
2001-02	Prem'ship	26 December	Won	**2**	**1**	8 September	Drew	**1**	**1**		1st	6th
2002-03	Prem'ship	1 January	Won	**3**	**2**	1 September	Drew	**1**	**1**		2nd	4th
2003-04	Prem'ship	18 October	Won	**2**	**1**	21 February	Won	**2**	**1**		1st	2nd

FA Cup

										Division	
1914-15	Round 2					30 January	Lost	**0**	**1**	Div 2	Div 1
1929-30	Round 3	11 January	Won	**2**	**0**					Div 1	Div 2
1930-31	Round 4					24 January	Lost	**1**	**2**	Div 1	Div 1
1938-39	Round 3					7 January	Lost	**1**	**2**	Div 1	Div 1
1946-47	Round 3	15 January	Drew	**1**	**1**	11 January	Drew	**1**	**1**	Div 1	Div 1
		20 January		Tottenham (2nd replay)			Lost	**0**	**2**		
1949-50	Semi Final	18 March		Tottenham			Drew	**2**	**2**	Div 1	Div 1
		22 March		Tottenham (replay)			Won*	**1**	**0**		
1951-52	Semi Final	5 April		Tottenham			Drew	**1**	**1**	Div 1	Div 1
		7 April		Tottenham (replay)			Won	**3**	**0**		
1972-73	Q'ter Final	20 March	Won	**2**	**1**	17 March	Drew	**2**	**2**	Div 1	Div 1
2000-01	Round 5	18 February	Won	**3**	**1**					Prem	Prem
2001-02	Final	4 May		Millennium Stadium			Won	**2**	**0**	Prem	Prem
2002-03	Q'ter Final	8 March	Drew	**2**	**2**	25 March	Won	**3**	**1**	Prem	Prem
2003-04	Round 5	15 February	Won	**2**	**1**					Prem	Prem

League Cup

1976-77	Round 4	26 October	Won	**2**	**1**					Div 1	Div 2
1997-98	Semi Final	28 January	Won	**2**	**1**	18 February	Lost	**1**	**3**	Prem	Prem
1998-99	Round 4	11 November	Lost	**0**	**5**					Prem	Prem

European Cup

2003-04	Q'ter Final	6 April	Lost	**1**	**2**	24 March	Drew	**1**	**1**	Prem	Prem

FACT FILE

- **Arsenal are undefeated in their last 17 league matches. They have also won four FA Cup ties in this time, but lost two league cup ties and one Champions' League tie.**
- **Arsenal have knocked Chelsea out of the FA Cup in each of the last four seasons.**
- **Chelsea's 5-0 win at Highbury in 1998 was Arsenal's worst home defeat since 1925 (when they lost to Huddersfield).**
- **In winning the title in 1990-91, Arsenal lost just one league match all season, the best such record since 1889 at the time. That one defeat came at the hands of Chelsea.**
- **In the 2002 FA Cup Final, Freddie Ljungberg became the first player for 40 years to score in two consecutive cup finals.**
- **Arsenal have not lost in their last 13 home league games.**
- **Arsenal lost six home games in a row from 1960 to 1965.**
- **Arsenal failed to win in 11 visits to Stamford Bridge between 1974 and 1993.**
- **Arsenal were undefeated in 15 games at home from 1919 to 1939.**
- **Arsenal's last ever Christmas Day fixture was against Chelsea in 1956.**

Summary	P	W	D	L	F	A
Arsenal's home league record:	67	34	17	16	111	83
Arsenal's away league record:	67	23	23	21	90	81
Arsenal's cup record:	24	10	7	7	36	33
TOTAL	**158**	**67**	**47**	**44**	**237**	**197**

Arsenal's top scorers vs Chelsea

Cliff Bastin, Ray Kennedy 9
Ted Drake, Thierry Henry, Ian Wright 8
Freddie Cox, Doug Lishman 6
Dennis Bergkamp, David Jack, Alf Kirchen 5

Arsenal hat-tricks vs Chelsea

29 Nov 1930 David Jack
24 Nov 1934 Ted Drake (4)
8 Mar 1958 David Herd
23 Oct 1999 Nwankwo Kanu

Played for both clubs

Jimmy Sharp	Arsenal 1905-08	Chelsea 1912-15
Bobby Turnbull	Arsenal 1921-25	Chelsea 1924-28
Tommy Lawton	Chelsea 1946-48	Arsenal 1953-56
Bill Dickson	Chelsea 1947-53	Arsenal 1953-56
Tommy Docherty	Arsenal 1958-61	Chelsea 1961-62
Alan Young	Arsenal 1960-61	Chelsea 1961-67
George Graham	Chelsea 1964-67	Arsenal 1966-73
Tommy Baldwin	Arsenal 1964-67	Chelsea 1966-75
Alan Hudson	Chelsea 1968-74	Arsenal 1976-78
John Hollins	Chelsea 1963-75/83-84	Arsenal 1979-83
Peter Nicholas	Arsenal 1980-83	Chelsea 1988-91
Colin Pates	Chelsea 1979-89	Arsenal 1989-92
David Rocastle	Arsenal 1985-92	Chelsea 1994-96
Emmanuel Petit	Arsenal 1997-2000	Chelsea 2001-04

v. Chester City

				Home				Away		Division	
League Cup		*Date*	*Result*	Arsenal	Chester C	*Date*	*Result*	Arsenal	Chester C	Arsenal	Chester C
1990-91	Round 2	9 October	Won	**5**	**0**	25 September	Won	**1**	**0**	Div 1	Div 3

Summary	P	W	D	L	F	A
Arsenal's cup record:	2	2	0	0	6	0
TOTAL	**2**	**2**	**0**	**0**	**6**	**0**

Arsenal's top scorers vs Chester

Perry Groves, Paul Merson 2

Played for both clubs

Brian Hornsby	Arsenal 1972-76	Chester City 1981-82
Lee Dixon	Chester City 1983-85	Arsenal 1987-2002

Having won the League Cup Round Two first leg 1-0, Arsenal comfortably swept aside Chester City and Paul Merson scored two of those goals against the Blues.

v. Chesterfield

		Home					Away			Final Positions	
Season	League	Date	Result	Arsenal	Chester'fd	Date	Result	Arsenal	Chester'fd	Arsenal	Chester'fd
1899-00	Division 2	10 February	Won	**2**	**0**	7 October	Lost	**1**	**3**	8th	7th
1900-01	Division 2	29 September	Won	**1**	**0**	19 February	Won	**1**	**0**	7th	14th
1901-02	Division 2	5 October	Won	**3**	**2**	1 February	Won	**3**	**1**	4th	16th
1902-03	Division 2	10 April	Won	**3**	**0**	14 March	Drew	**2**	**2**	3rd	6th
1903-04	Division 2	21 November	Won	**6**	**0**	19 March	Lost	**0**	**1**	2ndP	11th

FA Cup						Division	
1936-37	Round 3	16 January	Won	**5**	**1**	Div 1	Div 2

Summary	P	W	D	L	F	A
Arsenal's home league record:	5	5	0	0	15	2
Arsenal's away league record:	5	2	1	2	7	7
Arsenal's cup record:	1	1	0	0	5	1
TOTAL	**11**	**8**	**1**	**2**	**27**	**10**

FACT FILE

- **Arsenal have a 100% record at home.**

Arsenal's top scorers vs Chesterfield

Tim Coleman 3

Tommy Briercliffe, John Dick, Ted Drake, Bill Gooing, Alf Kirchen, Sandy Main, Tommy Shanks 2

Played for both clubs

Andy McCowie	Arsenal 1899-1901	Chesterfield 1901-02
Bill Gooing	Chesterfield 1899-1902	Arsenal 1901-05
Harry Thorpe	Chesterfield 1900-03	Arsenal 1903-04
Alfred Fletcher	Arsenal 1914-15	Chesterfield 1921-22
Jack Lee	Arsenal 1926-27	Chesterfield 1928-33
Jack Moody	Arsenal 1926-28	Chesterfield 1933-39
George Hunt	Chesterfield 1929-30	Arsenal 1937-38
Brian Hornsby	Arsenal 1972-76	Chesterfield 1983-84
John Matthews	Arsenal 1974-78	Chesterfield 1984-85

v. City Ramblers

FA Cup		Date	Result	Home Arsenal	Home Ramblers	Division Arsenal	Division Ramblers
1893	2nd Qual	29 October	Won	**10**	**1**	Non L	Non L

Summary	P	W	D	L	F	A
Arsenal's cup record:	1	1	0	0	10	1
TOTAL	**1**	**1**	**0**	**0**	**10**	**1**

FACT FILE

- **This is the only match in which three Arsenal players have claimed hat-tricks.**

Arsenal's top scorers vs City Ramblers

Charles Booth, Arthur Elliott, James Henderson 3

Arsenal hat-tricks vs City Ramblers

29 Oct 1892 Charles Booth (cup)
29 Oct 1892 Arthur Elliott (cup)
29 Oct 1892 James Henderson (cup)

v. Clapton

FA Cup		Date	Result	Home Arsenal	Home Clapton	Division Arsenal	Division Clapton
1893	4th Qual	10 December	Won	**3**	**0**	Non L	Non L

Summary	P	W	D	L	F	A
Arsenal's cup record:	1	1	0	0	3	0
TOTAL	**1**	**1**	**0**	**0**	**3**	**0**

FACT FILE

- **Clapton were drawn at home but gave up their right. Henderson, Booth and Crawford scored the goals.**

v. Colchester United

FA Cup		Home				Away				Division	
		Date	Result	Arsenal	Colchester	Date	Result	Arsenal	Colchester	Arsenal	Colchester
1958-59	Round 4	28 January	Won	**4**	**0**	24 January	Drew	**2**	**2**	Div 1	Div 3

Summary	P	W	D	L	F	A
Arsenal's cup record:	2	1	1	0	6	2
TOTAL	**2**	**1**	**1**	**0**	**6**	**2**

Arsenal's top scorers vs Colchester

Vic Groves, David Herd 2

Played for both clubs

Terry Anderson	Arsenal 1962-65	Colchester United 1973-74/75-76
Ian Allinson	Colchester United 1974-83/88-90	Arsenal 1983-87
Colin Hill	Arsenal 1982-85	Colchester United 1987-89
Perry Groves	Colchester United 1981-87	Arsenal 1986-92
Gus Caesar	Arsenal 1985-90	Colchester United 1994-97
Isaiah Rankin	Arsenal 1997-98	Colchester United 1997-98
Graham Barrett	Arsenal 1999-2000	Colchester United 2001-02

Gordon Banks makes an acrobatic stop for Leicester City at Highbury in February 1961. Arsenal centre-forward David Herd is to the extreme right of the picture and he tops the scoring chart, with Vic Groves, in their two clashes against Colchester United.

v. Coventry City

Season	League	Home Date	Home Result	Home Arsenal	Home Coventry	Away Date	Away Result	Away Arsenal	Away Coventry	Final Positions Arsenal	Final Positions Coventry
1967-68	Division 1	2 September	Drew	**1**	**1**	6 January	Drew	**1**	**1**	9th	20th
1968-69	Division 1	12 October	Won	**2**	**1**	14 December	Won	**1**	**0**	4th	20th
1969-70	Division 1	4 October	Lost	**0**	**1**	31 January	Lost	**0**	**2**	12th	6th
1970-71	Division 1	6 April	Won	**1**	**0**	24 October	Won	**3**	**1**	1st	10th
1971-72	Division 1	11 December	Won	**2**	**0**	1 May	Won	**1**	**0**	5th	18th
1972-73	Division 1	4 November	Lost	**0**	**2**	22 August	Drew	**1**	**1**	2nd	19th
1973-74	Division 1	1 December	Drew	**2**	**2**	27 April	Drew	**3**	**3**	10th	16th
1974-75	Division 1	8 April	Won	**2**	**0**	23 November	Lost	**0**	**3**	16th	14th
1975-76	Division 1	11 October	Won	**5**	**0**	13 March	Drew	**1**	**1**	17th	14th
1976-77	Division 1	23 April	Won	**2**	**0**	27 November	Won	**2**	**1**	8th	19th
1977-78	Division 1	12 November	Drew	**1**	**1**	17 December	Won	**2**	**1**	5th	7th
1978-79	Division 1	3 April	Drew	**1**	**1**	25 November	Drew	**1**	**1**	7th	10th
1979-80	Division 1	8 December	Won	**3**	**1**	3 May	Won	**1**	**0**	4th	15th
1980-81	Division 1	31 January	Drew	**2**	**2**	23 August	Lost	**1**	**3**	3rd	16th
1981-82	Division 1	31 October	Won	**1**	**0**	20 March	Lost	**0**	**1**	5th	14th
1982-83	Division 1	9 April	Won	**2**	**1**	11 September	Won	**2**	**0**	10th	19th
1983-84	Division 1	15 October	Lost	**0**	**1**	31 March	Won	**4**	**1**	6th	19th
1984-85	Division 1	2 February	Won	**2**	**1**	29 September	Won	**2**	**1**	7th	18th
1985-86	Division 1	23 March	Won	**3**	**0**	7 September	Won	**2**	**0**	7th	17th
1986-87	Division 1	18 January	Drew	**0**	**0**	26 August	Lost	**1**	**2**	4th	10th
1987-88	Division 1	2 May	Drew	**1**	**1**	13 December	Drew	**0**	**0**	6th	10th
1988-89	Division 1	29 October	Won	**2**	**0**	21 February	Lost	**0**	**1**	1st	7th
1989-90	Division 1	22 August	Won	**2**	**0**	9 December	Won	**1**	**0**	4th	12th
1990-91	Division 1	11 May	Won	**6**	**1**	3 November	Won	**2**	**0**	1st	16th
1991-92	Division 1	7 September	Lost	**1**	**2**	4 April	Won	**1**	**0**	4th	19th
1992-93	Prem'ship	7 November	Won	**3**	**0**	13 March	Won	**2**	**0**	10th	15th
1993-94	Prem'ship	14 August	Lost	**0**	**3**	4 December	Lost	**0**	**1**	4th	11th
1994-95	Prem'ship	23 October	Won	**2**	**1**	21 January	Won	**1**	**0**	12th	16th
1995-96	Prem'ship	3 February	Drew	**1**	**1**	26 August	Drew	**0**	**0**	5th	16th
1996-97	Prem'ship	19 October	Drew	**0**	**0**	21 April	Drew	**1**	**1**	3rd	17th
1997-98	Prem'ship	11 August	Won	**2**	**0**	17 January	Drew	**2**	**2**	1st	11th
1998-99	Prem'ship	21 March	Won	**2**	**0**	31 October	Won	**1**	**0**	2nd	15th
1999-00	Prem'ship	26 March	Won	**3**	**0**	26 December	Lost	**2**	**3**	2nd	14th
2000-01	Prem'ship	16 September	Won	**2**	**1**	3 February	Won	**1**	**0**	2nd	19thR

FA Cup

Season	Round	Home Date	Home Result	Arsenal	Coventry	Away Date	Away Result	Arsenal	Coventry	Division	
1974-75	Round 4	29 January	Won	**3**	**0**	25 January	Drew	**1**	**1**	Div 1	Div 1
1976-77	Round 4	29 January	Won	**3**	**1**					Div 1	Div 1

League Cup

Season	Round	Home Date	Home Result	Arsenal	Coventry	Away Date	Away Result	Arsenal	Coventry	Division	
1967-68	Round 2					12 September	Won	**2**	**1**	Div 1	Div 1
1991-92	Round 3					30 October	Lost	**0**	**1**	Div 1	Div 1
1997-98	Round 4	18 November	Won*	**1**	**0**					Prem	Prem

Summary	P	W	D	L	F	A
Arsenal's home league record:	34	20	9	5	59	25
Arsenal's away league record:	34	17	9	8	43	31
Arsenal's cup record:	6	4	1	1	10	4
TOTAL	**74**	**41**	**19**	**14**	**112**	**60**

FACT FILE

- **Arsenal have won their last five home matches, and are undefeated in their last eight.**
- **Arsenal lost one in 20 at home from 1973 to 1991.**
- **Arsenal have lost one of their last 15 matches with Coventry.**
- **Between 1989 and 1995, Arsenal conceded only one goal in seven league matches at Highfield Road.**

Arsenal's top scorers vs Coventry

Frank Stapleton 9
Ian Wright 7
Anders Limpar, John Radford, Tony Woodcock 5
Dennis Bergkamp, George Graham, Brian Kidd, Malcolm Macdonald 4

Arsenal hat-tricks vs Coventry

11 May 1991 Anders Limpar

Played for both clubs

Bill Henderson	Arsenal 1921-23	Coventry City 1928-29
Les Jones	Coventry City 1933-38	Arsenal 1937-40
Bobby Davidson	Arsenal 1934-38	Coventry City 1937-48
Gordon Nutt	Coventry City 1951-55	Arsenal 1955-60
Geoff Strong	Arsenal 1960-65	Coventry City 1970-72
Bobby Gould	Coventry City 1963-68	Arsenal 1967-70
Jeff Blockley	Coventry City 1968-73	Arsenal 1972-75
Chris Whyte	Arsenal 1981-86	Coventry City 1995-96
Stewart Robson	Arsenal 1981-87	Coventry City 1990-94
Kenny Sansom	Arsenal 1980-88	Coventry City 1990-93
Kevin Richardson	Arsenal 1987-90	Coventry City 1994-98
Alan Miller	Arsenal 1992-94	Coventry City 2000-01
John Hartson	Arsenal 1994-97	Coventry City 2000-01
Graham Barrett	Arsenal 1999-2000	Coventry City 2003-04

v. Crewe Alexandra

		Home				Away				Final Positions	
Season	*League*	*Date*	*Result*	Arsenal	Crewe	*Date*	*Result*	Arsenal	Crewe	Arsenal	Crewe
1893-94	Division 2	10 February	Won	**3**	**2**	3 March	Drew	**0**	**0**	9th	12th
1894-95	Division 2	6 April	Won	**7**	**0**	23 March	Drew	**0**	**0**	8th	16th
1895-96	Division 2	21 March	Won	**7**	**0**	23 December	Won	**1**	**0**	7th	16thF

Summary	P	W	D	L	F	A
Arsenal's home league record:	3	3	0	0	17	2
Arsenal's away league record:	3	1	2	0	1	0
TOTAL	**6**	**4**	**2**	**0**	**18**	**2**

FACT FILE

- **Arsenal have kept five clean sheets in six games, but the sides have not met since 1896.**

Arsenal's top scorers vs Crewe

Henry Boyd, James Henderson,
Peter Mortimer 3

Arsenal hat-tricks vs Crewe

10 Feb 1894 James Henderson
21 Mar 1896 Peter Mortimer

Played for both clubs

Wee Winship	Arsenal 1910-15	Crewe Alexandra 1926-27
Frank Hill	Arsenal 1932-36	Crewe Alexandra 1946-48
Peter Kane	Arsenal 1960-61	Crewe Alexandra 1963-67
Terry Anderson	Arsenal 1962-65	Crewe Alexandra 1974-75
Jimmy Robertson	Arsenal 1968-70	Crewe Alexandra 1978-79
Jimmy Harvey	Arsenal 1977-79	Crewe Alexandra 1992-93
David Platt	Crewe Alexandra 1984-88	Arsenal 1995-98
Graham Barrett	Arsenal 1999-2000	Crewe Alexandra 2001-02

v. Croydon Common

FA Cup		Home Date	Result	Arsenal	Croydon	Away Date	Result	Arsenal	Croydon	Division Arsenal	Croydon
1908-09	Round 1	20 January	Won	**2**	**0**	16 January	Drew	**1**	**1**	Div 1	Non L
1912-13	Round 1	15 January	Won	**2**	**1**	11 January	Drew	**0**	**0**	Div 1	Non L

1909 away match played at Crystal Palace

Summary	P	W	D	L	F	A
Arsenal's cup record:	4	2	2	0	5	2
TOTAL	**4**	**2**	**2**	**0**	**5**	**2**

v. Crusaders

FA Cup		Date	Result	Home Arsenal	Home Crusaders	Division Arsenal	Division Crusaders
1889-90	3rd Qual	16 November	Won*	**5**	**2**	Non L	Non L

Summary	P	W	D	L	F	A
Arsenal's cup record:	1	1	0	0	5	2
TOTAL	**1**	**1**	**0**	**0**	**5**	**2**

Arsenal's top scorers vs Crusaders

H.S. Robertson 2

FACT FILE

- **The Crusaders played in Leyton, Essex.**

v. Crystal Palace

Season	League	Home Date	Home Result	Arsenal	Palace	Away Date	Away Result	Arsenal	Palace	Final Positions Arsenal	Final Positions Palace
1969-70	Division 1	30 March	Won	2	0	1 November	Won	5	1	12th	20th
1970-71	Division 1	14 November	Drew	1	1	13 March	Won	2	0	1st	18th
1971-72	Division 1	27 November	Won	2	1	11 April	Drew	2	2	5th	20th
1972-73	Division 1	26 March	Won	1	0	21 October	Won	3	2	2nd	21stR
1979-80	Division 1	22 March	Drew	1	1	10 November	Lost	0	1	4th	13th
1980-81	Division 1	20 April	Won	3	2	26 December	Drew	2	2	3rd	22ndR
1989-90	Division 1	1 January	Won	4	1	14 April	Drew	1	1	4th	15th
1990-91	Division 1	23 February	Won	4	0	10 November	Drew	0	0	1st	3rd
1991-92	Division 1	11 April	Won	4	1	14 September	Won	4	1	4th	10th
1992-93	Prem'ship	8 May	Won	3	0	2 November	Won	2	1	10th	20thR
1994-95	Prem'ship	1 October	Lost	1	2	25 February	Won	3	0	12th	19thR
1997-98	Prem'ship	21 February	Won	1	0	18 October	Drew	0	0	1st	20thR

FA Cup

Season	Round	Home Date	Home Result	Arsenal	Palace	Away Date	Away Result	Arsenal	Palace	Division Arsenal	Division Palace
1933-34	Round 4	27 January	Won	7	0					Div 1	Div 3S
1997-98	Round 4	15 February	Drew	0	0	25 February	Won	2	1	Prem	Prem

League Cup

Season	Round	Home Date	Home Result	Arsenal	Palace	Away Date	Away Result	Arsenal	Palace	Division Arsenal	Division Palace
1970-71	Round 4	9 November	Lost	0	2	28 October	Drew	0	0	Div 1	Div 1
1992-93	Semi Final	10 March	Won	2	0	7 February	Won	3	1	Prem	Prem

Summary	P	W	D	L	F	A
Arsenal's home league record:	12	9	2	1	27	9
Arsenal's away league record:	12	6	5	1	24	11
Arsenal's cup record:	7	4	2	1	14	4
TOTAL	**31**	**19**	**9**	**3**	**65**	**24**

FACT FILE

- **Arsenal were undefeated in 10 home games from 1970 to 1993.**
- **Arsenal are undefeated in their last nine away games.**

Arsenal's top scorers vs Palace

John Radford 8

Paul Merson, Alan Smith 6

Kevin Campbell, Ian Wright 5

Arsenal hat-tricks vs Palace

1 Nov 1969 John Radford

11 Apr 1992 Paul Merson

Played for both clubs

Bobby Turnbull	Arsenal 1921-25	Crystal Palace 1932-33
Andy Kennedy	Crystal Palace 1920-22	Arsenal 1922-28
Len Thompson	Arsenal 1927-32	Crystal Palace 1933-34
Alfred Haynes	Arsenal 1929-34	Crystal Palace 1933-36
Ronnie Rooke	Crystal Palace 1933-37/49-51	Arsenal 1946-49
Dave Nelson	Arsenal 1936-47	Crystal Palace 1951-53
Noel Kelly	Arsenal 1949-50	Crystal Palace 1949-51
Laurie Scott	Arsenal 1946-52	Crystal Palace 1951-53
Cliff Holton	Arsenal 1950-59	Crystal Palace 1962-65
Tony Burns	Arsenal 1964-66	Crystal Palace 1974-78
George Graham	Arsenal 1966-73	Crystal Palace 1976-78
Kenny Sansom	Crystal Palace 1974-80	Arsenal 1980-88
Paul Barron	Arsenal 1978-80	Crystal Palace 1980-83
David Price	Arsenal 1972-81	Crystal Palace 1980-82
Peter Nicholas	Crystal Palace 1977-81/83-85	Arsenal 1980-83
George Wood	Arsenal 1980-83	Crystal Palace 1983-88
Brian Sparrow	Arsenal 1983-84	Crystal Palace 1984-87
David Madden	Arsenal 1983-84	Crystal Palace 1988-90
Chris Whyte	Arsenal 1981-86	Crystal Palace 1984-85
Rhys Wilmot	Arsenal 1985-87	Crystal Palace 1994-95
Ian Wright	Crystal Palace 1985-92	Arsenal 1991-98
Eddie McGoldrick	Crystal Palace 1988-93	Arsenal 1993-96
Andy Linighan	Arsenal 1990-97	Crystal Palace 1997-2001
Ashley Cole	Crystal Palace 1999-2000	Arsenal 1999-2004
Julian Gray	Arsenal 1999-2000	Crystal Palace 2000-04
Tommy Black	Arsenal 1999-2000	Crystal Palace 2000-04
Stuart Taylor	Crystal Palace 2000-01	Arsenal 2001-03
Matthew Upson	Arsenal 1997-2002	Crystal Palace 2000-01

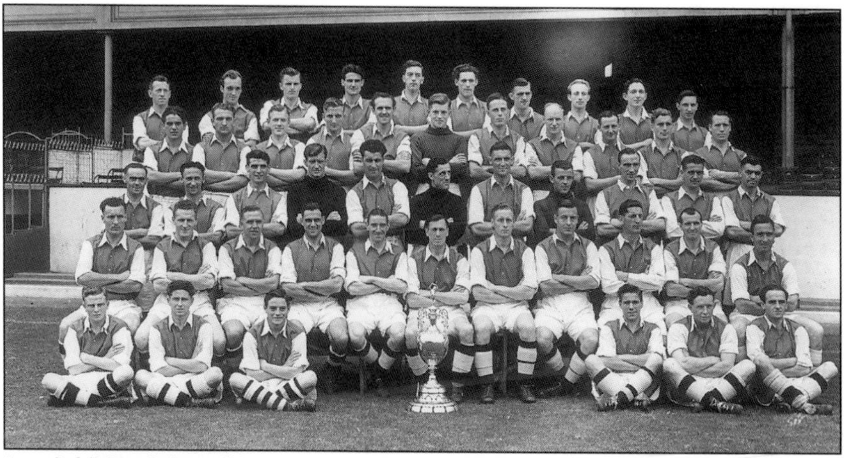

Arsenal's full-time playing staff in 1948 – some 49 players including four goalkeepers – pose proudly with the Football League championship trophy, won after the Gunners had recovered from a mediocre start to the post-war era. Many consider that the reasons for this transformation were the signing of the inspirational Joe Mercer (seen here sitting behind the trophy) and prolific goalscorer Ronnie Rooke (seated, third from the right) who left the Gunners to play for Palace.

v. Darlington

FA Cup	Date	Result	Away Arsenal	Away Darlington	Division Arsenal	Division Darlington
1964-65 Round 3	9 January	Won	2	0	Div 1	Div 4

Summary	P	W	D	L	F	A
Arsenal's cup record:	1	1	0	0	2	0
TOTAL	**1**	**1**	**0**	**0**	**2**	**0**

FACT FILE

- **John Radford and George Armstrong scored the goals.**

Played for both clubs

Wee Winship	Arsenal 1910-15	Darlington 1921-26
Eddie Carr	Arsenal 1937-39	Darlington 1953-54
Laurie Brown	Darlington 1958-59	Arsenal 1961-64
Willie Young	Arsenal 1976-82	Darlington 1984-85
David Cork	Arsenal 1983-84	Darlington 1990-92
Neil Heaney	Arsenal 1991-94	Darlington 1999-2000

David O'Leary hammers the ball clear, watched by Willie Young, who spent one season at the Quakers.

v. Darwen

			Home				Away			Final Positions	
Season	League	Date	Result	Arsenal	Darwen	Date	Result	Arsenal	Darwen	Arsenal	Darwen
1894-95	Division 2	8 December	Won	**4**	**0**	1 January	Lost	**1**	**3**	8th	6th
1895-96	Division 2	18 April	Lost	**1**	**3**	14 March	Drew	**1**	**1**	7th	9th
1896-97	Division 2	19 April	Won	**1**	**0**	1 January	Lost	**1**	**4**	10th	11th
1897-98	Division 2	9 April	Won	**3**	**1**	12 March	Won	**4**	**1**	5th	15th
1898-99	Division 2	14 January	Won	**6**	**0**	17 September	Won	**4**	**1**	7th	18thF

FA Cup										Division
1900-01	Int					5 January	Won	**2**	**0**	Div 2 Non L
1931-32	Round 3	9 January	Won	**11**	**1**					Div 1 Non L

Summary	P	W	D	L	F	A
Arsenal's home league record:	5	4	0	1	15	4
Arsenal's away league record:	5	2	1	2	11	10
Arsenal's cup record:	2	2	0	0	13	1
TOTAL	**12**	**8**	**1**	**3**	**39**	**14**

FACT FILE

- **Arsenal have won their last seven matches against Darwen.**

Arsenal's top scorers vs Darwen

Cliff Bastin 4

James Brock, Adam Haywood, Fergus Hunt, David Jack, Bill White 3

Arsenal hat-tricks vs Darwen

9 Jan 1932 Cliff Bastin (4) (cup)

9 Jan 1932 David Jack (cup)

Played for both clubs

Thomas Shrewsbury	Darwen 1895-96	Arsenal 1896-98
Fergus Hunt	Darwen 1895-97	Arsenal 1897-1903

Cliff Bastin, a prolific scoring winger whose total of goals for the club was a record until Ian Wright overhauled it some 60 years later. Four of those goals came against non-league Darwen during the cup tie in 1932.

v. Derby County

		Home					Away			Final Positions	
Season	League	Date	Result	Arsenal	Derby	Date	Result	Arsenal	Derby	Arsenal	Derby
1904-05	Division 1	18 March	Drew	0	0	19 November	Drew	0	0	10th	11th
1905-06	Division 1	17 March	Won	1	0	11 November	Lost	1	5	12th	15th
1906-07	Division 1	27 April	Won	3	2	22 December	Drew	0	0	7th	19thR
1912-13	Division 1	12 April	Lost	1	2	7 December	Lost	1	4	20thR	7th
1914-15	Division 2	27 February	Lost	1	2	24 October	Lost	0	4	5thP	1stP
1919-20	Division 1	26 December	Won	1	0	25 December	Lost	1	2	10th	18th
1920-21	Division 1	30 October	Won	2	0	23 October	Drew	1	1	9th	21stR
1926-27	Division 1	28 August	Won	2	1	15 January	Won	2	0	11th	12th
1927-28	Division 1	4 February	Lost	3	4	24 September	Lost	0	4	10th	4th
1928-29	Division 1	29 August	Lost	1	3	26 September	Drew	0	0	9th	6th
1929-30	Division 1	12 October	Drew	1	1	19 February	Lost	1	4	14th	2nd
1930-31	Division 1	14 February	Won	6	3	11 October	Lost	2	4	1st	6th
1931-32	Division 1	25 March	Won	2	1	28 March	Drew	1	1	2nd	15th
1932-33	Division 1	8 October	Drew	3	3	22 February	Drew	2	2	1st	7th
1933-34	Division 1	30 March	Won	1	0	2 April	Won	4	2	1st	4th
1934-35	Division 1	4 May	Lost	0	1	22 December	Lost	1	3	1st	6th
1935-36	Division 1	9 November	Drew	1	1	4 March	Won	4	0	6th	2nd
1936-37	Division 1	26 September	Drew	2	2	3 February	Lost	4	5	3rd	4th
1937-38	Division 1	5 February	Won	3	0	25 September	Lost	0	2	1st	13th
1938-39	Division 1	14 September	Lost	1	2	29 April	Won	2	1	5th	6th
1946-47	Division 1	21 September	Lost	0	1	10 May	Won	1	0	13th	14th
1947-48	Division 1	17 April	Lost	1	2	29 November	Lost	0	1	1st	4th
1948-49	Division 1	25 December	Drew	3	3	27 December	Lost	1	2	5th	3rd
1949-50	Division 1	18 February	Won	1	0	1 October	Won	2	1	6th	11th
1950-51	Division 1	28 October	Won	3	1	17 March	Lost	2	4	5th	11th
1951-52	Division 1	15 September	Won	3	1	19 January	Won	2	1	3rd	17th
1952-53	Division 1	18 February	Won	6	2	27 September	Lost	0	2	1st	22ndR
1969-70	Division 1	8 November	Won	4	0	21 February	Lost	2	3	12th	4th
1970-71	Division 1	31 October	Won	2	0	27 February	Lost	0	2	1st	9th
1971-72	Division 1	12 February	Won	2	0	23 October	Lost	1	2	5th	1st
1972-73	Division 1	31 March	Lost	0	1	25 November	Lost	0	5	2nd	7th
1973-74	Division 1	20 April	Won	2	0	8 December	Drew	1	1	10th	3rd
1974-75	Division 1	16 November	Won	3	1	22 February	Lost	1	2	16th	1st
1975-76	Division 1	8 November	Lost	0	1	18 February	Lost	0	2	17th	4th
1976-77	Division 1	3 May	Drew	0	0	15 December	Drew	0	0	8th	15th
1977-78	Division 1	26 November	Lost	1	3	9 May	Lost	0	3	5th	12th
1978-79	Division 1	16 December	Won	2	0	21 April	Lost	0	2	7th	19th
1979-80	Division 1	19 January	Won	2	0	8 September	Lost	2	3	4th	21stR
1987-88	Division 1	24 October	Won	2	1	26 March	Drew	0	0	6th	15th
1988-89	Division 1	13 May	Lost	1	2	26 November	Lost	1	2	1st	5th
1989-90	Division 1	28 October	Drew	1	1	24 March	Won	3	1	4th	16th
1990-91	Division 1	26 December	Won	3	0	30 March	Won	2	0	1st	20thR
1996-97	Prem'ship	7 December	Drew	2	2	11 May	Won	3	1	3rd	12th
1997-98	Prem'ship	28 April	Won	1	0	1 November	Lost	0	3	1st	9th

			Home				Away			Final Positions	
Season	League	Date	Result	Arsenal	Derby	Date	Result	Arsenal	Derby	Arsenal	Derby
1998-99	Prem'ship	2 May	Won	**1**	**0**	5 December	Drew	**0**	**0**	2nd	8th
1999-00	Prem'ship	28 November	Won	**2**	**1**	10 August	Won	**2**	**1**	2nd	16th
2000-01	Prem'ship	11 November	Drew	**0**	**0**	28 April	Won	**2**	**1**	2nd	17th
2001-02	Prem'ship	5 March	Won	**1**	**0**	29 September	Won	**2**	**0**	1st	19thR

FA Cup										*Division*	
1890-91	Round 1	17 January	Lost	**1**	**2**					Non L	Div 1
1898-99	Round 1	28 January	Lost	**0**	**6**					Div 2	Div 1
1933-34	Round 5	17 February	Won	**1**	**0**					Div 1	Div 1
1948-49	Round 4					29 January	Lost	**0**	**1**	Div 1	Div 1
1971-72	Round 5	29 February	Drew*	**0**	**0**	26 February	Drew	**2**	**2**	Div 1	Div 1
		13 March		Filbert Street			Won	**1**	**0**		
1998-99	Q'ter Final	6 March	Won	**1**	**0**					Prem	Prem

League Cup											
1992-93	Round 3	1 December	Won	**2**	**1**	28 October	Drew	**1**	**1**	Prem	Div 1
1998-99	Round 3					28 October	Won	**2**	**1**	Prem	Prem

Summary	P	W	D	L	F	A
Arsenal's home league record:	48	26	10	12	84	51
Arsenal's away league record:	48	13	10	25	57	89
Arsenal's cup record:	11	5	3	3	11	14
TOTAL	**107**	**44**	**23**	**40**	**152**	**154**

Cliff Bastin is held back by the arm of Derby County's England centre-half Jack Barker at Highbury in February 1938. Arsenal won 3-0 in front of a crowd of 47,000 and at the end of the season were League champions for the fifth time in eight years.

FACT FILE

- **Derby were the only side to take maximum points from Arsenal in their title-winning season of 1988-89.**
- **Arsenal won seven in a row at home from 1950 to 1972.**
- **Derby were unbeaten in 15 matches at home from 1952 to 1988.**
- **Nine league matches in succession (1952-72) resulted in home wins.**
- **Arsenal have not lost in their last 11 matches.**

Arsenal's top scorers vs Derby

Ted Drake 7
Cliff Bastin, Charlie George, Alan Smith 6
Reg Lewis 5
Thierry Henry, Cliff Holton, David Jack,
Jimmy Logie 4

Arsenal hat-tricks vs Derby

4 Feb 1928 Jimmy Brain
14 Feb 1931 Cliff Bastin

Played for both clubs

Samuel Mills	Derby County 1891-93	Arsenal 1895-96
Sam Raybould	Derby County 1894-95	Arsenal 1908-09
Tommy Shanks	Derby County 1898-1901	Arsenal 1902-04
Reg Stockill	Arsenal 1931-33	Derby County 1934-39
Frank Boulton	Arsenal 1936-38	Derby County 1938-40
Wilf Walsh	Arsenal 1938-39	Derby County 1939-47
Ray Swallow	Arsenal 1954-58	Derby County 1958-64
Charlie George	Arsenal 1969-75	Derby County 1975-79/81-82
Frank Stapleton	Arsenal 1974-81	Derby County 1987-88

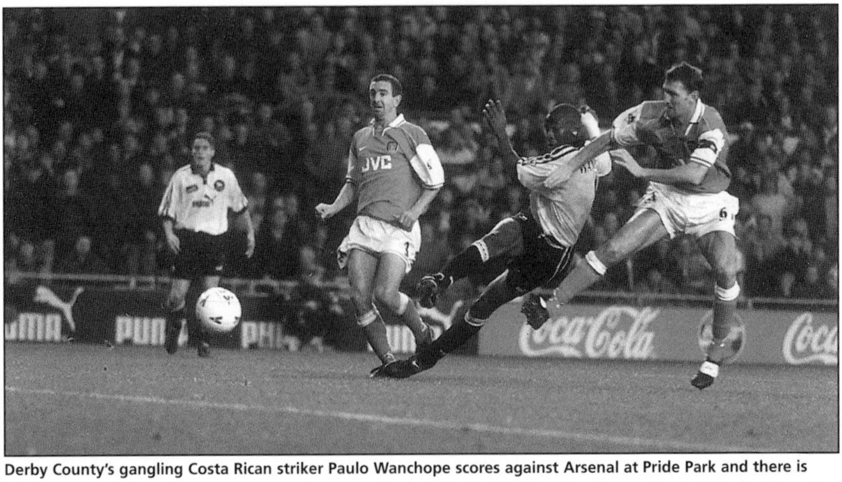

Derby County's gangling Costa Rican striker Paulo Wanchope scores against Arsenal at Pride Park and there is nothing that Tony Adams or Nigel Winterburn can do about it. Ian Wright missed a penalty that day in November 1997 and the Gunners went down 3-0. A league and cup Double at the end of the season was not even a dream at that stage.

v. Doncaster Rovers

		Home					Away			Final Positions	
Season	League	Date	Result	Arsenal	Doncaster	Date	Result	Arsenal	Doncaster	Arsenal	Doncaster
1901-02	Division 2	30 November	Won	**1**	**0**	29 March	Lost	**0**	**1**	4th	7th
1902-03	Division 2	21 March	Won	**3**	**0**	22 November	Won	**1**	**0**	3rd	16thF

FA Cup

						Division	
1952-53	Round 3	10 January	Won	**4**	**0**	Div 1	Div 2

League Cup

1987-88	Division 2	6 October	Won	**1**	**0**	23 September	Won	**3**	**0**	Div 1	Div 3

Summary	P	W	D	L	F	A
Arsenal's home league record:	2	2	0	0	4	0
Arsenal's away league record:	2	1	0	1	1	1
Arsenal's cup record:	3	3	0	0	8	0
TOTAL	**7**	**6**	**0**	**1**	**13**	**1**

FACT FILE

- **All 13 Arsenal goals have been scored by different men.**
- **Arsenal have won their last five matches.**

Played for both clubs

Jock Russell	Arsenal 1896-97	Doncaster Rovers 1904-05
Jack Aston	Arsenal 1899-1900	Doncaster Rovers 1902-03
Jack Lambert	Doncaster Rovers 1924-26	Arsenal 1926-34
Jack Moody	Arsenal 1926-28	Doncaster Rovers 1930-32
Alf Calverley	Arsenal 1946-47	Doncaster Rovers 1947-53
Tony Woodcock	Doncaster Rovers 1976-77	Arsenal 1982-86

Tony Woodcock was on Doncaster Rovers' books before he joined the Gunners in 1982 from Nottingham Forest.

v. Everton

Season	League	Home Date	Home Result	Home Arsenal	Home Everton	Away Date	Away Result	Away Arsenal	Away Everton	Final Positions Arsenal	Final Positions Everton
1904-05	Division 1	22 April	Won	**2**	**1**	5 April	Lost	**0**	**1**	10th	2nd
1905-06	Division 1	4 November	Lost	**1**	**2**	21 March	Won	**1**	**0**	12th	11th
1906-07	Division 1	15 December	Won	**3**	**1**	10 April	Lost	**1**	**2**	7th	3rd
1907-08	Division 1	18 April	Won	**2**	**1**	21 December	Drew	**1**	**1**	14th=	11th
1908-09	Division 1	2 September	Lost	**0**	**4**	7 September	Won	**3**	**0**	6th	2nd
1909-10	Division 1	23 October	Won	**1**	**0**	7 March	Lost	**0**	**1**	18th	10th
1910-11	Division 1	11 March	Won	**1**	**0**	5 November	Lost	**0**	**2**	10th	4th
1911-12	Division 1	4 November	Lost	**0**	**1**	27 March	Lost	**0**	**1**	10th	2nd
1912-13	Division 1	16 November	Drew	**0**	**0**	22 March	Lost	**0**	**3**	20thR	11th
1919-20	Division 1	18 October	Drew	**1**	**1**	11 October	Won	**3**	**2**	10th	16th
1920-21	Division 1	27 December	Drew	**1**	**1**	25 December	Won	**4**	**2**	9th	7th
1921-22	Division 1	1 October	Won	**1**	**0**	24 September	Drew	**1**	**1**	17th	20th
1922-23	Division 1	11 November	Lost	**1**	**2**	4 November	Lost	**0**	**1**	11th	5th
1923-24	Division 1	21 April	Lost	**0**	**1**	18 April	Lost	**1**	**3**	19th	7th
1924-25	Division 1	21 March	Won	**3**	**1**	15 November	Won	**3**	**2**	20th	17th
1925-26	Division 1	31 October	Won	**4**	**1**	13 March	Won	**3**	**2**	2nd	11th
1926-27	Division 1	19 March	Lost	**1**	**2**	30 October	Lost	**1**	**3**	11th	20th
1927-28	Division 1	24 December	Won	**3**	**2**	5 May	Drew	**3**	**3**	10th	1st
1928-29	Division 1	22 April	Won	**2**	**0**	6 October	Lost	**2**	**4**	9th	18th
1929-30	Division 1	8 February	Won	**4**	**0**	5 October	Drew	**1**	**1**	14th	22ndR
1931-32	Division 1	26 September	Won	**3**	**2**	6 February	Won	**3**	**1**	2nd	1st
1932-33	Division 1	24 September	Won	**2**	**1**	4 February	Drew	**1**	**1**	1st	11th
1933-34	Division 1	3 February	Lost	**1**	**2**	23 September	Lost	**1**	**3**	1st	14th
1934-35	Division 1	3 November	Won	**2**	**0**	16 March	Won	**2**	**0**	1st	8th
1935-36	Division 1	25 March	Drew	**1**	**1**	16 November	Won	**2**	**0**	6th	16th
1936-37	Division 1	29 August	Won	**3**	**2**	26 December	Drew	**1**	**1**	3rd	17th
1937-38	Division 1	1 January	Won	**2**	**1**	28 August	Won	**4**	**1**	1st	14th
1938-39	Division 1	10 September	Lost	**1**	**2**	14 January	Lost	**0**	**2**	5th	1st
1946-47	Division 1	31 May	Won	**2**	**1**	11 September	Lost	**2**	**3**	13th	10th
1947-48	Division 1	25 October	Drew	**1**	**1**	13 March	Won	**2**	**0**	1st	14th
1948-49	Division 1	23 October	Won	**5**	**0**	16 April	Drew	**0**	**0**	5th	18th
1949-50	Division 1	8 October	Won	**5**	**2**	25 February	Won	**1**	**0**	6th	18th
1950-51	Division 1	6 September	Won	**2**	**1**	13 September	Drew	**1**	**1**	5th	22ndR
1954-55	Division 1	31 August	Won	**2**	**0**	25 August	Lost	**0**	**1**	9th	11th
1955-56	Division 1	21 February	Won	**3**	**2**	8 October	Drew	**1**	**1**	5th	15th
1956-57	Division 1	23 February	Won	**2**	**0**	27 October	Lost	**0**	**4**	5th	15th
1957-58	Division 1	10 September	Lost	**2**	**3**	16 October	Drew	**2**	**2**	12th	16th
1958-59	Division 1	17 January	Won	**3**	**1**	6 September	Won	**6**	**1**	3rd	16th
1959-60	Division 1	20 February	Won	**2**	**1**	3 October	Lost	**1**	**3**	13th	15th
1960-61	Division 1	26 November	Won	**3**	**2**	29 April	Lost	**1**	**4**	11th	5th
1961-62	Division 1	1 May	Lost	**2**	**3**	30 September	Lost	**1**	**4**	10th	4th
1962-63	Division 1	26 March	Won	**4**	**3**	24 April	Drew	**1**	**1**	7th	1st
1963-64	Division 1	10 December	Won	**6**	**0**	2 October	Lost	**1**	**2**	8th	3rd
1964-65	Division 1	31 October	Won	**3**	**1**	24 April	Lost	**0**	**1**	13th	4th

Season	League	Home Date	Home Result	Home Arsenal	Home Everton	Away Date	Away Result	Away Arsenal	Away Everton	Final Positions Arsenal	Final Positions Everton
1965-66	Division 1	12 March	Lost	**0**	**1**	18 September	Lost	**1**	**3**	14th	11th
1966-67	Division 1	25 April	Won	**3**	**1**	12 November	Drew	**0**	**0**	7th	6th
1967-68	Division 1	11 November	Drew	**2**	**2**	6 April	Lost	**0**	**2**	9th	5th
1968-69	Division 1	7 December	Won	**3**	**1**	29 April	Lost	**0**	**1**	4th	3rd
1969-70	Division 1	9 April	Lost	**0**	**1**	14 February	Drew	**2**	**2**	12th	1st
1970-71	Division 1	17 October	Won	**4**	**0**	15 August	Drew	**2**	**2**	1st	14th
1971-72	Division 1	1 January	Drew	**1**	**1**	18 September	Lost	**1**	**2**	5th	15th
1972-73	Division 1	18 November	Won	**1**	**0**	21 April	Drew	**0**	**0**	2nd	17th
1973-74	Division 1	22 December	Won	**1**	**0**	29 September	Lost	**0**	**1**	10th	7th
1974-75	Division 1	1 March	Lost	**0**	**2**	31 August	Lost	**1**	**2**	16th	4th
1975-76	Division 1	20 September	Drew	**2**	**2**	10 April	Drew	**0**	**0**	17th	11th
1976-77	Division 1	18 September	Won	**3**	**1**	1 March	Lost	**1**	**2**	8th	9th
1977-78	Division 1	23 August	Won	**1**	**0**	31 December	Lost	**0**	**2**	5th	3rd
1978-79	Division 1	18 November	Drew	**2**	**2**	26 August	Lost	**0**	**1**	7th	4th
1979-80	Division 1	17 November	Won	**2**	**0**	28 March	Won	**1**	**0**	4th	19th
1980-81	Division 1	22 November	Won	**2**	**1**	10 January	Won	**2**	**1**	3rd	15th
1981-82	Division 1	28 November	Won	**1**	**0**	24 April	Lost	**1**	**2**	5th	8th
1982-83	Division 1	13 November	Drew	**1**	**1**	26 March	Won	**3**	**2**	10th	7th
1983-84	Division 1	19 November	Won	**2**	**1**	9 April	Drew	**0**	**0**	6th	7th
1984-85	Division 1	6 October	Won	**1**	**0**	23 March	Lost	**0**	**2**	7th	1st
1985-86	Division 1	12 April	Lost	**0**	**1**	9 November	Lost	**1**	**6**	7th	2nd
1986-87	Division 1	28 March	Lost	**0**	**1**	4 October	Won	**1**	**0**	4th	1st
1987-88	Division 1	19 December	Drew	**1**	**1**	7 May	Won	**2**	**1**	6th	4th
1988-89	Division 1	8 April	Won	**2**	**0**	14 January	Won	**3**	**1**	1st	8th
1989-90	Division 1	31 March	Won	**1**	**0**	21 October	Lost	**0**	**3**	4th	6th
1990-91	Division 1	19 January	Won	**1**	**0**	8 September	Drew	**1**	**1**	1st	9th
1991-92	Division 1	21 December	Won	**4**	**2**	20 August	Lost	**1**	**3**	4th	12th
1992-93	Prem'ship	24 October	Won	**2**	**0**	1 May	Drew	**0**	**0**	10th	13th
1993-94	Prem'ship	28 August	Won	**2**	**0**	19 February	Drew	**1**	**1**	4th	17th
1994-95	Prem'ship	14 January	Drew	**1**	**1**	29 October	Drew	**1**	**1**	12th	15th
1995-96	Prem'ship	20 January	Lost	**1**	**2**	23 August	Won	**2**	**0**	5th	6th
1996-97	Prem'ship	19 January	Won	**3**	**1**	1 March	Won	**2**	**0**	3rd	15th
1997-98	Prem'ship	3 May	Won	**4**	**0**	27 September	Drew	**2**	**2**	1st	17th
1998-99	Prem'ship	8 November	Won	**1**	**0**	13 March	Won	**2**	**0**	2nd	14th
1999-00	Prem'ship	16 October	Won	**4**	**1**	29 April	Won	**1**	**0**	2nd	13th
2000-01	Prem'ship	21 April	Won	**4**	**1**	18 November	Lost	**0**	**2**	2nd	16th
2001-02	Prem'ship	11 May	Won	**4**	**3**	10 February	Won	**1**	**0**	1st	15th
2002-03	Prem'ship	23 March	Won	**2**	**1**	19 October	Lost	**1**	**2**	2nd	7th
2003-04	Prem'ship	16 August	Won	**2**	**1**	7 January	Drew	**1**	**1**	1st	17th

FA Cup

Season	Round	Home Date	Home Result	Home Arsenal	Home Everton	Away Date	Away Result	Away Arsenal	Away Everton	Division Arsenal	Division Everton
1909-10	Round 2					5 February	Lost	**0**	**5**	Div 1	Div 1
1927-28	Round 4	28 January	Won	**4**	**3**					Div 1	Div 1
1980-81	Round 3					3 January	Lost	**0**	**2**	Div 1	Div 1

League Cup

Season	Round	Home Date	Home Result	Home Arsenal	Home Everton	Away Date	Away Result	Away Arsenal	Away Everton	Division Arsenal	Division Everton
1969-70	Round 3	24 September	Drew	**0**	**0**	1 October	Lost	**0**	**1**	Div 1	Div 1
1972-73	Round 2	5 September	Won	**1**	**0**					Div 1	Div 1

Season		Home Date	Home Result	Arsenal	Everton	Away Date	Away Result	Arsenal	Everton	Division Arsenal	Division Everton
1975-76	Round 2	23 September	Lost	**0**	**1**	9 September	Drew	**2**	**2**	Div 1	Div 1
1982-83	Round 3	23 November	Won	**3**	**0**	9 November	Drew	**1**	**1**	Div 1	Div 1
1987-88	Semi Final	24 February	Won	**3**	**1**	7 February	Won	**1**	**0**	Div 1	Div 1

Summary	P	W	D	L	F	A
Arsenal's home league record:	83	55	12	16	164	86
Arsenal's away league record:	83	24	23	36	100	123
Arsenal's cup record:	12	5	3	4	15	16
TOTAL	**178**	**84**	**38**	**56**	**279**	**225**

FACT FILE

- **Arsenal have lost only one of their last 18 matches at home. They have won their last eight of these.**
- **In October 2002, Arsenal went to Goodison Park with two Premiership record sequences in progress. They had not lost for 23 away matches (over 17 months), and had not lost at home or away for 30 matches. However, a stunning last-minute strike from 16-year-old Wayne Rooney ended both runs.**
- **Arsenal failed to win in 22 matches at Goodison from 1959 to 1978.**
- **Arsenal have won six or more in a row at home on three occasions.**
- **Arsenal lost one in 17 between 1991 and 2000.**

Reg Lewis heads goalwards for Arsenal against Everton. Lewis was 'ahead of his time', different in style to Rooke and, indeed, to most other centre-forwards, but he still scored 116 goals in only 175 games for the Gunners.

Arsenal's top scorers vs Everton

Ian Wright 12
Jimmy Brain, David Herd 9
Joe Hulme, Reg Lewis 7
Joe Baker, Vic Groves, Frank Stapleton 6
Cliff Bastin, Ted Drake, Alan Sunderland 5

Arsenal hat-tricks vs Everton

31 Oct 1925 Jimmy Brain
13 Mar 1926 Jimmy Brain
8 Feb 1930 Jack Lambert
28 Aug 1937 Ted Drake
6 Sep 1958 David Herd (4)
26 Nov 1960 David Herd
23 Nov 1982 Alan Sunderland (cup)
21 Dec 1991 Ian Wright (4)

Played for both clubs

Abe Hartley	Everton 1892-98	Arsenal 1899-1900
Dick Roose	Everton 1904-05	Arsenal 1911-12
Tim Coleman	Arsenal 1902-08	Everton 1907-10
Bertie Freeman	Arsenal 1905-08	Everton 1907-11
James Caldwell	Everton 1912-13	Arsenal 1913-14
Frank Bradshaw	Everton 1911-14	Arsenal 1914-23
Andy Kennedy	Arsenal 1922-28	Everton 1928-29
Archie Clark	Arsenal 1927-28	Everton 1931-35
Peter Dougal	Arsenal 1933-36	Everton 1937-38
Tommy Lawton	Everton 1936-39	Arsenal 1953-56
Joe Mercer	Everton 1932-47	Arsenal 1946-54
Geoff Barnett	Everton 1965-68	Arsenal 1969-76
Alan Ball	Everton 1966-72	Arsenal 1971-77
Brian Kidd	Arsenal 1974-76	Everton 1978-80
Trevor Ross	Arsenal 1974-78	Everton 1977-83
George Wood	Everton 1977-80	Arsenal 1980-83
Martin Keown	Arsenal 1985-86/92-2004	Everton 1989-93
Kevin Richardson	Everton 1981-87	Arsenal 1987-90
Kenny Sansom	Arsenal 1980-88	Everton 1992-93
Anders Limpar	Arsenal 1990-94	Everton 1993-97
Kevin Campbell	Arsenal 1987-95	Everton 1998-2004
Stephen Hughes	Arsenal 1994-2000	Everton 1999-2001
Francis Jeffers	Everton 1997-2001/03-04	Arsenal 2001-03
Richard Wright	Arsenal 2001-02	Everton 2002-04

In August 1954, Everton marked their return to the First Division with a visit from Arsenal at Goodison Park and over 69,000 fans saw the Merseysiders triumph 1-0 with this goal from Tommy Eglington. Jack Kelsey is the Arsenal goalkeeper.

v. Farnborough Town

FA Cup		Date	Result	Home Arsenal	Home Farn'brgh	Division Arsenal	Division Farn'brgh
2002-03	Round 4	25 January	Won	**5**	**1**	Prem	Non L

Summary	P	W	D	L	F	A
Arsenal's cup record:	1	1	0	0	5	1
TOTAL	**1**	**1**	**0**	**0**	**5**	**1**

FACT FILE

- **Farnborough were drawn at home but waived the right.**

Arsenal's top scorers vs Farnborough

Francis Jeffers 2

v. Fulham

Season	League	Home Date	Home Result	Arsenal	Fulham	Away Date	Away Result	Arsenal	Fulham	Final Positions Arsenal	Final Positions Fulham
1913-14	Division 2	14 March	Won	**2**	**0**	8 November	Lost	**1**	**6**	3rd	11th
1914-15	Division 2	12 September	Won	**3**	**0**	16 January	Won	**1**	**0**	5thP	12th
1949-50	Division 1	5 November	Won	**2**	**1**	25 March	Drew	**2**	**2**	6th	17th
1950-51	Division 1	25 November	Won	**5**	**1**	14 April	Lost	**2**	**3**	5th	18th
1951-52	Division 1	27 October	Won	**4**	**3**	15 March	Drew	**0**	**0**	3rd	22ndR
1959-60	Division 1	15 April	Won	**2**	**0**	18 April	Lost	**0**	**3**	13th	10th
1960-61	Division 1	3 April	Won	**4**	**2**	31 March	Drew	**2**	**2**	11th	17th
1961-62	Division 1	26 December	Won	**1**	**0**	11 April	Lost	**2**	**5**	10th	20th
1962-63	Division 1	14 May	Won	**3**	**0**	15 September	Won	**3**	**1**	7th	16th
1963-64	Division 1	18 January	Drew	**2**	**2**	14 September	Won	**4**	**1**	8th	15th
1964-65	Division 1	20 February	Won	**2**	**0**	5 December	Won	**4**	**3**	13th	20th
1965-66	Division 1	9 October	Won	**2**	**1**	1 January	Lost	**0**	**1**	14th	20th
1966-67	Division 1	19 November	Won	**1**	**0**	19 April	Drew	**0**	**0**	7th	18th
1967-68	Division 1	28 October	Won	**5**	**3**	23 March	Won	**3**	**1**	9th	22ndR
2001-02	Prem'ship	23 February	Won	**4**	**1**	15 September	Won	**3**	**1**	1st	13th
2002-03	Prem'ship	1 February	Won	**2**	**1**	3 November	Won	**1**	**0**	2nd	14th
2003-04	Prem'ship	30 November	Drew	**0**	**0**	9 May	Won	**1**	**0**	1st	9th

FA Cup

Season	Round	Date	Result	Arsenal	Fulham	Division
1903-04	Round 1	6 February	Won	**1**	**0**	Div 2 Non L

Summary	P	W	D	L	F	A
Arsenal's home league record:	17	15	2	0	44	15
Arsenal's away record:	17	8	4	5	29	29
Arsenal's cup record:	1	1	0	0	1	0
TOTAL	**35**	**24**	**6**	**5**	**74**	**44**

FACT FILE

- **Arsenal have the extraordinary record of 16 wins and two draws in 18 home games.**
- **Arsenal have lost one of their last 18 – on New Years Day 1966.**
- **Fulham last finished above Arsenal in 1960.**

Arsenal's top scorers vs Fulham

Joe Baker 10

Doug Lishman 6

John Radford 4

Jackie Henderson,Thierry Henry, David Herd, John MacLeod, Alan Skirton, Geoff Strong 3

Arsenal hat-tricks vs Fulham

25 Nov 1950 Doug Lishman

27 Oct 1951 Doug Lishman

14 May 1963 Joe Baker

Played for both clubs

Bobby Templeton	Arsenal 1904-06	Fulham 1914-15
Jim Bellamy	Arsenal 1904-07	Fulham 1914-15
Tim Coleman	Arsenal 1902-08	Fulham 1911-14
Jimmy Sharp	Arsenal 1905-08	Fulham 1908-13/19-20
Tom Fitchie	Arsenal 1901-09	Fulham 1912-13
Hugh McDonald	Arsenal 1905-10/12-13	Fulham 1913-14
Pat Flanagan	Fulham 1909-11	Arsenal 1910-15
Archie Gray	Arsenal 1904-12	Fulham 1911-15
Andy Ducat	Arsenal 1904-12	Fulham 1921-24
Gordon Hoare	Arsenal 1907-12	Fulham 1919-20
David Duncan	Fulham 1911-12	Arsenal 1912-13
Donald Slade	Arsenal 1913-14	Fulham 1914-15
Jim Smith	Fulham 1908-15	Arsenal 1920-21
Wee Winship	Arsenal 1910-15	Fulham 1912-13
Donald Cock	Fulham 1919-23	Arsenal 1924-26
Bert White	Arsenal 1919-23	Fulham 1925-26
Jack Lambert	Arsenal 1926-34	Fulham 1933-35
Bernard Joy	Fulham 1933-34	Arsenal 1935-47
George Cox	Arsenal 1933-36	Fulham 1936-37
Ernie Tuckett	Arsenal 1935-36	Fulham 1938-39
Pat Beasley	Arsenal 1931-37	Fulham 1946-50
Dave Nelson	Arsenal 1936-47	Fulham 1946-47
Ronnie Rooke	Fulham 1936-47	Arsenal 1946-49
Cyril Grant	Arsenal 1946-47	Fulham 1946-48
Archie Macaulay	Arsenal 1947-50	Fulham 1950-53
John Chenhall	Arsenal 1951-53	Fulham 1953-58
Bill Dodgin	Fulham 1951-53/60-64	Arsenal 1952-60
Alex Forbes	Arsenal 1947-56	Fulham 1957-58
Jackie Henderson	Arsenal 1958-62	Fulham 1961-64
John McClelland	Arsenal 1960-64	Fulham 1965-69
Roger Davidson	Arsenal 1967-68	Fulham 1970-71
George Johnston	Arsenal 1967-69	Fulham 1970-72
Malcolm Macdonald	Fulham 1968-69	Arsenal 1976-79
Malcolm Webster	Arsenal 1969-70	Fulham 1969-74
Peter Marinello	Arsenal 1969-73	Fulham 1978-80
Peter Storey	Arsenal 1965-77	Fulham 1976-78
Brian McDermott	Arsenal 1978-84	Fulham 1982-83
Brian Talbot	Arsenal 1978-85	Fulham 1990-91
Andy Cole	Arsenal 1990-91	Fulham 1991-92
Ian Selley	Arsenal 1992-97	Fulham 1997-98
Stephen Hughes	Arsenal 1994-2000	Fulham 1999-2000
Luis Boa Morte	Arsenal 1997-2000	Fulham 2000-03

Peter Storey, later to join Fulham.

v. Gainsborough Trinity

Season	League	Home Date	Home Result	Arsenal	Gainsbr'gh	Away Date	Away Result	Arsenal	Gainsbr'gh	Final Positions Arsenal	Final Positions Gainsbr'gh
1896-97	Division 2	24 October	Won	6	1	26 December	Lost	1	4	10th	7th
1897-98	Division 2	18 September	Won	4	0	26 March	Lost	0	1	5th	9th
1898-99	Division 2	24 September	Won	5	1	21 January	Won	1	0	7th	14th
1899-00	Division 2	14 October	Won	2	1	17 February	Drew	1	1	8th	13th
1900-01	Division 2	1 September	Won	2	1	29 December	Lost	0	1	7th	13th
1901-02	Division 2	8 February	Won	5	0	12 October	Drew	2	2	4th	18th
1902-03	Division 2	27 September	Won	6	1	24 January	Won	1	0	3rd	12th
1903-04	Division 2	9 January	Won	6	0	12 September	Won	2	0	2ndP	9th

Summary	P	W	D	L	F	A
Arsenal's home league record:	8	8	0	0	36	5
Arsenal's away league record:	8	3	2	3	8	9
TOTAL	**16**	**11**	**2**	**3**	**44**	**14**

FACT FILE

- **Arsenal have a 100% home record, and have averaged 4.5 goals per game in the process.**
- **Arsenal have won their last five matches in the series.**

Arsenal's top scorers vs Gainsborough

Bill Gooing 6
Archie McGeoch 5
Tim Coleman 4
Tommy Briercliffe, James Brock 3

Arsenal hat-tricks vs Gainsborough

18 Sep 1897 Archie McGeoch
27 Sep 1902 Bill Gooing

Played for both clubs

Abe Foxall	Gainsborough Town 1897-99/1903-06	Arsenal 1901-02
Ned Liddell	Gainsborough Town 1906-07	Arsenal 1914-15

v. Gillingham

FA Cup		Home Date	Home Result	Arsenal	Gillingham	Away Date	Away Result	Arsenal	Gillingham	Division Arsenal	Division Gillingham
1897-98	5thQual	11 December	Won	**4**	**2**					Div 2	Non L
1899-00	3rdQual	28 October	Drew	**1**	**1**	1 November	Drew	**0**	**0**	Div 2	Non L
		6 November				Millwall (2nd replay)	Drew	**2**	**2**		
		8 November				Tottenham (3rd replay)	Drew	**1**	**1**		
		14 November				Gravesend (4th replay)	Lost	**0**	**1**		
2001-02	Round 5	16 February	Won	**5**	**2**					Prem	Div 1

League Cup		Home Date	Home Result	Arsenal	Gillingham	Away Date	Away Result	Arsenal	Gillingham	Division Arsenal	Division Gillingham
1966-67	Round 2	13 September	Drew	**1**	**1**	21 September	Drew	**1**	**1**	Div 1	Div 3
		28 September	Won	**5**	**0**	(2nd replay)					

Summary	P	W	D	L	F	A
Arsenal's cup record:	10	3	6	1	20	11
TOTAL	**10**	**3**	**6**	**1**	**20**	**11**

FACT FILE

- **The first six meetings took place with Gillingham known as New Brompton.**
- **The 2002 meeting produced legendary captain Tony Adams' last ever goal for Arsenal.**
- **The 1966-67 tie was Arsenal's first-ever league cup tie. Having disposed of Gillingham (eventually), they lost to West Ham in the next round.**

Arsenal's top scorers vs Gillingham

Tommy Baldwin 4

Jack Aston, Fergus Hunt, Frank McLintock,
Sylvain Wiltord 2

Played for both clubs

Archie Roe	Gillingham 1920-21	Arsenal 1922-23
Joe North	Arsenal 1919-22	Gillingham 1923-24
James Shaw	Arsenal 1926-28	Gillingham 1931-32
Dan Lewis	Arsenal 1924-30	Gillingham 1931-32
Brian Sparrow	Gillingham 1983-84	Arsenal 1983-84
Steve Walford	Arsenal 1977-81	Gillingham 1988-89
Vince Bartram	Arsenal 1994-95	Gillingham 1997-2004
Paul Shaw	Arsenal 1994-97	Gillingham 2000-04

v. Glossop

		Home					Away			Final Positions	
Season	League	Date	Result	Arsenal	Glossop	Date	Result	Arsenal	Glossop	Arsenal	Glossop
1898-99	Division 2	13 February	Won	**3**	**0**	4 February	Lost	**0**	**2**	7th	2ndP
1900-01	Division 2	23 March	Won	**2**	**0**	17 November	Won	**1**	**0**	7th	5th
1901-02	Division 2	22 March	Won	**4**	**0**	23 November	Won	**1**	**0**	4th	8th
1902-03	Division 2	14 February	Drew	**0**	**0**	18 October	Won	**2**	**1**	3rd	11th
1903-04	Division 2	4 April	Won	**2**	**1**	10 October	Won	**3**	**1**	2ndP	17th
1913-14	Division 2	20 December	Won	**2**	**0**	25 April	Won	**2**	**0**	3rd	17th
1914-15	Division 2	1 September	Won	**3**	**0**	8 September	Won	**4**	**0**	5thP	20thF

Summary	P	W	D	L	F	A
Arsenal's home league record:	7	6	1	0	16	1
Arsenal's away league record:	7	6	0	1	13	4
TOTAL	**14**	**12**	**1**	**1**	**29**	**5**

FACT FILE

- **Arsenal are unbeaten in their last 13 meetings with Glossop, conceding only three goals in the process.**
- **Arsenal have conceded only one goal at home.**

Arsenal's top scorers vs Glossop

Tim Coleman, Bill Gooing, Harry King 4

Frank Bradshaw, Walter Place 2

Played for both clubs

Edward Lawrence	Arsenal 1902-03	Glossop 1904-05
Tom Fitchie	Arsenal 1901-09	Glossop 1909-12
Gordon Hoare	Arsenal 1907-12	Glossop 1909-14
Freddie Groves	Glossop 1911-12	Arsenal 1912-21
Alfred Fletcher	Glossop 1913-14	Arsenal 1914-15

Walter Place Junior scored in both matches against Glossop in the 1900-01 season.

v. Grimsby Town

Season	League	Date	Result	Home Arsenal	Home Grimsby	Date	Result	Away Arsenal	Away Grimsby	Final Positions Arsenal	Final Positions Grimsby
1893-94	Division 2	25 September	Won	3	1	26 December	Lost	1	3	9th	5th
1894-95	Division 2	10 September	Lost	1	3	26 December	Lost	2	4	8th	5th
1895-96	Division 2	2 September	Won	3	1	4 April	Drew	1	1	7th	3rd
1896-97	Division 2	28 November	Won	4	2	8 April	Lost	1	3	10th	3rd
1897-98	Division 2	1 September	Won	4	1	12 February	Won	4	1	5th	12th
1898-99	Division 2	25 March	Drew	1	1	26 November	Lost	0	1	7th	10th
1899-00	Division 2	16 April	Won	2	0	14 April	Lost	0	1	8th	6th
1900-01	Division 2	27 October	Drew	1	1	2 March	Lost	0	1	7th	1stP
1903-04	Division 2	19 December	Won	5	1	16 April	Drew	2	2	2ndP	6th
1913-14	Division 2	23 April	Won	2	0	15 November	Drew	1	1	3rd	15th
1914-15	Division 2	14 November	Won	6	0	20 March	Lost	0	1	5thP	17th
1929-30	Division 1	19 October	Won	4	1	22 February	Drew	1	1	14th	18th
1930-31	Division 1	28 January	Won	9	1	11 April	Won	1	0	1st	13th
1931-32	Division 1	17 February	Won	4	0	3 October	Lost	1	3	2nd	21stR
1934-35	Division 1	23 March	Drew	1	1	10 November	Drew	2	2	1st	5th
1935-36	Division 1	11 September	Won	6	0	3 September	Lost	0	1	6th	17th
1936-37	Division 1	24 October	Drew	0	0	27 February	Won	3	1	3rd	12th
1937-38	Division 1	19 March	Won	5	1	6 November	Lost	1	2	1st	20th
1938-39	Division 1	8 October	Won	2	0	21 February	Lost	1	2	5th	10th
1946-47	Division 1	26 April	Won	5	3	21 December	Drew	0	0	13th	16th
1947-48	Division 1	1 May	Won	8	0	13 December	Won	4	0	1st	22ndR

FA Cup

										Division	
1906-07	Round 1	16 January	Won	3	0	12 January	Drew	1	1	Div 1	Div 2
1935-36	Semi Final	21 March		Leeds Rd, Huddersfield			Won	1	0	Div 1	Div 1
1985-86	Round 3					4 January	Won	4	3	Div 1	Div 2

League Cup

2001-02	Round 4	27 November	Won	2	0					Prem	Div 1

Summary	P	W	D	L	F	A
Arsenal's home league record:	21	16	4	1	76	18
Arsenal's away league record:	21	4	6	11	26	31
Arsenal's cup record:	5	4	1	0	11	4
TOTAL	**47**	**24**	**11**	**12**	**113**	**53**

FACT FILE

- **Arsenal have twice hit eight goals past Grimsby.**
- **Between 1899 and 1931, 17 matches produced no away wins for either side.**
- **Arsenal are undefeated in their last 21 home games.**

Arsenal's top scorers vs Grimsby

Jack Lambert 9
Ronnie Rooke 6
Cliff Bastin, David Jack, Alf Kirchen 5
Reg Lewis, Paddy O'Brien, Tommy Shanks 4

Arsenal hat-tricks vs Grimsby

19 Dec 1903 Tommy Shanks (4)
14 Nov 1914 Harry King
19 Oct 1929 Jack Lambert
28 Jan 1931 David Jack (4)
28 Jan 1931 Jack Lambert
11 Sep 1935 Jackie Milne
27 Feb 1937 Alf Kirchen
26 Apr 1947 Reg Lewis (4)
1 May 1948 Ronnie Rooke (4)
4 Jan 1986 Charlie Nicholas (cup)

Played for both clubs

Tom Pratt	Grimsby Town 1895-96	Arsenal 1903-04
Alex McConnell	Arsenal 1897-99	Grimsby Town 1901-05
John McAvoy	Arsenal 1898-99	Grimsby Town 1899-1901
Isaac Owens	Arsenal 1901-02	Grimsby Town 1908-09
Gordon Coles	Arsenal 1900-04	Grimsby Town 1904-08
Joe Satterthwaite	Arsenal 1907-08	Grimsby Town 1908-09
Willis Rippon	Arsenal 1910-11	Grimsby Town 1913-14
Bill Seddon	Arsenal 1925-32	Grimsby Town 1931-33
Tim Coleman	Grimsby Town 1928-32	Arsenal 1931-34
Rhys Wilmot	Arsenal 1985-87	Grimsby Town 1992-93
Alan Miller	Arsenal 1992-94	Grimsby Town 1996-97
Isaiah Rankin	Arsenal 1997-98	Grimsby Town 2003-04

Ronnie Rooke scored four times against Grimsby Town in the 8-0 Division One thrashing in May 1948.

v. Hartlepool United

League Cup		Home Date	Home Result	Arsenal	Hartlepool	Away Date	Away Result	Arsenal	Hartlepool	Division Arsenal	Division Hartlepool
1994-95	Round 2	5 October	Won	**2**	**0**	21 September	Won	**5**	**0**	Prem	Div 3
1995-96	Round 2	3 October	Won	**5**	**0**	19 September	Won	**3**	**0**	Prem	Div 3

Summary	P	W	D	L	F	A
Arsenal's cup record:	4	4	0	0	15	0
TOTAL	**4**	**4**	**0**	**0**	**15**	**0**

FACT FILE

- **Hartlepool have never scored a goal against Arsenal.**
- **Only Reading have played Arsenal as many times without ever avoiding defeat.**

Arsenal's top scorers vs Hartlepool

Ian Wright 6
Tony Adams 3
Dennis Bergkamp 2

Arsenal hat-tricks vs Hartlepool

3 Oct 1995 Ian Wright (cup)

Played for both clubs

Jack Lee	Hartlepool United 1924-25	Arsenal 1926-27
Ralph Guthrie	Arsenal 1954-55	Hartlepool United 1956-58
Ray Kennedy	Arsenal 1969-74	Hartlepool United 1983-84
Andy Linighan	Hartlepool United 1980-84	Arsenal 1990-97
Neil Heaney	Hartlepool United 1990-91	Arsenal 1991-94

Ian Wright's hat-trick against Hartlepool in the League Cup Round 2 game gave them their second 5-0 victory in two years

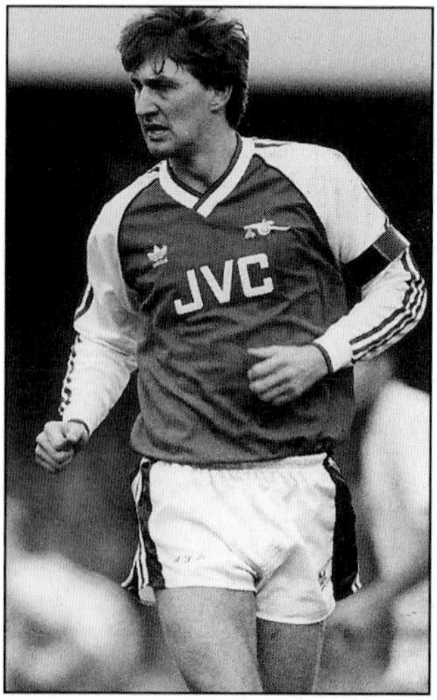

Also a goalscorer against Hartlepool was Tony Adams.

v. Hereford United

FA Cup		Date	Result	Home Arsenal	Home Hereford	Date	Result	Away Arsenal	Away Hereford	Division Arsenal	Division Hereford
1984-85	Round 3	22 January	Won	**7**	**2**	5 January	Drew	**1**	**1**	Div 1	Div 4

League Cup											
1985-86	Round 2	8 October	Won*	**2**	**1**	25 September	Drew	**0**	**0**	Div 1	Div 4

Summary	P	W	D	L	F	A
Arsenal's cup record:	4	2	2	0	10	4
TOTAL	**4**	**2**	**2**	**0**	**10**	**4**

FACT FILE

- **In four meetings in 1985 against fourth division Hereford, Arsenal won in 90 minutes only once.**

Arsenal's top scorers vs Hereford

Viv Anderson, Paul Mariner, Charlie Nicholas, Brian Talbot, Tony Woodcock 2

Played for both clubs

Colin Addison	Arsenal 1966-68	Hereford United 1972-74
George Johnston	Arsenal 1967-69	Hereford United 1972-73
David Jenkins	Arsenal 1967-69	Hereford United 1972-74
Bobby Gould	Arsenal 1967-70	Hereford United 1978-80
Jimmy Harvey	Arsenal 1977-79	Hereford United 1979-87
George Wood	Arsenal 1980-83	Hereford United 1990-91
Rhys Wilmot	Hereford United 1982-83	Arsenal 1985-87

On the books at Hereford in the early seventies, Arsenal's David Jenkins and Liverpool's Chris Lawler challenge for the ball at Highbury in August 1968. The sides drew 1-1.

v. Highland Light Infantry

FA Cup		Date	Result	Home Arsenal	Home Highland In	Division Arsenal	Division Highland In
1893	1st Qual	15 October	Won	**3**	**0**	Non L	Non L

Summary	P	W	D	L	F	A
Arsenal's cup record:	1	1	0	0	3	0
TOTAL	**1**	**1**	**0**	**0**	**3**	**0**

FACT FILE

- **The goalscorers were Elliott, Davie and Booth.**

v. Huddersfield Town

Season	League	Home Date	Home Result	Home Arsenal	Home Hudd'fd	Away Date	Away Result	Away Arsenal	Away Hudd'fd	Final Positions Arsenal	Final Positions Hudd'fd
1913-14	Division 2	14 February	Lost	0	1	11 October	Won	2	1	3rd	13th
1914-15	Division 2	27 March	Lost	0	3	21 November	Lost	0	3	5thP	8th
1920-21	Division 1	27 November	Won	2	0	20 November	Won	4	0	9th	17th
1921-22	Division 1	29 October	Lost	1	3	22 October	Lost	0	2	17th	14th
1922-23	Division 1	16 December	Drew	1	1	23 December	Lost	0	4	11th	3rd
1923-24	Division 1	15 December	Lost	1	3	22 December	Lost	1	6	19th	1st
1924-25	Division 1	14 February	Lost	0	5	11 October	Lost	0	4	20th	1st
1925-26	Division 1	17 April	Won	3	1	5 December	Drew	2	2	2nd	1st
1926-27	Division 1	2 April	Lost	0	2	13 November	Drew	3	3	11th	2nd
1927-28	Division 1	14 April	Drew	0	0	3 December	Lost	1	2	10th	2nd
1928-29	Division 1	29 September	Won	2	0	9 February	Won	1	0	9th	16th
1929-30	Division 1	14 December	Won	2	0	19 April	Drew	2	2	14th	10th
1930-31	Division 1	7 March	Drew	0	0	1 November	Drew	1	1	1st	5th
1931-32	Division 1	12 December	Drew	1	1	27 April	Won	2	1	2nd	4th
1932-33	Division 1	29 April	Drew	2	2	17 December	Won	1	0	1st	6th
1933-34	Division 1	7 April	Won	3	1	25 November	Won	1	0	1st	2nd
1934-35	Division 1	20 April	Won	1	0	8 December	Drew	1	1	1st	16th
1935-36	Division 1	7 March	Drew	1	1	30 November	Drew	0	0	6th	3rd
1936-37	Division 1	2 January	Drew	1	1	5 September	Drew	0	0	3rd	15th
1937-38	Division 1	1 September	Won	3	1	8 September	Lost	1	2	1st	15th
1938-39	Division 1	31 December	Won	1	0	3 September	Drew	1	1	5th	19th
1946-47	Division 1	4 April	Lost	1	2	7 April	Drew	0	0	13th	20th
1947-48	Division 1	22 November	Won	2	0	10 April	Drew	1	1	1st	19th
1948-49	Division 1	18 December	Won	3	0	21 August	Drew	1	1	5th	20th
1949-50	Division 1	14 January	Won	1	0	10 September	Drew	2	2	6th	15th
1950-51	Division 1	16 September	Won	6	2	20 January	Drew	2	2	5th	19th
1951-52	Division 1	18 August	Drew	2	2	15 December	Won	3	2	3rd	21stR
1953-54	Division 1	22 August	Drew	0	0	19 December	Drew	2	2	12th	3rd
1954-55	Division 1	13 November	Lost	3	5	2 April	Won	1	0	9th	12th
1955-56	Division 1	2 April	Won	2	0	3 April	Won	1	0	5th	21stR
1970-71	Division 1	25 August	Won	1	0	16 January	Lost	1	2	1st	15th
1971-72	Division 1	22 January	Won	1	0	17 August	Won	1	0	5th	22ndR

FA Cup

Season	Round	Home Date	Home Result	Home Arsenal	Home Hudd'fd	Away Date	Away Result	Away Arsenal	Away Hudd'fd	Division Arsenal	Division Hudd'fd
1929-30	Final	26 April	Wembley				Won	2	0	Div 1	Div 1
1931-32	Q'ter Final					27 February	Won	1	0	Div 1	Div 1

League Cup

Season	Round	Home Date	Home Result	Home Arsenal	Home Hudd'fd	Away Date	Away Result	Away Arsenal	Away Hudd'fd	Division Arsenal	Division Hudd'fd
1967-68	Semi Final	17 January	Won	3	2	6 February	Won	3	1	Div 1	Div 2
1982-83	Round 4	30 November	Won	1	0					Div 1	Div 3
1986-87	Round 2	23 September	Won	2	0	7 October	Drew	1	1	Div 1	Div 2
1993-94	Round 2	5 October	Drew	1	1	21 September	Won	5	0	Prem	Div 2

Summary	P	W	D	L	F	A
Arsenal's home league record:	32	15	9	8	47	37
Arsenal's away league record:	32	10	14	8	39	47
Arsenal's cup record:	9	7	2	0	19	5
TOTAL	**73**	**32**	**25**	**16**	**105**	**89**

FACT FILE

- **Jack Lambert and Alex James scored the goals in 1930 as Arsenal won the FA Cup for the first time. They have won it eight times since, a record bettered only by Manchester United.**
- **Between 1934 and 1951, Arsenal failed to win in 10 visits to Huddersfield, although it should be pointed out that they drew nine of these!**
- **Arsenal were unbeaten in 12 home games from 1928 to 1938.**
- **The meeting in February 1925 was the last occasion Arsenal lost a home league game by five goals.**
- **Arsenal have won all six cup ties.**

Arsenal's top scorers vs Huddersfield

Cliff Bastin, Reg Lewis, Ronnie Rooke 5
Peter Goring, David Jack, Fred Pagnam, Don Roper 4

Arsenal hat-tricks vs Huddersfield

18 Dec 1948 Ronnie Rooke
16 Sep 1950 Peter Goring
21 Sep 1993 Ian Wright (cup)

Played for both clubs

Dick Roose	Huddersfield Town 1910-11	Arsenal 1911-12
Joey Williams	Huddersfield Town 1924-26	Arsenal 1929-32
Pat Beasley	Arsenal 1931-37	Huddersfield Town 1936-40
Joe Hulme	Arsenal 1925-38	Huddersfield Town 1937-38
Eddie Carr	Arsenal 1937-39	Huddersfield Town 1946-47
Peter Goy	Arsenal 1958-59	Huddersfield Town 1966-67
Bob McNab	Huddersfield Town 1963-67	Arsenal 1966-75
Jimmy McGill	Arsenal 1965-67	Huddersfield Town 1967-72
Frank Stapleton	Arsenal 1974-81	Huddersfield Town 1991-92
Steve Walford	Arsenal 1977-81	Huddersfield Town 1987-88
Brian McDermott	Arsenal 1978-84	Huddersfield Town 1986-87
David Cork	Arsenal 1983-84	Huddersfield Town 1985-88
Vince Bartram	Arsenal 1994-95	Huddersfield Town 1997-98

v. Hull City

			Home				Away			Final Positions	
Season	*League*	*Date*	*Result*	Arsenal	Hull City	*Date*	*Result*	Arsenal	Hull City	Arsenal	Hull City
1913-14	Division 2	20 September	Drew	**0**	**0**	17 January	Won	**2**	**1**	3rd	7th
1914-15	Division 2	26 September	Won	**2**	**1**	2 April	Lost	**0**	**1**	5thP	7th

FA Cup

										Division	
1907-08	Round 1	11 January	Drew	**0**	**0**	16 January	Lost	**1**	**4**	Div 1	Div 2
1929-30	Semi Final	22 March		Elland Road			Drew	**2**	**2**	Div 1	Div 2
	26 March			Villa Park (replay)			Won	**1**	**0**		

League Cup

1977-78	Round 4	29 November	Won	**5**	**1**					Div 1	Div 2
1988-89	Round 2	12 October	Won	**3**	**0**	28 September	Won	**2**	**1**	Div 1	Div 2

Summary	P	W	D	L	F	A
Arsenal's home league record:	2	1	1	0	2	1
Arsenal's away league record:	2	1	0	1	2	2
Arsenal's cup record:	7	4	2	1	14	8
TOTAL	**11**	**6**	**3**	**2**	**18**	**11**

FACT FILE

- **Hull have not won in their five visits to Highbury.**
- **Arsenal have won their last four matches of the series.**

Arsenal's top scorers vs Hull

Pat Flanagan, Wally Hardinge, David Jack,
John Matthews, Alan Smith 2

Played for both clubs

Horace Cumner	Hull City 1937-38	Arsenal 1938-40
Ian McKechnie	Arsenal 1961-64	Hull City 1966-74
Jimmy McGill	Arsenal 1965-67	Hull City 1971-76
Terry Neill	Arsenal 1960-70	Hull City 1970-73
John Roberts	Arsenal 1969-73	Hull City 1980-81
John Hawley	Hull City 1972-78/82-83	Arsenal 1981-83
Brian Marwood	Hull City 1979-84	Arsenal 1987-90
David Rocastle	Arsenal 1985-92	Hull City 1997-98

v. Ipswich Town

		Home					Away			Final Positions	
Season	*League*	*Date*	*Result*	Arsenal	Ipswich	*Date*	*Result*	Arsenal	Ipswich	Arsenal	Ipswich
1961-62	Division 1	23 April	Lost	**0**	**3**	20 April	Drew	**2**	**2**	10th	1st
1962-63	Division 1	24 November	Won	**3**	**1**	30 March	Drew	**1**	**1**	7th	17th
1963-64	Division 1	5 October	Won	**6**	**0**	18 February	Won	**2**	**1**	8th	22ndR
1968-69	Division 1	18 February	Lost	**0**	**2**	24 August	Won	**2**	**1**	4th	12th
1969-70	Division 1	25 October	Drew	**0**	**0**	31 March	Lost	**1**	**2**	12th	18th
1970-71	Division 1	20 February	Won	**3**	**2**	21 November	Won	**1**	**0**	1st	19th
1971-72	Division 1	30 October	Won	**2**	**1**	19 February	Won	**1**	**0**	5th	13th
1972-73	Division 1	14 October	Won	**1**	**0**	10 March	Won	**2**	**1**	2nd	4th
1973-74	Division 1	20 October	Drew	**1**	**1**	16 March	Drew	**2**	**2**	10th	4th
1974-75	Division 1	20 August	Lost	**0**	**1**	27 August	Lost	**0**	**3**	16th	3rd
1975-76	Division 1	17 April	Lost	**1**	**2**	26 December	Lost	**0**	**2**	17th	6th
1976-77	Division 1	5 March	Lost	**1**	**4**	25 September	Lost	**1**	**3**	8th	3rd
1977-78	Division 1	2 January	Won	**1**	**0**	20 August	Lost	**0**	**1**	5th	18th
1978-79	Division 1	4 November	Won	**4**	**1**	17 March	Lost	**0**	**2**	7th	6th
1979-80	Division 1	21 August	Lost	**0**	**2**	9 October	Won	**2**	**1**	4th	3rd
1980-81	Division 1	27 December	Drew	**1**	**1**	18 April	Won	**2**	**0**	3rd	2nd
1981-82	Division 1	13 March	Won	**1**	**0**	24 October	Lost	**1**	**2**	5th	2nd
1982-83	Division 1	22 March	Drew	**2**	**2**	9 October	Won	**1**	**0**	10th	9th
1983-84	Division 1	10 March	Won	**4**	**1**	12 November	Lost	**0**	**1**	6th	12th
1984-85	Division 1	19 March	Drew	**1**	**1**	15 September	Lost	**1**	**2**	7th	17th
1985-86	Division 1	19 October	Won	**1**	**0**	11 March	Won	**2**	**1**	7th	20thR
1992-93	Prem'ship	26 December	Drew	**0**	**0**	10 April	Won	**2**	**1**	10th	16th
1993-94	Prem'ship	11 September	Won	**4**	**0**	5 March	Won	**5**	**1**	4th	19th
1994-95	Prem'ship	15 April	Won	**4**	**1**	28 December	Won	**2**	**0**	12th	22ndR
2000-01	Prem'ship	10 February	Won	**1**	**0**	23 September	Drew	**1**	**1**	2nd	5th
2001-02	Prem'ship	21 April	Won	**2**	**0**	1 December	Won	**2**	**0**	1st	18thR

FA Cup										*Division*	
1977-78	Final	6 May				Wembley	Lost	**0**	**1**	Div 1	Div 1
1992-93	Q'ter Final					6 March	Won	**4**	**2**	Prem	Prem

League Cup											
1970-71	Round 2	28 September	Won	**4**	**0**	8 September	Drew	**0**	**0**	Div 1	Div 1
2000-01	Round 3	1 November	Lost	**1**	**2**					Prem	Prem

Summary	P	W	D	L	F	A
Arsenal's home league record:	26	14	6	6	44	26
Arsenal's away league record:	26	13	4	9	36	31
Arsenal's cup record:	5	2	1	2	9	5
TOTAL	**57**	**29**	**11**	**17**	**89**	**62**

FACT FILE

- **Arsenal players claimed three hat-tricks in two seasons against Ipswich between 1993 and 1995.**
- **2000-01 was the first time for 22 years that Arsenal fell at the first hurdle in the League Cup (since 1996 they have had a bye to Round 3 due to European participation).**
- **This was Ipswich's only win in the last 14 games.**
- **Arsenal lost seven in a row between 1974 and 1977.**

Arsenal's top scorers vs Ipswich

Ian Wright 9
Kevin Campbell 5
Charlie George, John Radford,
Frank Stapleton, Geoff Strong 4

Arsenal hat-tricks vs Ipswich

5 Oct 1963 Geoff Strong
4 Nov 1978 Frank Stapleton
11 Sep 1993 Kevin Campbell
5 Mar 1994 Ian Wright
15 Apr 1995 Ian Wright

Played for both clubs

Jimmy Robertson	Arsenal 1968-70	Ipswich Town 1969-72
Brian Talbot	Ipswich Town 1973-79	Arsenal 1978-85
Paul Mariner	Ipswich Town 1976-84	Arsenal 1983-86
Alan Sunderland	Arsenal 1977-84	Ipswich Town 1983-86
Lee Chapman	Arsenal 1982-84	Ipswich Town 1994-96
Raphael Meade	Arsenal 1981-85	Ipswich Town 1989-90
Chris Kiwomya	Ipswich Town 1988-95	Arsenal 1994-95
Richard Wright	Ipswich Town 1994-2001	Arsenal 2001-02
Paulo Vernazza	Arsenal 1997-2001	Ipswich Town 1998-99

Irish international Frank Stapleton, seen here scoring against Ipswich at Highbury in April 1976, hit 108 goals for Arsenal in 299 senior games.

v. Leeds City

Season	League	Date	Result	Home Arsenal	Home Leeds City	Date	Result	Away Arsenal	Away Leeds City	Final Positions Arsenal	Final Positions Leeds City
1913-14	Division 2	6 December	Won	**1**	**0**	11 April	Drew	**0**	**0**	3rd	4th
1914-15	Division 2	6 February	Won	**2**	**0**	3 October	Drew	**2**	**2**	5thP	15th

Summary	P	W	D	L	F	A
Arsenal's home league record:	2	2	0	0	3	0
Arsenal's away league record:	2	0	2	0	2	2
TOTAL	**4**	**2**	**2**	**0**	**5**	**2**

FACT FILE

- **The expulsion from the league of Leeds City in 1919 led to the formation of Leeds United.**

Arsenal's top scorers vs Leeds City

Frank Bradshaw 2

Played for both clubs

Bob Watson	Arsenal 1903-05	Leeds City 1905-08
Thomas Drain	Leeds City 1905-06	Arsenal 1909-10
Tommy Hynds	Arsenal 1906-07	Leeds City 1907-08

Frank Bradshaw tops the scoring chart against Leeds City for Arsenal.

v. Leeds United

		Home					Away				Final Positions	
Season	*League*	*Date*	*Result*	Arsenal	Leeds Utd	*Date*	*Result*	Arsenal	Leeds Utd		Arsenal	Leeds Utd
1924-25	Division 1	20 December	Won	**6**	**1**	25 April	Lost	**0**	**1**		20th	18th
1925-26	Division 1	26 September	Won	**4**	**1**	6 February	Lost	**2**	**4**		2nd	19th
1926-27	Division 1	12 February	Won	**1**	**0**	25 September	Lost	**1**	**4**		11st	21stR
1928-29	Division 1	27 April	Won	**1**	**0**	15 December	Drew	**1**	**1**		9th	13th
1929-30	Division 1	31 August	Won	**4**	**0**	28 December	Lost	**0**	**2**		14th	5th
1930-31	Division 1	6 September	Won	**3**	**1**	11 March	Won	**2**	**1**		1st	21stR
1932-33	Division 1	26 December	Lost	**1**	**2**	27 December	Drew	**0**	**0**		1st	8th
1933-34	Division 1	26 December	Won	**2**	**0**	25 December	Won	**1**	**0**		1st	9th
1934-35	Division 1	19 January	Won	**3**	**0**	8 September	Drew	**1**	**1**		1st	18th
1935-36	Division 1	2 May	Drew	**2**	**2**	18 September	Drew	**1**	**1**		6th	11th
1936-37	Division 1	7 November	Won	**4**	**1**	13 March	Won	**4**	**3**		3rd	19th
1937-38	Division 1	27 November	Won	**4**	**1**	9 April	Won	**1**	**0**		1st	9th
1938-39	Division 1	5 November	Lost	**2**	**3**	11 March	Lost	**2**	**4**		5th	13th
1946-47	Division 1	16 November	Won	**4**	**2**	22 March	Drew	**1**	**1**		13th	22ndR
1956-57	Division 1	6 April	Won	**1**	**0**	24 November	Drew	**3**	**3**		5th	8th
1957-58	Division 1	28 September	Won	**2**	**1**	19 March	Lost	**0**	**2**		12th	17th
1958-59	Division 1	24 February	Won	**1**	**0**	27 September	Lost	**1**	**2**		3rd	15th
1959-60	Division 1	26 March	Drew	**1**	**1**	7 November	Lost	**2**	**3**		13th	21stR
1964-65	Division 1	13 February	Lost	**1**	**2**	11 November	Lost	**1**	**3**		13th	2nd
1965-66	Division 1	5 May	Lost	**0**	**3**	13 November	Lost	**0**	**2**		14th	2nd
1966-67	Division 1	5 November	Lost	**0**	**1**	15 October	Lost	**1**	**3**		7th	4th
1967-68	Division 1	7 May	Won	**4**	**3**	4 November	Lost	**1**	**3**		9th	4th
1968-69	Division 1	12 April	Lost	**1**	**2**	21 September	Lost	**0**	**2**		4th	1st
1969-70	Division 1	19 August	Drew	**1**	**1**	13 August	Drew	**0**	**0**		12th	2nd
1970-71	Division 1	1 September	Drew	**0**	**0**	26 April	Lost	**0**	**1**		1st	2nd
1971-72	Division 1	11 September	Won	**2**	**0**	25 March	Lost	**0**	**3**		5th	2nd
1972-73	Division 1	2 December	Won	**2**	**1**	9 May	Lost	**1**	**6**		2nd	3rd
1973-74	Division 1	28 August	Lost	**1**	**2**	5 February	Lost	**1**	**3**		10th	1st
1974-75	Division 1	12 April	Lost	**1**	**2**	5 October	Lost	**0**	**2**		16th	9th
1975-76	Division 1	6 December	Lost	**1**	**2**	27 March	Lost	**0**	**3**		17th	5th
1976-77	Division 1	3 January	Drew	**1**	**1**	30 October	Lost	**1**	**2**		8th	10th
1977-78	Division 1	10 December	Drew	**1**	**1**	22 April	Won	**3**	**1**		5th	9th
1978-79	Division 1	19 August	Drew	**2**	**2**	11 November	Won	**1**	**0**		7th	5th
1979-80	Division 1	12 January	Lost	**0**	**1**	1 September	Drew	**1**	**1**		4th	11th
1980-81	Division 1	11 April	Drew	**0**	**0**	8 November	Won	**5**	**0**		3rd	9th
1981-82	Division 1	30 January	Won	**1**	**0**	19 September	Drew	**0**	**0**		5th	20thR
1990-91	Division 1	17 March	Won	**2**	**0**	29 September	Drew	**2**	**2**		1st	4th
1991-92	Division 1	22 March	Drew	**1**	**1**	3 September	Drew	**2**	**2**		4th	1st
1992-93	Prem'ship	24 February	Drew	**0**	**0**	21 November	Lost	**0**	**3**		10th	17th
1993-94	Prem'ship	24 August	Won	**2**	**1**	18 December	Lost	**1**	**2**		4th	5th
1994-95	Prem'ship	17 December	Lost	**1**	**3**	23 August	Lost	**0**	**1**		12th	5th
1995-96	Prem'ship	6 April	Won	**2**	**1**	14 October	Won	**3**	**0**		5th	13th
1996-97	Prem'ship	26 October	Won	**3**	**0**	1 February	Drew	**0**	**0**		3rd	11th
1997-98	Prem'ship	10 January	Won	**2**	**1**	9 August	Drew	**1**	**1**		1st	5th

Season	League	Home Date	Home Result	Arsenal	Leeds Utd	Away Date	Away Result	Arsenal	Leeds Utd	Final Positions Arsenal	Leeds Utd
1998-99	Prem'ship	20 December	Won	**3**	**1**	11 May	Lost	**0**	**1**	2nd	4th
1999-00	Prem'ship	28 December	Won	**2**	**0**	16 April	Won	**4**	**0**	2nd	3rd
2000-01	Prem'ship	5 May	Won	**2**	**1**	26 November	Lost	**0**	**1**	2nd	4th
2001-02	Prem'ship	21 August	Lost	**1**	**2**	20 January	Drew	**1**	**1**	1st	5th
2002-03	Prem'ship	4 May	Lost	**2**	**3**	28 September	Won	**4**	**1**	2nd	15th
2003-04	Prem'ship	16 April	Won	**5**	**0**	1 November	Won	**4**	**1**	1st	19thR

FA Cup										Division	
1949-50	Q'ter Final	4 March	Won	**1**	**0**					Div 1	Div 2
1971-72	Final	6 May		Wembley			Lost	**0**	**1**	Div 1	Div 1
1982-83	Round 4	29 January	Drew	**1**	**1**	2 February		**1**	**1**	Div 1	Div 2
		9 February	Won	**2**	**1**	(2nd replay)					
1990-91	Round 4	27 January	Drew	**0**	**0**	30 January	Drew*	**1**	**1**	Div 1	Div 1
		13 February	Drew*	**0**	**0**	(2nd replay)					
				(3rd replay)		16 February	Won	**2**	**1**		
1992-93	Round 4	25 January	Drew	**2**	**2**	3 February	Won*	**3**	**2**	Prem	Prem
1996-97	Round 4	4 February	Lost	**0**	**1**					Prem	Prem
2003-04	Round 3					4 January	Won	**4**	**1**	Prem	Prem

League Cup											
1967-68	Final	2 March		Wembley			Lost	**0**	**1**	Div 1	Div 1
1979-80	Round 2	4 September	Won	**7**	**0**	29 August	Drew	**1**	**1**	Div 1	Div 1

Summary	P	W	D	L	F	A
Arsenal's home league record:	50	27	10	13	93	54
Arsenal's away league record:	50	11	14	25	61	84
Arsenal's cup record:	16	6	7	3	25	14
TOTAL	**116**	**44**	**31**	**41**	**179**	**152**

FACT FILE

- **Arsenal's biggest league cup win was the 7-0 win over Leeds in 1979.**
- **Between 1939 and 1976, Arsenal failed to win in 17 games at Elland Road. This included runs of eight and seven consecutive defeats.**
- **Arsenal failed to win in eight home games from 1973 to 1981.**
- **Arsenal won six Premiership home games in succession from 1996 to 2001. They also won their first six home games with Leeds.**
- **Arsenal lost seven games in a row from 1974 to 1977.**
- **Arsenal have won 4-1 on their last three visits to Elland Road.**
- **Leeds' FA Cup win at Highbury in 1997 was Arsenal's last FA Cup exit at home. It was also the last time Arsenal lost any FA Cup match prior to the semi-finals.**

Arsenal's top scorers vs Leeds

Thierry Henry 11
Jimmy Brain 8
Cliff Bastin, Ted Drake, David Herd, Ian Wright 7
Liam Brady, Alf Kirchen, Paul Merson, Alan Sunderland 5

Arsenal hat-tricks vs Leeds

20 Dec 1924 Jimmy Brain (4)
4 Sep 1979 Alan Sunderland (cup)
16 Apr 2004 Thierry Henry (4)

Wilf Copping's career was curtailed by World War Two and he enjoyed two spells at Leeds United.

Played for both clubs

Jack Lambert	Leeds United 1923-24	Arsenal 1926-34
Wilf Copping	Leeds United 1930-34/38-40	Arsenal 1934-39
John Hawley	Leeds United 1978-80	Arsenal 1981-83
John Lukic	Leeds United 1979-83/90-96	Arsenal 1983-90/96-2001
Lee Chapman	Arsenal 1982-84	Leeds United 1989-93/95-96
Chris Whyte	Arsenal 1981-86	Leeds United 1990-93
Andy Linighan	Leeds United 1984-86	Arsenal 1990-97
David Rocastle	Arsenal 1985-92	Leeds United 1992-94
David O'Leary	Arsenal 1975-93	Leeds United 1993-94
Jermaine Pennant	Arsenal 2002-03	Leeds United 2003-04

Liam Brady in full flight against Leeds United at Highbury on the opening day of the 1978-79 season, pursued by Brian Flynn and Tony Currie. Brady scored both Arsenal goals in the 2-2 draw.

v. Leicester City

		Home					Away				
										Final Positions	
Season	*League*	*Date*	*Result*	Arsenal	Leicester	*Date*	*Result*	Arsenal	Leicester	Arsenal	Leicester
1894-95	Division 2	9 March	Drew	**3**	**3**	7 January	Lost	**1**	**3**	8th	4th
1895-96	Division 2	7 December	Drew	**1**	**1**	25 January	Lost	**0**	**1**	7th	8th
1896-97	Division 2	17 April	Won	**2**	**1**	13 February	Lost	**3**	**6**	10th	9th
1897-98	Division 2	23 October	Lost	**0**	**3**	4 December	Lost	**1**	**2**	5th	7th
1898-99	Division 2	10 September	Won	**4**	**0**	7 January	Lost	**1**	**2**	7th	3rd
1899-00	Division 2	2 September	Lost	**0**	**2**	30 December	Drew	**0**	**0**	8th	5th
1900-01	Division 2	3 November	Won	**2**	**1**	15 December	Lost	**0**	**1**	7th	11th
1901-02	Division 2	7 September	Won	**2**	**0**	4 January	Lost	**1**	**2**	4th	15th
1902-03	Division 2	13 April	Drew	**0**	**0**	11 April	Won	**2**	**0**	3rd	15th
1903-04	Division 2	26 October	Won	**8**	**0**	26 December	Drew	**0**	**0**	2ndP	18th
1908-09	Division 1	26 December	Won	**2**	**1**	25 December	Drew	**1**	**1**	6th	20thR
1913-14	Division 2	6 September	Won	**2**	**1**	27 December	Won	**2**	**1**	3rd	18th
1914-15	Division 2	26 December	Won	**6**	**0**	25 December	Won	**4**	**1**	5thP	19th
1925-26	Division 1	31 August	Drew	**2**	**2**	7 September	Won	**1**	**0**	2nd	17th
1926-27	Division 1	11 September	Drew	**2**	**2**	10 February	Lost	**1**	**2**	11th	7th
1927-28	Division 1	15 October	Drew	**2**	**2**	25 February	Lost	**2**	**3**	10th	3rd
1928-29	Division 1	13 April	Drew	**1**	**1**	1 December	Drew	**1**	**1**	9th	2nd
1929-30	Division 1	18 April	Drew	**1**	**1**	21 April	Drew	**6**	**6**	14th	8th
1930-31	Division 1	20 September	Won	**4**	**1**	5 February	Won	**7**	**2**	1st	16th
1931-32	Division 1	5 March	Won	**2**	**1**	24 October	Won	**2**	**1**	2nd	19th
1932-33	Division 1	29 October	Won	**8**	**2**	11 March	Drew	**1**	**1**	1st	19th
1933-34	Division 1	21 October	Won	**2**	**0**	8 March	Lost	**1**	**4**	1st	17th
1934-35	Division 1	15 December	Won	**8**	**0**	27 April	Won	**5**	**3**	1st	21stR
1937-38	Division 1	2 February	Won	**3**	**1**	11 September	Drew	**1**	**1**	1st	16th
1938-39	Division 1	19 November	Drew	**0**	**0**	25 March	Won	**2**	**0**	5th	22ndR
1954-55	Division 1	19 February	Drew	**1**	**1**	2 October	Drew	**3**	**3**	9th	21stR
1957-58	Division 1	14 September	Won	**3**	**1**	18 January	Won	**1**	**0**	12th	18th
1958-59	Division 1	30 August	Won	**5**	**1**	3 January	Won	**3**	**2**	3rd	19th
1959-60	Division 1	15 March	Drew	**1**	**1**	24 October	Drew	**2**	**2**	13th	12th
1960-61	Division 1	25 February	Lost	**1**	**3**	8 October	Lost	**1**	**2**	11th	6th
1961-62	Division 1	29 August	Drew	**4**	**4**	23 August	Won	**1**	**0**	10th	14th
1962-63	Division 1	22 September	Drew	**1**	**1**	9 February	Lost	**0**	**2**	7th	4th
1963-64	Division 1	21 December	Lost	**0**	**1**	31 August	Lost	**2**	**7**	8th	11th
1964-65	Division 1	23 January	Won	**4**	**3**	19 September	Won	**3**	**2**	13th	18th
1965-66	Division 1	7 May	Won	**1**	**0**	30 October	Lost	**1**	**3**	14th	7th
1966-67	Division 1	1 October	Lost	**2**	**4**	11 February	Lost	**1**	**2**	7th	8th
1967-68	Division 1	13 April	Won	**2**	**1**	18 November	Drew	**2**	**2**	9th	13th
1968-69	Division 1	13 August	Won	**3**	**0**	8 April	Drew	**0**	**0**	4th	21stR
1971-72	Division 1	25 September	Won	**3**	**0**	4 April	Drew	**0**	**0**	5th	12th
1972-73	Division 1	17 February	Won	**1**	**0**	12 August	Won	**1**	**0**	2nd	16th
1973-74	Division 1	8 September	Lost	**0**	**2**	29 December	Lost	**0**	**2**	10th	9th
1974-75	Division 1	14 December	Drew	**0**	**0**	17 August	Won	**1**	**0**	16th	18th
1975-76	Division 1	6 September	Drew	**1**	**1**	17 January	Lost	**1**	**2**	17th	7th
1976-77	Division 1	2 April	Won	**3**	**0**	23 October	Lost	**1**	**4**	8th	11th

Season	League	Home Date	Result	Arsenal	Leicester	Away Date	Result	Arsenal	Leicester	Final Positions Arsenal	Leicester
1977-78	Division 1	17 September	Won	**2**	**1**	11 February	Drew	**1**	**1**	5th	22ndR
1980-81	Division 1	4 October	Won	**1**	**0**	7 March	Lost	**0**	**1**	3rd	21stR
1983-84	Division 1	28 April	Won	**2**	**1**	26 November	Lost	**0**	**3**	6th	15th
1984-85	Division 1	16 March	Won	**2**	**0**	13 October	Won	**4**	**1**	7th	15th
1985-86	Division 1	31 August	Won	**1**	**0**	18 January	Drew	**2**	**2**	7th	19th
1986-87	Division 1	20 April	Won	**4**	**1**	26 December	Drew	**1**	**1**	4th	20thR
1994-95	Prem'ship	11 February	Drew	**1**	**1**	23 November	Lost	**1**	**2**	12th	21stR
1996-97	Prem'ship	12 April	Won	**2**	**0**	24 August	Won	**2**	**0**	3rd	9th
1997-98	Prem'ship	26 December	Won	**2**	**1**	27 August	Drew	**3**	**3**	1st	9th
1998-99	Prem'ship	20 February	Won	**5**	**0**	12 September	Drew	**1**	**1**	2nd	10th
1999-00	Prem'ship	7 August	Won	**2**	**1**	4 December	Won	**3**	**0**	2nd	8th
2000-01	Prem'ship	26 December	Won	**6**	**1**	20 January	Drew	**0**	**0**	2nd	13th
2001-02	Prem'ship	25 August	Won	**4**	**0**	23 January	Won	**3**	**1**	1st	20thR
2003-04	Prem'ship	15 May	Won	**2**	**1**	6 December	Drew	**1**	**1**	1st	18thR

FA Cup

Season	Round	Home Date	Result	Arsenal	Leicester	Away Date	Result	Arsenal	Leicester	Division	
1921-22	Round 3	18 February	Won	**3**	**0**					Div 1	Div 2
1934-35	Round 3					26 January	Won	**1**	**0**	Div 1	Div 1
1970-71	Q'ter Final	15 March	Won	**1**	**0**	6 March	Drew	**0**	**0**	Div 1	Div 2
1972-73	Round 3	13 January	Drew	**2**	**2**	17 January	Won	**2**	**1**	Div 1	Div 1
1974-75	Round 5	15 February	Drew	**0**	**0**	19 February	Drew*	**1**	**1**	Div 1	Div 1
			(2nd replay)			24 February	Won*	**1**	**0**		
1999-00	Round 4	9 January	Drew	**0**	**0**	19 January	Drew*	**0**	**0**	Prem	Prem
			lost 5-6 pens								

League Cup

Season	Round	Home Date	Result	Arsenal	Leicester	Away Date	Result	Arsenal	Leicester	Division	
1974-75	Round 2	10 September	Drew	**1**	**1**	18 September	Lost	**1**	**2**	Div 1	Div 1
1991-92	Round 2	8 October	Won	**2**	**0**	25 September	Drew	**1**	**1**	Div 1	Div 2

Summary	P	W	D	L	F	A	
Arsenal's home league record:	58	36	16	6	139	58	
Arsenal's away league record:	58	18	19	21	92	96	
Arsenal's cup record:	15	6	8	1	16	8	
TOTAL	**131**	**60**	**43**	**28**	**247**	**162**	(+one penalty shoot-out defeat)

The 1971 Double winners. Back row (left to right): Bob McNab, Ray Kennedy, Bob Wilson, John Roberts, Geoff Barnett, Peter Simpson, Peter Marinello. Front row: Sammy Nelson, Peter Storey, John Radford, Eddie Kelly, Frank McLintock, Pat Rice, George Graham, George Armstrong. Captain Frank McLintock was an inspired signing from Leicester City in 1964.

FACT FILE

- **On 15 May 2004, Arsenal matched the feat of the 1889 Preston 'Invincibles', when victory over Leicester ensured they completed the entire league season unbeaten. No club has acheived this in any division of the Football League since Liverpool in 1894.**
- **Between 1900 and 1960, Arsenal were unbeaten in 24 home games. They scored eight in a match three times in this sequence.**
- **Arsenal failed to win in their first eight away games.**
- **Arsenal are unbeaten in their last 17 matches, but were eliminated from the FA Cup on penalties in this time.**
- **In 1930, the sides produced one of only two 6-6 draws in Football League history (and the only one in the top flight). It included three goals in five minutes by Arsenal's Dave Halliday.**
- **The match in September 1913 was Arsenal's first ever match at Highbury.**

Arsenal's top scorers vs Leicester

Cliff Bastin, Joe Hulme 11
Jimmy Brain, Ted Drake, John Radford 6
Dennis Bergkamp, Thierry Henry,
Jack Lambert 5

Arsenal hat-tricks vs Leicester

26 Oct 1903 Tommy Shanks
26 Dec 1914 Reg Lewis
21 Apr 1930 Dave Halliday (4)
5 Feb 1931 Jack Lambert
29 Oct 1932 Joe Hulme
15 Dec 1934 Joe Hulme
15 Dec 1934 Ted Drake
27 Aug 1997 Dennis Bergkamp
20 Feb 1999 Nicolas Anelka
26 Dec 2000 Thierry Henry

Played for both clubs

Robert Gordon	Leicester City 1894-95	Arsenal 1895-96
Tommy Shanks	Arsenal 1902-04	Leicester City 1906-09
Billy Bannister	Arsenal 1902-04/10-12	Leicester City 1904-10
Harry Thorpe	Arsenal 1903-04	Leicester City 1907-08
Billy Spittle	Arsenal 1912-14	Leicester City 1919-21
George Jobey	Arsenal 1913-14	Leicester City 1919-20
Harry King	Arsenal 1914-15	Leicester City 1919-20
Mal Griffiths	Arsenal 1937-38	Leicester City 1938-56
Frank McLintock	Leicester City 1959-65	Arsenal 1964-73
Jon Sammels	Arsenal 1962-71	Leicester City 1971-78
Jeff Blockley	Arsenal 1972-75	Leicester City 1974-78
Eddie Kelly	Arsenal 1969-76	Leicester City 1977-80/81-83
George Armstrong	Arsenal 1961-77	Leicester City 1977-79
Colin Hill	Arsenal 1982-85	Leicester City 1991-97
Alan Smith	Leicester City 1982-87	Arsenal 1987-95
Kevin Campbell	Arsenal 1987-95	Leicester City 1989-90
Paul Dickov	Arsenal 1992-97	Leicester City 2001-03

v. Leyton

FA Cup		Date	Result	Home Arsenal	Home Leyton	Division Arsenal	Division Leyton
1896-97	4th Qual	12 December	Won	**5**	**0**	Div 2	Non L

Summary	P	W	D	L	F	A
Arsenal's cup record:	1	1	0	0	5	0
TOTAL	**1**	**1**	**0**	**0**	**5**	**0**

FACT FILE

- **Arsenal fielded a reserve side for this fixture, as the first team had to fulfil a league fixture at Loughborough. Strangely, the reserves won 5-0 whilst the first team lost 8-0!**

Arsenal's top scorers vs Leyton

Frank McAvoy 2

v. Leyton Orient

			Home					Away			Final Positions	
Season	*League*	*Date*	*Result*	Arsenal	Orient	*Date*	*Result*	Arsenal	Orient		Arsenal	Orient
1913-14	Division 2	18 April	Drew	**2**	**2**	13 December	Lost	**0**	**1**		3rd	6th
1914-15	Division 2	10 October	Won	**2**	**1**	13 February	Lost	**0**	**1**		5thP	9th
1962-63	Division 1	15 December	Won	**2**	**0**	18 August	Won	**2**	**1**		7th	22ndR

FA Cup										*Division*	
1893-94	2nd Qual	4 November	Won	**6**	**2**					Div 2	Non L
1910-11	Round 1					16 January	Won	**2**	**1**	Div 1	Div 2
1951-52	Round 5					23 February	Won	**3**	**0**	Div 1	Div 3S
1971-72	Q'ter Final					18 March	Won	**1**	**0**	Div 1	Div 2
1977-78	Semi Final	8 April				Stamford Bridge	Won	**3**	**0**	Div 1	Div 2

Summary	P	W	D	L	F	A
Arsenal's home league record:	3	2	1	0	6	3
Arsenal's away league record:	3	1	0	2	2	3
Arsenal's cup record:	5	5	0	0	15	3
TOTAL	**11**	**8**	**1**	**2**	**23**	**9**

FACT FILE

- **Arsenal have won their last five matches against the O's.**

Later to become an Orient player, Cliff Holton gets in a header against Spurs at Highbury in February 1954. The other Arsenal player is Doug Lishman. Arsenal lost 3-0.

Arsenal's top scorers vs Orient

Joe Baker 3

Joseph Cooper, Pat Flanagan, Jackie Henderson, Doug Lishman, Malcolm Macdonald 2

Played for both clubs

Ned Liddell	Leyton Orient 1907-13	Arsenal 1914-15
Edward King	Arsenal 1912-13	Leyton Orient 1914-15
Stan Earle	Arsenal 1921-24	Leyton Orient 1932-33
Bobby Turnbull	Arsenal 1921-25	Leyton Orient 1927-30
Jock Rutherford	Arsenal 1913-26	Leyton Orient 1926-27
Donald Cock	Arsenal 1924-26	Leyton Orient 1925-27
Sid Hoar	Arsenal 1924-29	Leyton Orient 1929-30
Reg Tricker	Arsenal 1926-29	Leyton Orient 1928-33
Dave Halliday	Arsenal 1929-30	Leyton Orient 1933-35
Henry Waller	Arsenal 1946-47	Leyton Orient 1947-48
Alan Smith	Arsenal 1946-47	Leyton Orient 1949-50
Stan Morgan	Arsenal 1946-47	Leyton Orient 1953-56
Alex Forbes	Arsenal 1947-56	Leyton Orient 1956-57
Stan Charlton	Leyton Orient 1952-56/58-65	Arsenal 1955-59
Vic Groves	Leyton Orient 1954-56	Arsenal 1955-64
Len Julians	Leyton Orient 1955-59	Arsenal 1958-60
Cliff Holton	Arsenal 1950-59	Leyton Orient 1966-68
Anthony Biggs	Arsenal 1957-59	Leyton Orient 1958-60
Jimmy Bloomfield	Arsenal 1954-61	Leyton Orient 1967-69
Gerry Ward	Arsenal 1953-63	Leyton Orient 1963-65
John Snedden	Arsenal 1959-65	Leyton Orient 1966-68
Gordon Ferry	Arsenal 1964-65	Leyton Orient 1965-66
Tom Walley	Arsenal 1965-67	Leyton Orient 1971-76
Terry Mancini	Leyton Orient 1967-72	Arsenal 1974-76
David Price	Arsenal 1972-81	Leyton Orient 1982-83
John Hawley	Arsenal 1981-83	Leyton Orient 1982-83
Rhys Wilmot	Leyton Orient 1984-85	Arsenal 1985-87
Kwame Ampadu	Arsenal 1989-90	Leyton Orient 1998-2000
Kevin Campbell	Arsenal 1987-95	Leyton Orient 1988-89

Stan Charlton (left) returned to Orient after transferring to Arsenal in 1955 and long-serving Jock Rutherford (right) left the Gunners in 1926 to join the O's after a 13-year association.

v. Lincoln City

		Home					Away			Final Positions	
Season	League	Date	Result	Arsenal	Lincoln	Date	Result	Arsenal	Lincoln	Arsenal	Lincoln
1893-94	Division 2	17 February	Won	4	0	3 February	Lost	0	3	9th	8th
1894-95	Division 2	6 October	Won	5	2	1 September	Lost	2	5	8th	13th
1895-96	Division 2	21 September	Won	4	0	14 September	Drew	1	1	7th	13th
1896-97	Division 2	25 December	Won	6	2	3 December	Won	3	2	10th	16th
1897-98	Division 2	11 September	Drew	2	2	27 December	Won	3	2	5th	14th
1898-99	Division 2	17 December	Won	4	2	15 April	Lost	0	2	7th	12th
1899-00	Division 2	24 March	Won	2	1	25 December	Lost	0	5	8th	9th
1900-01	Division 2	9 March	Drew	0	0	26 January	Drew	3	3	7th	8th
1901-02	Division 2	5 April	Won	2	0	7 December	Drew	0	0	4th	5th
1902-03	Division 2	29 November	Won	2	1	28 March	Drew	2	2	3rd	10th
1903-04	Division 2	7 November	Won	4	0	5 March	Won	2	0	2ndP	12th
1913-14	Division 2	18 October	Won	3	0	21 February	Lost	2	5	3th	19th
1914-15	Division 2	31 October	Drew	1	1	6 March	Lost	0	1	5thP	16th

Summary	P	W	D	L	F	A
Arsenal's home league record:	13	10	3	0	39	11
Arsenal's away league record:	13	3	4	6	18	31
TOTAL	**26**	**13**	**7**	**6**	**57**	**42**

FACT FILE

- **Lincoln have never beaten Arsenal away in 13 attempts.**
- **Arsenal have not won in their last three meetings.**

Arsenal's top scorers vs Lincoln

Paddy O'Brien 5
Tommy Shanks 4
Henry Boyd, Ralph Gaudie, Fergus Hunt 3
Peter Mortimer 3

Arsenal hat-tricks vs Lincoln

7 Nov 1903 Tommy Shanks

Played for both clubs

Andrew Swann	Lincoln City 1898-99	Arsenal 1901-02
Donald Slade	Lincoln City 1912-14	Arsenal 1913-14
Archie Roe	Arsenal 1922-23	Lincoln City 1923-25
Tom Rudkin	Lincoln City 1938-39	Arsenal 1946-47
John McClelland	Arsenal 1960-64	Lincoln City 1968-69
Roger Davidson	Arsenal 1967-68	Lincoln City 1971-72
Tony Woodcock	Lincoln City 1975-76	Arsenal 1982-86

v. Liverpool

		Home					Away			Final Positions	
Season	League	Date	Result	Arsenal	Liverpool	Date	Result	Arsenal	Liverpool	Arsenal	Liverpool
1893-94	Division 2	28 October	Lost	0	5	1 January	Lost	0	2	9th	1stP
1895-96	Division 2	16 November	Lost	0	2	11 January	Lost	0	3	7th	1stP
1905-06	Division 1	2 September	Won	3	1	30 December	Lost	0	3	12th	1st
1906-07	Division 1	6 October	Won	2	1	9 February	Lost	0	4	7th	15th
1907-08	Division 1	19 October	Won	2	1	15 February	Lost	1	4	14th=	8th
1908-09	Division 1	20 February	Won	5	0	17 October	Drew	2	2	6th	16th
1909-10	Division 1	27 December	Drew	1	1	1 January	Lost	1	5	18th	2nd
1910-11	Division 1	14 April	Drew	0	0	17 April	Drew	1	1	10th	13th
1911-12	Division 1	2 September	Drew	2	2	30 December	Lost	1	4	10th	17th
1912-13	Division 1	28 December	Drew	1	1	7 September	Lost	0	3	20thR	12th
1919-20	Division 1	8 September	Won	1	0	1 September	Won	3	2	10th	4th
1920-21	Division 1	2 May	Drew	0	0	7 May	Lost	0	3	9th	4th
1921-22	Division 1	22 March	Won	1	0	25 February	Lost	0	4	17th	1st
1922-23	Division 1	2 September	Won	1	0	26 August	Lost	2	5	11th	1st
1923-24	Division 1	1 March	Won	3	1	2 April	Drew	0	0	19th	12th
1924-25	Division 1	6 September	Won	2	0	3 January	Lost	1	2	20th	4th
1925-26	Division 1	12 September	Drew	1	1	23 January	Lost	0	3	2nd	7th
1926-27	Division 1	18 September	Won	2	0	5 February	Lost	0	3	11th	9th
1927-28	Division 1	7 March	Won	6	3	27 December	Won	2	0	10th	16th
1928-29	Division 1	27 October	Drew	4	4	9 March	Won	4	2	9th	5th
1929-30	Division 1	2 April	Lost	0	1	21 December	Lost	0	1	14th	12th
1930-31	Division 1	18 April	Won	3	1	13 December	Drew	1	1	1st	9th
1931-32	Division 1	28 November	Won	6	0	9 April	Lost	1	2	2nd	10th
1932-33	Division 1	4 March	Lost	0	1	22 October	Won	3	2	1st	14th
1933-34	Division 1	2 December	Won	2	1	14 April	Won	3	2	1st	18th
1934-35	Division 1	1 September	Won	8	1	5 January	Won	2	0	1st	7th
1935-36	Division 1	26 December	Lost	1	2	25 December	Won	1	0	6th	19th
1936-37	Division 1	10 March	Won	1	0	31 October	Lost	1	2	3rd	18th
1937-38	Division 1	30 April	Won	1	0	18 December	Lost	0	2	1st	11th
1938-39	Division 1	18 March	Won	2	0	12 November	Drew	2	2	5th	11th
1946-47	Division 1	24 May	Lost	1	2	23 November	Lost	2	4	13th	1st
1947-48	Division 1	27 December	Lost	1	2	25 December	Won	3	1	1st	11th
1948-49	Division 1	8 September	Drew	1	1	15 September	Won	1	0	5th	12th
1949-50	Division 1	3 September	Lost	1	2	31 December	Lost	0	2	6th	8th
1950-51	Division 1	7 April	Lost	1	2	18 November	Won	3	1	5th	9th
1951-52	Division 1	5 September	Drew	0	0	12 September	Drew	0	0	3rd	11th
1952-53	Division 1	4 April	Won	5	3	15 November	Won	5	1	1st	17th
1953-54	Division 1	10 April	Won	3	0	21 November	Won	2	1	12th	22ndR
1962-63	Division 1	9 March	Drew	2	2	14 November	Lost	1	2	7th	8th
1963-64	Division 1	7 December	Drew	1	1	18 April	Lost	0	5	8th	1st
1964-65	Division 1	12 December	Drew	0	0	22 August	Lost	2	3	13th	7th
1965-66	Division 1	8 January	Lost	0	1	11 December	Lost	2	4	14th	1st
1966-67	Division 1	28 March	Drew	1	1	27 March	Drew	0	0	7th	5th
1967-68	Division 1	28 August	Won	2	0	22 August	Lost	0	2	9th	3rd

		Home					Away			Final Positions	
Season	*League*	*Date*	*Result*	Arsenal	Liverpool	*Date*	*Result*	Arsenal	Liverpool	Arsenal	Liverpool
1968-69	Division 1	17 August	Drew	**1**	**1**	31 March	Drew	**1**	**1**	4th	2nd
1969-70	Division 1	14 March	Won	**2**	**1**	29 November	Won	**1**	**0**	12th	5th
1970-71	Division 1	28 November	Won	**2**	**0**	30 January	Lost	**0**	**2**	1st	5th
1971-72	Division 1	8 May	Drew	**0**	**0**	6 November	Lost	**2**	**3**	5th	3rd
1972-73	Division 1	16 September	Drew	**0**	**0**	10 February	Won	**2**	**0**	2nd	1st
1973-74	Division 1	3 November	Lost	**0**	**2**	24 April	Won	**1**	**0**	10th	2nd
1974-75	Division 1	1 February	Won	**2**	**0**	9 November	Won	**3**	**1**	16th	2nd
1975-76	Division 1	24 February	Won	**1**	**0**	2 December	Drew	**2**	**2**	17th	1st
1976-77	Division 1	20 November	Drew	**1**	**1**	16 April	Lost	**0**	**2**	8th	1st
1977-78	Division 1	4 October	Drew	**0**	**0**	25 March	Lost	**0**	**1**	5th	2nd
1978-79	Division 1	2 December	Won	**1**	**0**	7 April	Lost	**0**	**3**	7th	1st
1979-80	Division 1	24 November	Drew	**0**	**0**	19 April	Drew	**1**	**1**	4th	1st
1980-81	Division 1	28 March	Won	**1**	**0**	25 October	Drew	**1**	**1**	3rd	5th
1981-82	Division 1	11 May	Drew	**1**	**1**	5 September	Lost	**0**	**2**	5th	1st
1982-83	Division 1	4 September	Lost	**0**	**2**	3 January	Lost	**1**	**3**	10th	1st
1983-84	Division 1	10 September	Lost	**0**	**2**	11 February	Lost	**1**	**2**	6th	1st
1984-85	Division 1	8 September	Won	**3**	**1**	12 February	Lost	**0**	**3**	7th	2nd
1985-86	Division 1	14 December	Won	**2**	**0**	17 August	Lost	**0**	**2**	7th	1st
1986-87	Division 1	10 March	Lost	**0**	**1**	30 August	Lost	**1**	**2**	4th	2nd
1987-88	Division 1	15 August	Lost	**1**	**2**	16 January	Lost	**0**	**2**	6th	1st
1988-89	Division 1	4 December	Drew	**1**	**1**	26 May	Won	**2**	**0**	1st	2nd
1989-90	Division 1	18 April	Drew	**1**	**1**	26 November	Lost	**1**	**2**	4th	1st
1990-91	Division 1	2 December	Won	**3**	**0**	3 March	Won	**1**	**0**	1st	2nd
1991-92	Division 1	20 April	Won	**4**	**0**	29 January	Lost	**0**	**2**	4th	6th
1992-93	Prem'ship	31 January	Lost	**0**	**1**	23 August	Won	**2**	**0**	10th	6th
1993-94	Prem'ship	26 March	Won	**1**	**0**	2 October	Drew	**0**	**0**	4th	8th
1994-95	Prem'ship	12 April	Lost	**0**	**1**	28 August	Lost	**0**	**3**	12th	4th
1995-96	Prem'ship	1 May	Drew	**0**	**0**	23 December	Lost	**1**	**3**	5th	3rd
1996-97	Prem'ship	24 March	Lost	**1**	**2**	19 August	Lost	**0**	**2**	3rd	4th
1997-98	Prem'ship	30 November	Lost	**0**	**1**	6 May	Lost	**0**	**4**	1st	3rd
1998-99	Prem'ship	9 January	Drew	**0**	**0**	22 August	Drew	**0**	**0**	2nd	7th
1999-00	Prem'ship	13 February	Lost	**0**	**1**	28 August	Lost	**0**	**2**	2nd	4th
2000-01	Prem'ship	21 August	Won	**2**	**0**	23 December	Lost	**0**	**4**	2nd	3rd
2001-02	Prem'ship	13 January	Drew	**1**	**1**	23 December	Won	**2**	**1**	1st	2nd
2002-03	Prem'ship	29 December	Drew	**1**	**1**	29 January	Drew	**2**	**2**	2nd	5th
2003-04	Prem'ship	9 April	Won	**4**	**2**	4 October	Won	**2**	**1**	Ist	4th

FA Cup										*Division*	
1912-13	Round 2	1 February	Lost	**1**	**4**					Div 1	Div 1
1922-23	Division 1	17 January	Lost	**1**	**4**	13 January	Drew	**0**	**0**	Div 1	Div 1
1926-27	Round 5	19 February	Won	**2**	**0**					Div 1	Div 1
1935-36	Round 4					25 January	Won	**2**	**0**	Div 1	Div 1
1949-50	Final	29 April		Wembley			Won	**2**	**0**	Div 1	Div 1
1962-63	Round 5	19 March	Lost	**1**	**2**					Div 1	Div 1
1963-64	Round 5	15 February	Lost	**0**	**1**					Div 1	Div 1
1970-71	Final	8 May		Wembley			Won*	**2**	**1**	Div 1	Div 1
1979-80	Semi Final	12 April		Hillsborough			Drew	**0**	**0**	Div 1	Div 1
		16 April		Villa Park (replay)			Drew*	**1**	**1**		

Season		Date	Result	Home Arsenal	Home Liverpool	Date	Result	Away Arsenal	Away Liverpool	Division Arsenal	Division Liverpool
		28 April		Villa Park (2nd replay)			Drew*	1	1		
		1 May		Highfield Rd (3rd replay)			Won	1	0		
2000-01	Final	12 May		Millennium Stadium			Lost	1	2	Prem	Prem
2001-02	Round 4	27 January	Won	1	0					Prem	Prem

League Cup

Season		Date	Result	Home Arsenal	Home Liverpool	Date	Result	Away Arsenal	Away Liverpool	Division Arsenal	Division Liverpool
1968-69	Round 4	15 October	Won	2	1					Div 1	Div 1
1977-78	Semi Final	14 February	Drew	0	0	7 February	Lost	1	2	Div 1	Div 1
1981-82	Round 4	1 December	Drew	0	0	8 December	Lost	0	3	Div 1	Div 1
1986-87	Final	5 April		Wembley			Won	2	1	Div 1	Div 1
1988-89	Round 3	9 November	Drew*	0	0	2 November	Drew	1	1	Div 1	Div 1
			(2nd replay)			23 November	Lost	1	2		
1989-90	Round 3	25 October	Won	1	0					Div 1	Div 1
1994-95	Q'ter Final					11 January	Lost	0	1	Prem	Prem
1996-97	Round 4					27 November	Lost	2	4	Prem	Prem

Summary	P	W	D	L	F	A
Arsenal's home league record:	80	34	26	20	117	73
Arsenal's away league record:	80	21	14	45	83	154
Arsenal's cup record:	27	9	8	10	26	31
TOTAL	**187**	**64**	**48**	**75**	**226**	**258**

FACT FILE

- **The meeting in May 1989 is probably the most famous league match in English history. In the final game of the season, the two title contenders came head to head at Anfield with Arsenal needing to win by two goals. Arsenal had not won at Anfield since 1974, and no one had won by two at Anfield since February 1986. However, a goal from Alan Smith made things interesting, and in the final minute Michael Thomas scored the title-winning goal. Ironically, Thomas later joined Liverpool.**
- **Arsenal cliched their first double against Liverpool in the 1971 FA Cup Final, with an extra-time winner from Charlie George.**
- **The sides have met in three FA Cup finals. Arsenal won the first two, and looked set to win the third (in 2001) until Michael Owen scored twice in the last 10 minutes to deny them.**
- **The 1980 FA Cup semi-final is the only one that has gone to three replays.**
- **Arsenal failed to win in 14 games between 1994 and 2000. All four Arsenal goals in this run were scored by Ian Wright, and three of them were penalties.**

FACT FILE

- **Arsenal won only one of their first 19 matches at Anfield.**
- **Between 1905 and 1928, Arsenal were undefeated for 18 home league matches, although they lost twice there in the FA Cup.**
- **Arsenal have played Liverpool more than any other team, largely due to an astonishing 27 cup matches.**

Arsenal's top scorers vs Liverpool

Joe Hulme 10
Jimmy Brain 8
John Radford, Ian Wright 7
Alan Ball, Ted Drake, Jack Lambert 6
Reg Lewis, Paul Merson, Don Roper, Alan Smith, Alan Sunderland, Brian Talbot 5

Arsenal hat-tricks vs Liverpool

20 Feb 1909 Albert Beney
7 Mar 1928 Jimmy Brain
28 Nov 1931 Jack Lambert
1 Sep 1934 Ray Bowden
1 Sep 1934 Ted Drake
15 Nov 1952 Cliff Holton
9 Apr 2004 Thierry Henry

Played for both clubs

Harry Storer	Arsenal 1894-96	Liverpool 1895-1900
David Hannah	Liverpool 1894-97	Arsenal 1897-99
Abe Hartley	Liverpool 1897-98	Arsenal 1899-1900
Andy McCowie	Liverpool 1896-99	Arsenal 1899-1901
Bill White	Arsenal 1897-99	Liverpool 1901-02
Abe Foxall	Liverpool 1899-1900	Arsenal 1901-02
Sailor Hunter	Liverpool 1899-1902	Arsenal 1904-05
Charlie Satterthwaite	Liverpool 1899-1902	Arsenal 1904-10
Sam Raybould	Liverpool 1899-1907	Arsenal 1908-09
Fred Pagnam	Liverpool 1914-20	Arsenal 1919-21
Jim Furnell	Liverpool 1961-64	Arsenal 1963-68
Geoff Strong	Arsenal 1960-65	Liverpool 1964-70
Ray Kennedy	Arsenal 1969-74	Liverpool 1974-82
Jimmy Carter	Liverpool 1990-91	Arsenal 1991-95
Michael Thomas	Arsenal 1986-92	Liverpool 1991-98
Nicolas Anelka	Arsenal 1996-99	Liverpool 2001-02

In 1950, Joe Mercer led Arsenal to a famous FA Cup Final victory when they beat Liverpool 2-0. Here, Arsenal goalkeeper George Swindin and full-back Wally Barnes watch the ball go wide after Liverpool forward Albert Stubbins tries a diving header.

v. Loughborough Town

		Home					Away				Final Positions	
Season	League	Date	Result	Arsenal	Loughb'gh	Date	Result	Arsenal	Loughb'gh	Arsenal	Loughb'gh
1895-96	Division 2	4 January	Won	**5**	**0**	29 February	Lost	**1**	**2**	7th	12th
1896-97	Division 2	19 September	Won	**2**	**0**	12 December	Lost	**0**	**8**	10th	13th
1897-98	Division 2	19 March	Won	**4**	**0**	18 December	Won	**3**	**1**	5th	16th
1898-99	Division 2	13 March	Won	**3**	**1**	12 November	Drew	**0**	**0**	7th	17th
1899-00	Division 2	12 March	Won	**12**	**0**	3 March	Won	**3**	**2**	8th	18thF

Summary	P	W	D	L	F	A
Arsenal's home league record:	5	5	0	0	26	1
Arsenal's away league record:	5	2	1	2	7	13
TOTAL	**10**	**7**	**1**	**2**	**33**	**14**

FACT FILE

- **Bizarrely, both Arsenal's biggest league win and biggest league defeat both came against Loughborough, in the space of just over three years.**
- **Arsenal are undefeated in their last six matches.**

Arsenal's top scorers vs Loughborough

Ralph Gaudie 4

Henry Boyd, Ernest Cottrell, Jimmy Tennant 3

Arsenal hat-tricks vs Loughborough

12 Mar 1900 Ralph Gaudie

v. Luton Town

Season	League	Date (Home)	Result	Arsenal	Luton	Date (Away)	Result	Arsenal	Luton	Final Positions Arsenal	Luton
1897-98	Division 2	9 October	Won	3	0	2 October	Won	2	0	5th	8th
1898-99	Division 2	31 December	Won	6	2	3 September	Won	1	0	7th	15th
1899-00	Division 2	6 January	Won	3	1	9 September	Won	2	1	8th	17thF
1955-56	Division 1	31 March	Won	3	0	22 October	Drew	0	0	5th	10th
1956-57	Division 1	9 March	Lost	1	3	8 December	Won	2	1	5th	16th
1957-58	Division 1	31 August	Won	2	0	28 December	Lost	0	4	12th	8th
1958-59	Division 1	27 December	Won	1	0	26 December	Lost	3	6	3rd	17th
1959-60	Division 1	26 December	Lost	0	3	28 December	Won	1	0	13th	22ndR
1974-75	Division 1	21 September	Drew	2	2	25 March	Lost	0	2	16th	20thR
1982-83	Division 1	19 March	Won	4	1	6 November	Drew	2	2	10th	18th
1983-84	Division 1	27 August	Won	2	1	14 January	Won	2	1	6th	16th
1984-85	Division 1	1 December	Won	3	1	4 May	Lost	1	3	7th	13th
1985-86	Division 1	1 February	Won	2	1	27 August	Drew	2	2	7th	9th
1986-87	Division 1	20 December	Won	3	0	13 September	Drew	0	0	4th	7th
1987-88	Division 1	13 February	Won	2	1	31 August	Drew	1	1	6th	9th
1988-89	Division 1	25 February	Won	2	0	25 October	Drew	1	1	1st	16th
1989-90	Division 1	16 December	Won	3	2	21 April	Lost	0	2	4th	17th
1990-91	Division 1	29 August	Won	2	1	8 December	Drew	1	1	1st	18th
1991-92	Division 1	27 August	Won	2	0	26 December	Lost	0	1	4th	20thR

FA Cup

Season	Round	Date	Result	Arsenal	Luton	Date	Result	Arsenal	Luton	Division Arsenal	Luton
1901-02	Intermed'te	14 December	Drew	1	1	18 December	Won	2	0	Div 2	Non L
1923-24	Round 1	12 January	Won	4	1					Div 1	Div 3S
1933-34	Round 3					13 January	Won	1	0	Div 1	Div 3S
1951-52	Q'ter Final					8 March	Won	3	2	Div 1	Div 2
1985-86	Round 5	3 March	Drew*	0	0	15 February	Drew	2	2	Div 1	Div 1
			(2nd replay)			5 March	Lost	0	3		

League Cup

Season	Round	Date	Result	Arsenal	Luton	Date	Result	Arsenal	Luton	Arsenal	Luton
1970-71	Round 3					6 October	Won	1	0	Div 1	Div 2
1987-88	Final	24 April		Wembley			Lost	2	3	Div 1	Div 1

Summary	P	W	D	L	F	A
Arsenal's home league record:	19	16	1	2	46	19
Arsenal's away league record:	19	6	7	6	21	28
Arsenal's cup record:	10	5	3	2	16	12
TOTAL	**48**	**27**	**11**	**10**	**83**	**59**

FACT FILE

- **Arsenal have won their last 10 home league games.**
- **Arsenal won the first six matches betwen the sides.**
- **Arsenal have not won in their last 11 matches away from Highbury.**

Welsh international Peter Nicholas (left) joined the Gunners from Crystal Palace. He played for several London clubs, including Luton Town in 1984. Malcolm MacDonald (right) was thought of as a full-back when with Luton Town, but transformed into one of the finest centre-forwards in Arsenal's history when signed from Newcastle United.

Arsenal's top scorers vs Luton

Tony Woodcock 7
Alan Smith 6
Ian Allinson, Adam Haywood, Cliff Holton, Fergus Hunt, Paul Merson 3

Arsenal hat-tricks vs Luton

31 Dec 1898 Adam Haywood
31 Dec 1898 Fergus Hunt
19 Mar 1983 Tony Woodcock

Played for both clubs

Bill Henderson	Arsenal 1921-23	Luton Town 1922-24
Arthur Roe	Luton Town 1920-25	Arsenal 1924-25
Sid Hoar	Luton Town 1920-25	Arsenal 1924-29
John Clark	Arsenal 1922-25	Luton Town 1926-27
Reg Tricker	Luton Town 1924-25	Arsenal 1926-29
Harry Woods	Arsenal 1923-26	Luton Town 1926-30
Bert Lawson	Arsenal 1925-26	Luton Town 1933-34
Archie Clark	Arsenal 1927-28	Luton Town 1928-31
Charlie Preedy	Arsenal 1929-33	Luton Town 1934-35
Reg Stockill	Arsenal 1931-33	Luton Town 1939-40
Jim Standen	Arsenal 1957-61	Luton Town 1960-63
Danny Clapton	Arsenal 1954-62	Luton Town 1962-63
David Court	Arsenal 1962-70	Luton Town 1970-72
Malcolm Macdonald	Luton Town 1969-71	Arsenal 1976-79
Brian Chambers	Arsenal 1973-74	Luton Town 1974-77
Peter Nicholas	Arsenal 1980-83	Luton Town 1984-87
Raphael Meade	Arsenal 1981-85	Luton Town 1988-89
Ian Allinson	Arsenal 1983-87	Luton Town 1987-89
Steve Williams	Arsenal 1984-88	Luton Town 1988-91
John Hartson	Luton Town 1993-95	Arsenal 1994-97
Paul Dickov	Arsenal 1992-97	Luton Town 1993-94
Matthew Upson	Luton Town 1996-97	Arsenal 1997-2002
Gavin McGowan	Arsenal 1992-98	Luton Town 1996-2001

v. Lyndhurst

FA Cup		Date	Result	Home Arsenal	Home Lyndhurst	Division Arsenal	Division Lyndhurst
1889-90	1st Qual	5 October	Won	**11**	**0**	Non L	Non L

Summary	P	W	D	L	F	A
Arsenal's cup record:	1	1	0	0	11	0
TOTAL	**1**	**1**	**0**	**0**	**11**	**0**

FACT FILE

- **This was Arsenal's first-ever FA Cup match, and evidently one of their easiest.**
- **Lyndhurst played in Denmark Hill, South London.**

Arsenal's top scorers vs Lyndhurst

H. Barbour 3, W Scott 3

Arsenal hat-tricks vs Lyndhurst

5 Oct 1889 H. Barbour (cup)

5 Oct 1889 W. Scott (cup)

v. Manchester City

				Home				Away		Final Positions	
Season	*League*	*Date*	*Result*	Arsenal	Man City	*Date*	*Result*	Arsenal	Man City	Arsenal	Man City
1893-94	Division 2	11 November	Won	**1**	**0**	30 December	Won	**1**	**0**	9th	13th
1894-95	Division 2	29 September	Won	**4**	**2**	15 December	Lost	**1**	**4**	8th	9th
1895-96	Division 2	7 September	Lost	**0**	**1**	28 September	Lost	**0**	**1**	7th	2nd
1896-97	Division 2	28 April	Lost	**1**	**2**	5 September	Drew	**1**	**1**	10th	6th
1897-98	Division 2	5 February	Drew	**2**	**2**	25 September	Lost	**1**	**4**	5th	3rd
1898-99	Division 2	3 April	Lost	**0**	**1**	1 October	Lost	**1**	**3**	7th	1stP
1902-03	Division 2	1 November	Won	**1**	**0**	20 December	Lost	**1**	**4**	3rd	1stP
1904-05	Division 1	10 December	Won	**1**	**0**	8 April	Lost	**0**	**1**	10th	3rd
1905-06	Division 1	2 December	Won	**2**	**0**	7 April	Won	**2**	**1**	12th	5th
1906-07	Division 1	29 December	Won	**4**	**1**	1 September	Won	**4**	**1**	7th	17th
1907-08	Division 1	21 September	Won	**2**	**1**	18 January	Lost	**0**	**4**	14th=	3rd
1908-09	Division 1	10 October	Won	**3**	**0**	13 February	Drew	**2**	**2**	6th	19thR
1910-11	Division 1	29 October	Lost	**0**	**1**	4 March	Drew	**1**	**1**	10th	17th
1911-12	Division 1	2 March	Won	**2**	**0**	28 October	Drew	**3**	**3**	10th	15th
1912-13	Division 1	2 November	Lost	**0**	**4**	8 March	Won	**1**	**0**	20thR	6th
1919-20	Division 1	3 January	Drew	**2**	**2**	17 January	Lost	**1**	**4**	10th	7th
1920-21	Division 1	11 September	Won	**2**	**1**	18 September	Lost	**1**	**3**	9th	2nd
1921-22	Division 1	17 September	Lost	**0**	**1**	10 September	Lost	**0**	**2**	17th	10th
1922-23	Division 1	20 January	Won	**1**	**0**	27 January	Drew	**0**	**0**	11th	8th
1923-24	Division 1	13 October	Lost	**1**	**2**	6 October	Lost	**0**	**1**	19th	11th
1924-25	Division 1	1 September	Won	**1**	**0**	17 September	Lost	**0**	**2**	20th	10th
1925-26	Division 1	20 March	Won	**1**	**0**	7 November	Won	**5**	**2**	2nd	21stR
1928-29	Division 1	2 February	Drew	**0**	**0**	22 September	Lost	**1**	**4**	9th	8th
1929-30	Division 1	11 September	Won	**3**	**2**	4 September	Lost	**1**	**3**	14th	3rd
1930-31	Division 1	26 December	Won	**3**	**1**	25 December	Won	**4**	**1**	1st	8th
1931-32	Division 1	30 January	Won	**4**	**0**	19 September	Won	**3**	**1**	2nd	14th
1932-33	Division 1	21 January	Won	**2**	**1**	10 September	Won	**3**	**2**	1st	16th
1933-34	Division 1	9 September	Drew	**1**	**1**	20 January	Lost	**1**	**2**	1st	5th
1934-35	Division 1	13 October	Won	**3**	**0**	23 February	Drew	**1**	**1**	1st	4th
1935-36	Division 1	21 September	Lost	**2**	**3**	11 March	Lost	**0**	**1**	6th	9th
1936-37	Division 1	5 December	Lost	**1**	**3**	10 April	Lost	**0**	**2**	3rd	1st
1937-38	Division 1	2 October	Won	**2**	**1**	16 February	Won	**2**	**1**	1st	21stR
1947-48	Division 1	6 December	Drew	**1**	**1**	24 April	Drew	**0**	**0**	1st	10th
1948-49	Division 1	4 December	Drew	**1**	**1**	27 April	Won	**3**	**0**	5th	7th
1949-50	Division 1	1 April	Won	**4**	**1**	12 November	Won	**2**	**0**	6th	21stR
1951-52	Division 1	26 January	Drew	**2**	**2**	22 September	Won	**2**	**0**	3rd	15th
1952-53	Division 1	22 November	Won	**3**	**1**	11 April	Won	**4**	**2**	1st	20th
1953-54	Division 1	19 September	Drew	**2**	**2**	6 February	Drew	**0**	**0**	12th	17th
1954-55	Division 1	14 September	Lost	**2**	**3**	8 September	Lost	**1**	**2**	9th	7th
1955-56	Division 1	6 September	Drew	**0**	**0**	31 August	Drew	**2**	**2**	5th	4th
1956-57	Division 1	6 October	Won	**7**	**3**	20 March	Won	**3**	**2**	5th	18th
1957-58	Division 1	2 November	Won	**2**	**1**	15 March	Won	**4**	**2**	12th	5th
1958-59	Division 1	20 September	Won	**4**	**1**	7 February	Drew	**0**	**0**	3rd	20th
1959-60	Division 1	12 September	Won	**3**	**1**	23 January	Won	**2**	**1**	13th	16th

		Home				Away					Final Positions	
Season	*League*	*Date*	*Result*	Arsenal	Man City	*Date*	*Result*	Arsenal	Man City	Arsenal	Man City
1960-61	Division 1	14 January	Won	**5**	**4**	3 September	Drew	**0**	**0**	11th	13th
1961-62	Division 1	9 September	Won	**3**	**0**	20 January	Lost	**2**	**3**	10th	12th
1962-63	Division 1	20 April	Lost	**2**	**3**	1 December	Won	**4**	**2**	7th	21stR
1966-67	Division 1	14 January	Won	**1**	**0**	10 September	Drew	**1**	**1**	7th	15th
1967-68	Division 1	23 September	Won	**1**	**0**	3 February	Drew	**1**	**1**	9th	1st
1968-69	Division 1	27 August	Won	**4**	**1**	9 October	Drew	**1**	**1**	4th	13th
1969-70	Division 1	22 November	Drew	**1**	**1**	18 February	Drew	**1**	**1**	12th	10th
1970-71	Division 1	6 February	Won	**1**	**0**	5 December	Won	**2**	**0**	1st	11th
1971-72	Division 1	13 November	Lost	**1**	**2**	4 March	Lost	**0**	**2**	5th	4th
1972-73	Division 1	28 October	Drew	**0**	**0**	24 March	Won	**2**	**1**	2nd	11th
1973-74	Division 1	23 March	Won	**2**	**0**	10 November	Won	**2**	**1**	10th	14th
1974-75	Division 1	24 August	Won	**4**	**0**	16 October	Lost	**1**	**2**	16th	8th
1975-76	Division 1	4 October	Lost	**2**	**3**	24 April	Lost	**1**	**3**	17th	8th
1976-77	Division 1	4 September	Drew	**0**	**0**	12 February	Lost	**0**	**1**	8th	2nd
1977-78	Division 1	4 March	Won	**3**	**0**	8 October	Lost	**1**	**2**	5th	4th
1978-79	Division 1	24 March	Drew	**1**	**1**	22 August	Drew	**1**	**1**	7th	15th
1979-80	Division 1	6 October	Drew	**0**	**0**	15 March	Won	**3**	**0**	4th	17th
1980-81	Division 1	24 February	Won	**2**	**0**	6 September	Drew	**1**	**1**	3rd	12th
1981-82	Division 1	17 October	Won	**1**	**0**	6 March	Drew	**0**	**0**	5th	10th
1982-83	Division 1	23 April	Won	**3**	**0**	4 December	Lost	**1**	**2**	10th	20thR
1985-86	Division 1	2 November	Won	**1**	**0**	5 April	Won	**1**	**0**	7th	15th
1986-87	Division 1	22 November	Won	**3**	**0**	25 April	Lost	**0**	**3**	4th	21stR
1989-90	Division 1	14 October	Won	**4**	**0**	10 March	Drew	**1**	**1**	4th	14th
1990-91	Division 1	17 April	Drew	**2**	**2**	1 January	Won	**1**	**0**	1st	5th
1991-92	Division 1	31 August	Won	**2**	**1**	28 December	Lost	**0**	**1**	4th	5th
1992-93	Prem'ship	28 September	Won	**1**	**0**	16 January	Won	**1**	**0**	10th	9th
1993-94	Prem'ship	16 October	Drew	**0**	**0**	15 January	Drew	**0**	**0**	4th	16th
1994-95	Prem'ship	20 August	Won	**3**	**0**	12 December	Won	**2**	**1**	12th	17th
1995-96	Prem'ship	5 March	Won	**3**	**1**	10 September	Won	**1**	**0**	5th	18thR
2000-01	Prem'ship	28 October	Won	**5**	**0**	11 April	Won	**4**	**0**	2nd	18thR
2002-03	Prem'ship	10 September	Won	**2**	**1**	22 February	Won	**5**	**1**	2nd	9th
2003-04	Prem'ship	1 February	Won	**2**	**1**	31 August	Won	**2**	**1**	1st	16th

FA Cup										*Division*	
1903-04	Round 2	20 February	Lost	**0**	**2**					Div 2	Div 1
1931-32	Semi Final	12 March		Villa Park			Won	**1**	**0**	Div 1	Div 1
1970-71	Round 5					17 February	Won	**2**	**1**	Div 1	Div 1

League Cup											
1977-78	Q'ter Final	24 January	Won	**1**	**0**	18 January	Drew	**0**	**0**	Div 1	Div 1
1985-86	Round 3					30 October	Won	**2**	**1**	Div 1	Div 1
1986-87	Round 3	28 October	Won	**3**	**1**					Div 1	Div 1
1990-91	Round 3					30 October	Won	**2**	**1**	Div 1	Div 1

Summary	P	W	D	L	F	A
Arsenal's home league record:	76	47	16	13	148	71
Arsenal's away league record:	76	29	20	27	108	106
Arsenal's cup record:	8	6	1	1	11	6
TOTAL	**160**	**82**	**37**	**41**	**267**	**183**

FACT FILE

- **City's last win at Highbury was in October 1975. They have failed 21 times since. This included seven successive failures to register a league goal there.**
- **Arsenal have won their last 10 matches, and are unbeaten in their last 14.**
- **There were four consecutive 1-1 draws at Maine Road from 1966 to 1970.**
- **City's longest unbeaten run is nine matches, from 1894 to 1899.**

Arsenal's top scorers vs Man City

Doug Lishman 11
John Radford 10
Cliff Bastin, Jimmy Bloomfield, David Jack 7
David Herd 6
Thierry Henry, Cliff Holton 5
Tim Coleman, Jimmy Logie, Charlie Satterthwaite, Brian Talbot, Sylvain Wiltord 4

Arsenal hat-tricks vs Man City

29 Sep 1894 Henry Boyd
30 Jan 1932 Ray Parkin
6 Oct 1956 Cliff Holton (4)
15 Mar 1958 Jimmy Bloomfield
14 Jan 1961 David Herd
23 Apr 1983 Brian Talbot

Played for both clubs

Charlie Williams	Arsenal 1893-94	Manchester City 1894-1902
James Buchan	Arsenal 1904-05	Manchester City 1904-11
Tommy Hynds	Manchester City 1901-06	Arsenal 1906-07
Jimmy Blair	Arsenal 1905-07	Manchester City 1906-10
Dave Halliday	Arsenal 1929-30	Manchester City 1930-34
Dave Bacuzzi	Arsenal 1960-64	Manchester City 1964-66
Brian Kidd	Arsenal 1974-76	Manchester City 1976-79
Tommy Caton	Manchester City 1979-84	Arsenal 1983-86
Niall Quinn	Arsenal 1985-90	Manchester City 1989-96
David Rocastle	Arsenal 1985-92	Manchester City 1993-94
Neil Heaney	Arsenal 1991-94	Manchester City 1996-98
Eddie McGoldrick	Arsenal 1993-96	Manchester City 1996-98
Paul Dickov	Arsenal 1992-97	Manchester City 1996-2002
Nicolas Anelka	Arsenal 1996-99	Manchester City 2002-03
David Seaman	Arsenal 1990-2003	Manchester City 2003-04

v. Manchester United

		Home					Away			Final Positions	
Season	League	Date	Result	Arsenal	Man Utd	Date	Result	Arsenal	Man Utd	Arsenal	Man Utd
1894-95	Division 2	30 March	Won	3	2	13 October	Drew	3	3	8th	3rd
1895-96	Division 2	9 November	Won	2	1	30 November	Lost	1	5	7th	6th
1896-97	Division 2	3 April	Lost	0	2	22 March	Drew	1	1	10th	2nd
1897-98	Division 2	8 January	Won	5	1	26 February	Lost	1	5	5th	4th
1898-99	Division 2	3 December	Won	5	1	1 April	Drew	2	2	7th	4th
1899-00	Division 2	10 March	Won	2	1	4 November	Lost	0	2	8th	4th
1900-01	Division 2	10 November	Won	2	1	16 March	Lost	0	1	7th	10th
1901-02	Division 2	16 November	Won	2	0	15 March	Won	1	0	4th	15th
1902-03	Division 2	25 October	Lost	0	1	9 March	Lost	0	3	3rd	5th
1903-04	Division 2	3 October	Won	4	0	30 January	Lost	0	1	2ndP	3rd
1906-07	Division 1	16 March	Won	4	0	10 November	Lost	0	1	7th	8th
1907-08	Division 1	21 March	Won	1	0	23 November	Lost	2	4	14th=	1st
1908-09	Division 1	19 December	Lost	0	1	27 April	Won	4	1	6th	13th
1909-10	Division 1	12 March	Drew	0	0	30 October	Lost	0	1	18th	5th
1910-11	Division 1	1 September	Lost	1	2	26 December	Lost	0	5	10th	1st
1911-12	Division 1	5 April	Won	2	1	1 January	Lost	0	2	10th	13th
1912-13	Division 1	2 September	Drew	0	0	21 March	Lost	0	2	20thR	4th
1919-20	Division 1	21 February	Lost	0	3	28 February	Won	1	0	10th	12th
1920-21	Division 1	30 August	Won	2	0	6 September	Drew	1	1	9th	13th
1921-22	Division 1	5 April	Won	3	1	11 March	Lost	0	1	17th	22ndR
1925-26	Division 1	16 January	Won	3	2	5 September	Won	1	0	2nd	9th
1926-27	Division 1	28 December	Won	1	0	15 September	Drew	2	2	11th	15th
1927-28	Division 1	28 April	Lost	0	1	17 December	Lost	1	4	10th	18th
1928-29	Division 1	8 December	Won	3	1	20 April	Lost	1	4	9th	12th
1929-30	Division 1	12 March	Won	4	2	26 October	Lost	0	1	14th	17th
1930-31	Division 1	21 February	Won	4	1	18 October	Won	2	1	1st	22ndR
1936-37	Division 1	6 February	Drew	1	1	3 October	Lost	0	2	3rd	21stR
1938-39	Division 1	15 April	Won	2	1	10 December	Lost	0	1	5th	14th
1946-47	Division 1	1 February	Won	6	2	28 September	Lost	2	5	13th	2nd
1947-48	Division 1	6 September	Won	2	1	17 January	Drew	1	1	1st	2nd
1948-49	Division 1	28 August	Lost	0	1	1 January	Lost	0	2	5th	2nd
1949-50	Division 1	27 December	Drew	0	0	26 December	Lost	0	2	6th	4th
1950-51	Division 1	14 October	Won	3	0	3 March	Lost	1	3	5th	2nd
1951-52	Division 1	8 December	Lost	1	3	26 April	Lost	1	6	3rd	1st
1952-53	Division 1	27 August	Won	2	1	3 September	Drew	0	0	1st	8th
1953-54	Division 1	27 March	Won	3	1	7 November	Drew	2	2	12th	4th
1954-55	Division 1	23 April	Lost	2	3	20 November	Lost	1	2	9th	5th
1955-56	Division 1	17 March	Drew	1	1	5 November	Drew	1	1	5th	1st
1956-57	Division 1	29 September	Lost	1	2	9 February	Lost	2	6	5th	1st
1957-58	Division 1	1 February	Lost	4	5	21 September	Lost	2	4	12th	9th
1958-59	Division 1	28 February	Won	3	2	11 October	Drew	1	1	3rd	2nd
1959-60	Division 1	23 April	Won	5	2	10 October	Lost	2	4	13th	7th
1960-61	Division 1	29 October	Won	2	1	18 March	Drew	1	1	11th	7th
1961-62	Division 1	21 October	Won	5	1	16 April	Won	3	2	10th	15th

		Home					Away			Final Positions	
Season	*League*	*Date*	*Result*	Arsenal	Man Utd	*Date*	*Result*	Arsenal	Man Utd	Arsenal	Man Utd
1962-63	Division 1	25 August	Lost	**1**	**3**	6 May	Won	**3**	**2**	7th	19th
1963-64	Division 1	21 September	Won	**2**	**1**	1 February	Lost	**1**	**3**	8th	2nd
1964-65	Division 1	28 November	Lost	**2**	**3**	26 April	Lost	**1**	**3**	13th	1st
1965-66	Division 1	25 September	Won	**4**	**2**	19 March	Lost	**1**	**2**	14th	4th
1966-67	Division 1	3 March	Drew	**1**	**1**	29 October	Lost	**0**	**1**	7th	1st
1967-68	Division 1	24 February	Lost	**0**	**2**	7 October	Lost	**0**	**1**	9th	2nd
1968-69	Division 1	26 December	Won	**3**	**0**	5 October	Drew	**0**	**0**	4th	11th
1969-70	Division 1	20 September	Drew	**2**	**2**	10 January	Lost	**1**	**2**	12th	8th
1970-71	Division 1	22 August	Won	**4**	**0**	19 December	Won	**3**	**1**	1st	8th
1971-72	Division 1	25 April	Won	**3**	**0**	20 August	Lost	**1**	**3**	5th	8th
1972-73	Division 1	6 January	Won	**3**	**1**	26 August	Drew	**0**	**0**	2nd	18th
1973-74	Division 1	25 August	Won	**3**	**0**	19 January	Drew	**1**	**1**	10th	21stR
1975-76	Division 1	22 November	Won	**3**	**1**	18 October	Lost	**1**	**3**	17th	3rd
1976-77	Division 1	18 December	Won	**3**	**1**	14 May	Lost	**2**	**3**	8th	6th
1977-78	Division 1	1 April	Won	**3**	**1**	5 November	Won	**2**	**1**	5th	10th
1978-79	Division 1	23 September	Drew	**1**	**1**	3 February	Won	**2**	**0**	7th	9th
1979-80	Division 1	25 August	Drew	**0**	**0**	29 December	Lost	**0**	**3**	4th	2nd
1980-81	Division 1	20 December	Won	**2**	**1**	11 October	Drew	**0**	**0**	3rd	8th
1981-82	Division 1	26 September	Drew	**0**	**0**	20 February	Drew	**0**	**0**	5th	3rd
1982-83	Division 1	2 May	Won	**3**	**0**	25 September	Drew	**0**	**0**	10th	3rd
1983-84	Division 1	6 September	Lost	**2**	**3**	17 March	Lost	**0**	**4**	6th	4th
1984-85	Division 1	23 February	Lost	**0**	**1**	2 November	Lost	**2**	**4**	7th	4th
1985-86	Division 1	24 August	Lost	**1**	**2**	21 December	Won	**1**	**0**	7th	4th
1986-87	Division 1	23 August	Won	**1**	**0**	24 January	Lost	**0**	**2**	4th	11th
1987-88	Division 1	24 January	Lost	**1**	**2**	19 August	Drew	**0**	**0**	6th	2nd
1988-89	Division 1	17 December	Won	**2**	**1**	2 April	Drew	**1**	**1**	1st	11th
1989-90	Division 1	3 December	Won	**1**	**0**	19 August	Lost	**1**	**4**	4th	13th
1990-91	Division 1	6 May	Won	**3**	**1**	20 October	Won	**1**	**0**	1st	6th
1991-92	Division 1	1 February	Drew	**1**	**1**	19 October	Drew	**1**	**1**	4th	2nd
1992-93	Prem'ship	28 November	Lost	**0**	**1**	24 March	Drew	**0**	**0**	10th	1st
1993-94	Prem'ship	22 March	Drew	**2**	**2**	19 September	Lost	**0**	**1**	4th	1st
1994-95	Prem'ship	26 November	Drew	**0**	**0**	22 March	Lost	**0**	**3**	12th	2nd
1995-96	Prem'ship	4 November	Won	**1**	**0**	20 March	Lost	**0**	**1**	5th	1st
1996-97	Prem'ship	19 February	Lost	**1**	**2**	16 November	Lost	**0**	**1**	3rd	1st
1997-98	Prem'ship	9 November	Won	**3**	**2**	14 March	Won	**1**	**0**	1st	2nd
1998-99	Prem'ship	20 September	Won	**3**	**0**	17 February	Drew	**1**	**1**	2nd	1st
1999-00	Prem'ship	22 August	Lost	**1**	**2**	24 January	Drew	**1**	**1**	2nd	1st
2000-01	Prem'ship	1 October	Won	**1**	**0**	25 February	Lost	**1**	**6**	2nd	1st
2001-02	Prem'ship	25 November	Won	**3**	**1**	8 May	Won	**1**	**0**	1st	3rd
2002-03	Prem'ship	16 April	Drew	**2**	**2**	8 December	Lost	**0**	**2**	2nd	1st
2003-04	Prem'ship	28 March	Drew	**1**	**1**	21 September	Drew	**0**	**0**	1st	3rd

FA Cup										*Division*	
1905-06	Q'ter Final					10 March	Won	**3**	**2**	Div 1	Div 2
1936-37	Round 4	30 January	Won	**5**	**0**					Div 1	Div 1
1950-51	Round 5					10 February	Lost	**0**	**1**	Div 1	Div 1
1961-62	Round 4					31 January	Lost	**0**	**1**	Div 1	Div 1
1978-79	Final	12 May			Wembley		Won	**3**	**2**	Div 1	Div 1

				Home				Away		Division	
FA Cup cont.		*Date*	*Result*	Arsenal	Man Utd	*Date*	*Result*	Arsenal	Man Utd	Arsenal	Man Utd
1982-83	Semi Final	16 April				Villa Park	Lost	**1**	**2**	Div 1	Div 1
1987-88	Round 5	20 February	Won	**2**	**1**					Div 1	Div 1
1998-99	Semi Final	11 April				Villa Park	Drew*	**0**	**0**	Prem	Prem
		14 April				Villa Park (replay)	Lost*	**1**	**2**		
2002-03	Round 5					15 February	Won	**2**	**0**	Prem	Prem
2003-04	Semi Final	15 February				Villa Park	Lost	**0**	**1**	Prem	Prem

League Cup

1977-78	Round 2	30 August	Won	**3**	**2**					Div 1	Div 1
1982-83	Semi Final	15 February	Lost	**2**	**4**	23 February	Lost	**1**	**2**	Div 1	Div 1
1990-91	Round 4	28 November	Lost	**2**	**6**					Div 1	Div 1
2001-02	Round 3	5 November	Won	**4**	**0**					Prem	Prem

Summary	P	W	D	L	F	A
Arsenal's home league record:	85	49	15	21	169	97
Arsenal's away league record:	85	14	24	47	75	159
Arsenal's cup record:	16	7	1	8	29	26
TOTAL	**186**	**70**	**40**	**76**	**273**	**282**

FACT FILE

- **Four games stand out from this epic series. The league match in February 1958 was United's last match in England prior to the Munich disaster, and proved to be a thriller. 3-0 down at half-time, Arsenal looked beaten, but scored three goals in three minutes to equalise, only for United to clinch the match 5-4.**
- **In the 1979 FA Cup final, the first 85 minutes were fairly uneventful, with Arsenal looking comfortable at 2-0 up. Suddenly United scored twice in two minutes, but with the United fans still cheering their unlikely comeback, Alan Sunderland fired home and Arsenal won the cup.**
- **In a fantastic FA Cup semi-final replay at Villa Park in 1999, United led 1-0 at half-time after a fine strike from David Beckham. However, in the space of a few second-half minutes, Dennis Bergkamp equalised, Nicolas Anelka had a goal disallowed after a tight offside decision and United were reduced to 10 men after their captain Roy Keane was dismissed. Arsenal were well on top now, and seemed to have won it when they were awarded an injury time penalty. However, Schmeichel saved from Bergkamp and Ryan Giggs's outrageous solo goal in extra-time won the tie for United.**

FACT FILE

- **In May 2002, Arsenal sealed their third double with a win at Old Trafford over the reigning league champions. It also confirmed their record of going the whole league season without losing away.**
- **Arsenal failed to win in 19 away games between 1936 and 1962.**
- **Arsenal won eight games in a row at home from 1970 to 1978.**
- **Neither side has finished outside the top three since 1996.**
- **Incidentally, the August 1971 away league match was played at Anfield, as Old Trafford was closed.**

Arsenal's top scorers vs Man United

Jimmy Brain, Thierry Henry, David Herd,
Malcolm Macdonald, John Radford 7
George Eastham, Alan Smith 6
Jimmy Bloomfield, Ray Kennedy,
Sylvain Wiltord 5

Arsenal hat-tricks vs Man United

3 Dec 1898 Bill White
1 Feb 1947 Ronnie Rooke
23 Apr 1960 Jimmy Bloomfield
22 Aug 1970 John Radford
6 May 1991 Alan Smith
5 Nov 2001 Sylvain Wiltord (cup)

Played for both clubs

Henry Boyd	Arsenal 1894-97	Manchester United 1896-99
Caesar Jenkyns	Arsenal 1895-96	Manchester United 1896-98
Ralph Gaudie	Arsenal 1899-1901	Manchester United 1903-04
Jack Moody	Arsenal 1926-28	Manchester United 1931-33
David Herd	Arsenal 1954-61	Manchester United 1961-68
Tommy Baldwin	Arsenal 1964-67	Manchester United 1974-75
Ian Ure	Arsenal 1963-70	Manchester United 1969-71
George Graham	Arsenal 1966-73	Manchester United 1972-75
Jimmy Rimmer	Manchester United 1967-73	Arsenal 1973-77
Brian Kidd	Manchester United 1967-74	Arsenal 1974-76
Frank Stapleton	Arsenal 1974-81	Manchester United 1981-87
Viv Anderson	Arsenal 1984-87	Manchester United 1987-91
Andy Cole	Arsenal 1990-91	Manchester United 1994-2002

David Herd scores Arsenal's first goal in the memorable game against Manchester United at Arsenal in February 1958. It was United's last League game before the Munich air disaster. The Gunners went down 5-4. David Herd was later to transfer to United, in 1961, and spent seven successful years there.

v. Mansfield Town

FA Cup		Date	Result	Home Arsenal	Home Mansfield	Division Arsenal	Division Mansfield
1928-29	Round 4	26 January	Won	**2**	**0**	Div 1	Non L

Summary	P	W	D	L	F	A
Arsenal's cup record:	1	1	0	0	2	0
TOTAL	**1**	**1**	**0**	**0**	**2**	**0**

FACT FILE

- **The scorers were David Jack and Harold Peel.**

Played for both clubs

Alf Calverley	Mansfield Town 1946-47	Arsenal 1946-47
Bill Dickson	Arsenal 1953-56	Mansfield Town 1956-57
John Matthews	Arsenal 1974-78	Mansfield Town 1982-84

Mansfield Town's goalkeeper Staples punches clear from an Arsenal attack in the fourth-round FA Cup game at Highbury in January 1929. The Gunners beat Mansfield, who were then in the Midland League, 2-0, and eventually reached the quarter-finals where they lost 1-0 to Aston Villa.

v. Merthyr Town

FA Cup		Date	Result	Home Arsenal	Home Merthyr	Division Arsenal	Division Merthyr
1914-15	Round 1	9 January	Won	**3**	**0**	Div 2	Non L

Summary	P	W	D	L	F	A
Arsenal's cup record:	1	1	0	0	3	0
TOTAL	**1**	**1**	**0**	**0**	**3**	**0**

FACT FILE

- **This is a defunct side, not the current non-league outfit Merthyr Tydfil.**

Arsenal's top scorers vs Merthyr

Harry King 3

Arsenal hat-tricks vs Merthyr

9 Jan 1915 Harry King (cup)

v. Middlesbrough

Season	League	Home Date	Home Result	Home Arsenal	Home Middlesb'gh	Away Date	Away Result	Away Arsenal	Away Middlesb'gh	Final Positions Arsenal	Final Positions Middlesb'gh
1899-00	Division 2	30 September	Won	3	0	3 February	Lost	0	1	8th	14th
1900-01	Division 2	24 November	Won	1	0	30 March	Drew	1	1	7th	6th
1901-02	Division 2	19 October	Lost	0	3	15 February	Lost	0	1	4th	2ndP
1904-05	Division 1	14 January	Drew	1	1	17 September	Lost	0	1	10th	15th
1905-06	Division 1	16 December	Drew	2	2	21 April	Lost	0	2	12th	18th
1906-07	Division 1	8 September	Won	2	0	5 January	Lost	3	5	7th	11th
1907-08	Division 1	22 February	Won	4	1	26 October	Drew	0	0	14th=	6th
1908-09	Division 1	17 March	Drew	1	1	3 October	Drew	1	1	6th	9th
1909-10	Division 1	22 January	Won	3	0	11 September	Lost	2	5	18th	17th
1910-11	Division 1	10 December	Lost	0	2	15 April	Drew	1	1	10th	16th
1911-12	Division 1	16 December	Won	3	1	24 February	Won	2	0	10th	7th
1912-13	Division 1	26 April	Drew	1	1	21 December	Lost	0	2	20thR	16th
1919-20	Division 1	27 March	Won	2	1	20 March	Lost	0	1	10th	13th
1920-21	Division 1	25 September	Drew	2	2	2 October	Lost	1	2	9th	8th
1921-22	Division 1	1 April	Drew	2	2	8 April	Lost	2	4	17th	8th
1922-23	Division 1	10 March	Won	3	0	3 March	Lost	0	2	11th	18th
1923-24	Division 1	3 November	Won	2	1	10 November	Drew	0	0	19th	22ndR
1927-28	Division 1	12 November	Won	3	1	18 April	Drew	2	2	10th	22ndR
1929-30	Division 1	27 November	Lost	1	2	9 April	Drew	1	1	14th	16th
1930-31	Division 1	22 November	Won	5	3	28 March	Won	5	2	1st	7th
1931-32	Division 1	30 April	Won	5	0	19 December	Won	5	2	2nd	18th
1932-33	Division 1	26 November	Won	4	2	8 April	Won	4	3	1st	17th
1933-34	Division 1	30 September	Won	6	0	10 February	Won	2	0	1st	16th
1934-35	Division 1	19 April	Won	8	0	22 April	Won	1	0	1st	20th
1935-36	Division 1	9 December	Won	2	0	11 April	Drew	2	2	6th	14th
1936-37	Division 1	21 November	Won	5	3	27 March	Drew	1	1	3rd	7th
1937-38	Division 1	30 October	Lost	1	2	12 March	Lost	1	2	1st	5th
1938-39	Division 1	1 April	Lost	1	2	26 November	Drew	1	1	5th	4th
1946-47	Division 1	12 April	Won	4	0	7 December	Lost	0	2	13th	11th
1947-48	Division 1	26 March	Won	7	0	29 March	Drew	1	1	1st	16th
1948-49	Division 1	9 April	Drew	1	1	13 November	Won	1	0	5th	19th
1949-50	Division 1	8 March	Drew	1	1	15 October	Drew	1	1	6th	9th
1950-51	Division 1	13 January	Won	3	1	9 September	Lost	1	2	5th	6th
1951-52	Division 1	22 March	Won	3	1	3 November	Won	3	0	3rd	18th
1952-53	Division 1	8 November	Won	2	1	28 March	Lost	0	2	1st	13th
1953-54	Division 1	24 April	Won	3	1	5 December	Lost	0	2	12th	21stR
1974-75	Division 1	30 November	Won	2	0	18 January	Drew	0	0	16th	7th
1975-76	Division 1	25 October	Won	2	1	28 February	Won	1	0	17th	13th
1976-77	Division 1	7 May	Drew	1	1	15 February	Lost	0	3	8th	12th
1977-78	Division 1	29 April	Won	1	0	3 December	Won	1	0	5th	14th
1978-79	Division 1	10 February	Drew	0	0	30 September	Won	3	2	7th	12th
1979-80	Division 1	15 September	Won	2	0	19 May	Lost	0	5	4th	9th
1980-81	Division 1	28 February	Drew	2	2	20 September	Lost	1	2	3rd	14th
1981-82	Division 1	16 February	Won	1	0	8 May	Won	3	1	5th	22ndR

				Home				Away		Final Positions	
Season	*League*	*Date*	*Result*	Arsenal	Middlesb'gh	*Date*	*Result*	Arsenal	Middlesb'gh	Arsenal	Middlesb'gh
1988-89	Division 1	19 November	Won	**3**	**0**	6 May	Won	**1**	**0**	1st	18thR
1992-93	Prem'ship	19 December	Drew	**1**	**1**	6 April	Lost	**0**	**1**	10th	21stR
1995-96	Prem'ship	20 August	Drew	**1**	**1**	13 January	Won	**3**	**2**	5th	12th
1996-97	Prem'ship	1 January	Won	**2**	**0**	21 September	Won	**2**	**0**	3rd	19thR
1998-99	Prem'ship	29 November	Drew	**1**	**1**	24 April	Won	**6**	**1**	2nd	9th
1999-00	Prem'ship	20 November	Won	**5**	**1**	12 March	Lost	**1**	**2**	2nd	12th
2000-01	Prem'ship	14 April	Lost	**0**	**3**	4 November	Won	**1**	**0**	2nd	14th
2001-02	Prem'ship	29 December	Won	**2**	**1**	18 August	Won	**4**	**0**	1st	12th
2002-03	Prem'ship	21 December	Won	**2**	**0**	19 April	Won	**2**	**0**	2nd	11th
2003-04	Prem'ship	10 January	Won	**4**	**1**	24 August	Won	**4**	**0**	1st	11th

FA Cup										*Division*	
1929-30	Round 5					15 February	Won	**2**	**0**	Div 1	Div 1
1976-77	Round 5					26 February	Lost	**1**	**4**	Div 1	Div 1
1982-83	Round 5	28 February	Won	**3**	**2**	19 February	Drew	**1**	**1**	Div 1	Div 2
1983-84	Round 3					7 January	Lost	**2**	**3**	Div 1	Div 2
1997-98	Round 4					24 January	Won	**2**	**1**	Prem	Div 1
2001-02	Semi Final	14 April		Old Trafford			Won	**1**	**0**	Prem	Prem
2003-04	Round 4	24 January	Won	**4**	**1**					Prem	Prem

League Cup											
1999-00	Round 4					30 November	Drew*	**2**	**2**	Prem	Prem
							lost 1-3 pens				
2003-04	Semi Final	20 January	Lost	**0**	**1**	3 February	Lost	**1**	**2**	Prem	Prem

Summary	P	W	D	L	F	A	
Arsenal's home league record:	54	34	14	6	129	52	
Arsenal's away league record:	54	20	13	21	78	74	
Arsenal's cup record:	11	5	2	4	19	17	
TOTAL	**119**	**59**	**29**	**31**	**226**	**143**	(+one penalty shoot-out defeat)

FACT FILE

- **In 29 post-war visits to Highbury, Middlesbrough have won just twice. The first was a game in which Middlesbrough had just two shots on target but, thanks to two own goals, won 3-0 to end Arsenal's mathematical interest in the title race.**
- **In 1999-2000, Middlesbrough eliminated Arsenal from the League Cup on penalties. Arsenal were to be knocked out of three cups that season on penalties.**
- **Arsenal won 11 games in a row from 1930 to 1935. They won the last five of these with a 19-0 goal aggregate.**
- **Arsenal won on only one of their first 18 visits to Teesside.**
- **Arsenal have won eight of their last 10 meetings. The two exceptions came in a league cup tie, in which Arsenal fielded an under-strength side.**

Arsenal's top scorers vs Middlesbrough

Cliff Bastin 13

Jack Lambert 10

David Jack, Ronnie Rooke 8

Dennis Bergkamp, Joe Hulme 7

Ted Drake, Thierry Henry 6

Ray Bowden, Doug Lishman, Marc Overmars 5

Frank Stapleton 5

Arsenal hat-tricks vs Middlesbrough

10 Mar 1923 Bobby Turnbull

22 Nov 1930 Jack Lambert

28 Mar 1931 Jack Lambert

8 Apr 1933 Joe Hulme

19 Apr 1935 Ted Drake (4)

12 Apr 1947 Ronnie Rooke (4)

26 Mar 1948 Ronnie Rooke

20 Nov 1999 Marc Overmars

Played for both clubs

Andy McCowie	Arsenal 1899-1901	Middlesbrough 1900-01
Jimmy Tennant	Arsenal 1899-1901	Middlesbrough 1901-02
Peter Turner	Arsenal 1900-01	Middlesbrough 1901-02
Bob Watson	Middlesbrough 1901-03	Arsenal 1903-05
Jackie Mordue	Arsenal 1906-08	Middlesbrough 1920-22
Alf Common	Middlesbrough 1904-10	Arsenal 1910-13
Joey Williams	Arsenal 1929-32	Middlesbrough 1931-35
Tim Coleman	Arsenal 1931-34	Middlesbrough 1934-37
Ralph Birkett	Arsenal 1933-35	Middlesbrough 1934-38
Ray Parkin	Arsenal 1928-36	Middlesbrough 1935-37
Jackie Milne	Arsenal 1935-38	Middlesbrough 1937-40
John Kay	Arsenal 1982-84	Middlesbrough 1984-85
Viv Anderson	Arsenal 1984-87	Middlesbrough 1994-95
Brian Marwood	Arsenal 1987-90	Middlesbrough 1991-92
Michael Thomas	Arsenal 1986-92	Middlesbrough 1997-98
Alan Miller	Arsenal 1992-94	Middlesbrough 1994-97
Paul Merson	Arsenal 1986-97	Middlesbrough 1997-99

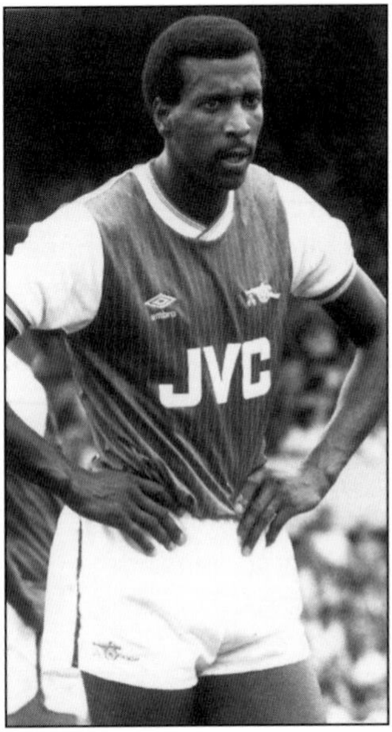

Viv Anderson (left) and Michael Thomas (right) were players who played for both Middlesbrough and Arsenal.

v. Middlesbrough Ironopolis

		Home					Away			Final Positions	
Season	*League*	*Date*	*Result*	Arsenal	Midd. Iron	*Date*	*Result*	Arsenal	Midd. Iron	Arsenal	Midd. Iron
1893-94	Division 2	10 March	Won	**1**	**0**	24 February	Won	**6**	**3**	9th	11thF

Summary	P	W	D	L	F	A
Arsenal's home league record:	1	1	0	0	1	0
Arsenal's away league record:	1	1	0	0	6	3
TOTAL	**2**	**2**	**0**	**0**	**7**	**3**

FACT FILE

- **This was Ironopolis' only season of league football.**

Arsenal's top scorers vs The Iron

Walter Shaw 4

James Henderson 2

Arsenal hat-tricks vs The Iron

24 Feb 1894 Walter Shaw

Played for both clubs

Roger Ord	Middlesbrough Ironopolis 1893-94	Arsenal 1897-1900
Fergus Hunt	Middlesbrough Ironopolis 1893-94	Arsenal 1897-1903

v. Millwall

Season	League	Date	Result	Home Arsenal	Home Millwall	Date	Result	Away Arsenal	Away Millwall	Final Positions Arsenal	Final Positions Millwall
1988-89	Division 1	28 February	Drew	**0**	**0**	11 February	Won	**2**	**1**	1st	10th
1989-90	Division 1	28 April	Won	**2**	**0**	11 November	Won	**2**	**1**	4th	20thR

FA Cup										Division	
1893	3rd Qual	19 November	Won	**3**	**2**					Non L	Non L
1893-94	3rd Qual	25 November	Won	**2**	**0**					Div 2	Non L
1896-97	Intermed'te					16 January	Lost	**2**	**4**	Div 2	Non L
1908-09	Round 2	6 February	Drew	**1**	**1**	10 February	Lost	**0**	**1**	Div 1	Non L
1987-88	Round 3	9 January	Won	**2**	**0**					Div 1	Div 2
1993-94	Round 3					10 January	Won	**1**	**0**	Prem	Div 1
1994-95	Round 3	18 January	Lost	**0**	**2**	7 January	Drew	**0**	**0**	Prem	Div 1

League Cup											
1992-93	Round 2	22 September	Drew	**1**	**1**	7 October	Drew*	**1**	**1**	Prem	Div 1
							won 3-1 pens				

Summary	P	W	D	L	F	A	
Arsenal's home league record:	2	1	1	0	2	0	
Arsenal's away record:	2	2	0	0	4	2	
Arsenal's cup record:	11	4	4	3	13	12	
TOTAL	**15**	**7**	**5**	**3**	**19**	**14**	(+one penalty shoot-out victory)

FACT FILE

- **Arsenal went nine matches unbeaten from 1988 to 1995.**

Arsenal's top scorers vs Millwall

Kevin Campbell 2

Played for both clubs

Sidney Crawford	Arsenal 1911-13	Millwall 1922-25
Stan Morgan	Arsenal 1946-47	Millwall 1948-53
Len Julians	Arsenal 1958-60	Millwall 1963-67
Joe Haverty	Arsenal 1954-61	Millwall 1962-64
Jim Standen	Arsenal 1957-61	Millwall 1968-70
Billy McCullough	Arsenal 1958-66	Millwall 1966-67
Tommy Baldwin	Arsenal 1964-67	Millwall 1974-75
Brian Chambers	Arsenal 1973-74	Millwall 1977-79
Brian Sparrow	Millwall 1983-84	Arsenal 1983-84
Jimmy Carter	Millwall 1986-91/98-99	Arsenal 1991-95
Paul Shaw	Arsenal 1994-97	Millwall 1997-2000

v. New Brighton Tower

		Home					Away			Final Positions	
Season	League	Date	Result	Arsenal	Tower	Date	Result	Arsenal	Tower	Arsenal	Tower
1898-99	Division 2	8 April	Won	**4**	**0**	10 December	Lost	**1**	**3**	7th	5th
1899-00	Division 2	7 April	Won	**5**	**0**	2 December	Won	**2**	**0**	8th	10th
1900-01	Division 2	22 December	Won	**2**	**1**	27 April	Lost	**0**	**1**	7th	4thF

Summary	P	W	D	L	F	A
Arsenal's home league record:	3	3	0	0	11	1
Arsenal's away league record:	3	1	0	2	3	4
TOTAL	**6**	**4**	**0**	**2**	**14**	**5**

Arsenal's top scorers vs New Brighton

Ralph Gaudie 3

Ernest Cottrell, Sandy Main, Andy McCowie 2

Played for both clubs

Sam Raybould	New Brighton Tower 1899-1900	Arsenal 1908-09

Woolwich Arsenal, 1900-01. Back row (left to right): Dr Clark (chairman), F. Warman (assistant trainer), Fred Coles, Duncan McNichol, Andy Main, Tom Spicer, Jimmy Jackson, Walter Place, J. Hindle (trainer), Harry Bradshaw (manager). Middle row: Tom Low, John Dick, John Blackwood, Peter Turner, James Tennant. Front row: Alex McCowie, John Anderson, Tom Grieve.

v. Newcastle United

		Home					Away			Final Positions	
Season	League	Date	Result	Arsenal	Newcastle	Date	Result	Arsenal	Newcastle	Arsenal	Newcastle
1893-94	Division 2	2 September	Drew	**2**	**2**	30 September	Lost	**0**	**6**	9th	4th
1894-95	Division 2	12 January	Won	**3**	**2**	24 November	Won	**4**	**2**	8th	10th
1895-96	Division 2	6 April	Won	**2**	**1**	18 January	Lost	**1**	**3**	7th	5th
1896-97	Division 2	16 April	Won	**5**	**1**	23 January	Lost	**0**	**2**	10th	5th
1897-98	Division 2	16 October	Drew	**0**	**0**	4 September	Lost	**1**	**4**	5th	2ndP
1904-05	Division 1	31 December	Lost	**0**	**2**	3 September	Lost	**0**	**3**	10th	1st
1905-06	Division 1	25 December	Won	**4**	**3**	16 April	Drew	**1**	**1**	12th	4th
1906-07	Division 1	22 September	Won	**2**	**0**	26 January	Lost	**0**	**1**	7th	1st
1907-08	Division 1	25 December	Drew	**2**	**2**	17 April	Lost	**1**	**2**	14th=	4th
1908-09	Division 1	12 September	Lost	**1**	**2**	9 January	Lost	**1**	**3**	6th	1st
1909-10	Division 1	25 December	Lost	**0**	**3**	25 March	Drew	**1**	**1**	18th	4th
1910-11	Division 1	26 November	Lost	**1**	**2**	1 April	Won	**1**	**0**	10th	8th
1911-12	Division 1	16 September	Won	**2**	**0**	20 January	Won	**2**	**1**	10th	3rd
1912-13	Division 1	28 September	Drew	**1**	**1**	25 January	Lost	**1**	**3**	20thR	14th
1919-20	Division 1	30 August	Lost	**0**	**1**	6 September	Lost	**1**	**3**	10th	8th
1920-21	Division 1	23 April	Drew	**1**	**1**	30 April	Lost	**0**	**1**	9th	5th
1921-22	Division 1	4 February	Won	**2**	**1**	11 February	Lost	**1**	**3**	17th	7th
1922-23	Division 1	28 October	Lost	**1**	**2**	21 October	Drew	**1**	**1**	11th	4th
1923-24	Division 1	25 August	Lost	**1**	**4**	1 September	Lost	**0**	**1**	19th	9th
1924-25	Division 1	17 January	Lost	**0**	**2**	13 September	Drew	**2**	**2**	20th	6th
1925-26	Division 1	13 February	Won	**3**	**0**	3 October	Lost	**0**	**7**	2nd	10th
1926-27	Division 1	2 October	Drew	**2**	**2**	6 April	Lost	**1**	**6**	11th	1st
1927-28	Division 1	10 December	Won	**4**	**1**	21 April	Drew	**1**	**1**	10th	9th
1928-29	Division 1	2 April	Lost	**1**	**2**	20 October	Won	**3**	**0**	9th	10th
1929-30	Division 1	30 November	Lost	**0**	**1**	5 April	Drew	**1**	**1**	14th	19th
1930-31	Division 1	20 December	Lost	**1**	**2**	25 April	Won	**3**	**1**	1st	17th
1931-32	Division 1	19 March	Won	**1**	**0**	7 November	Lost	**2**	**3**	2nd	11th
1932-33	Division 1	12 November	Won	**1**	**0**	25 March	Lost	**1**	**2**	1st	5th
1933-34	Division 1	14 October	Won	**3**	**0**	24 February	Won	**1**	**0**	1st	21stR
1948-49	Division 1	20 November	Lost	**0**	**1**	19 March	Lost	**2**	**3**	5th	4th
1949-50	Division 1	15 April	Won	**4**	**2**	29 October	Won	**3**	**0**	6th	5th
1950-51	Division 1	3 February	Drew	**0**	**0**	23 September	Lost	**1**	**2**	5th	4th
1951-52	Division 1	16 April	Drew	**1**	**1**	17 November	Lost	**0**	**2**	3rd	8th
1952-53	Division 1	25 October	Won	**3**	**0**	14 March	Drew	**2**	**2**	1st	16th
1953-54	Division 1	28 November	Won	**2**	**1**	17 April	Lost	**2**	**5**	12th	15th
1954-55	Division 1	21 August	Lost	**1**	**3**	18 December	Lost	**1**	**5**	9th	8th
1955-56	Division 1	15 October	Won	**1**	**0**	25 February	Lost	**0**	**2**	5th	11th
1956-57	Division 1	15 September	Lost	**0**	**1**	19 January	Lost	**1**	**3**	5th	17th
1957-58	Division 1	30 November	Lost	**2**	**3**	12 April	Drew	**3**	**3**	12th	19th
1958-59	Division 1	1 November	Won	**3**	**2**	21 March	Lost	**0**	**1**	3rd	11th
1959-60	Division 1	27 February	Won	**1**	**0**	5 December	Lost	**1**	**4**	13th	8th
1960-61	Division 1	17 September	Won	**5**	**0**	4 February	Drew	**3**	**3**	11th	21stR
1965-66	Division 1	26 March	Lost	**1**	**3**	2 October	Won	**1**	**0**	14th	15th
1966-67	Division 1	8 October	Won	**2**	**0**	25 February	Lost	**1**	**2**	7th	20th

				Home				Away		Final Positions	
Season	*League*	*Date*	*Result*	Arsenal	Newcastle	*Date*	*Result*	Arsenal	Newcastle	Arsenal	Newcastle
1967-68	Division 1	10 February	Drew	**0**	**0**	30 September	Lost	**1**	**2**	9th	10th
1968-69	Division 1	9 November	Drew	**0**	**0**	18 January	Lost	**1**	**2**	4th	9th
1969-70	Division 1	27 December	Drew	**0**	**0**	30 August	Lost	**1**	**3**	12th	7th
1970-71	Division 1	17 April	Won	**1**	**0**	10 October	Drew	**1**	**1**	1st	12th
1971-72	Division 1	9 October	Won	**4**	**2**	11 March	Lost	**0**	**2**	5th	11th
1972-73	Division 1	27 January	Drew	**2**	**2**	9 September	Lost	**1**	**2**	2nd	9th
1973-74	Division 1	1 January	Lost	**0**	**1**	1 September	Drew	**1**	**1**	10th	15th
1974-75	Division 1	18 March	Won	**3**	**0**	23 April	Lost	**1**	**3**	16th	15th
1975-76	Division 1	16 March	Drew	**0**	**0**	1 November	Lost	**0**	**2**	17th	15th
1976-77	Division 1	4 December	Won	**5**	**3**	30 April	Won	**2**	**0**	8th	5th
1977-78	Division 1	15 April	Won	**2**	**1**	19 November	Won	**2**	**1**	5th	21stR
1984-85	Division 1	4 September	Won	**2**	**0**	29 December	Won	**3**	**1**	7th	14th
1985-86	Division 1	28 September	Drew	**0**	**0**	1 March	Lost	**0**	**1**	7th	11th
1986-87	Division 1	14 April	Lost	**0**	**1**	18 October	Won	**2**	**1**	4th	17th
1987-88	Division 1	19 March	Drew	**1**	**1**	31 October	Won	**1**	**0**	6th	8th
1988-89	Division 1	15 April	Won	**1**	**0**	12 November	Won	**1**	**0**	1st	20thR
1993-94	Prem'ship	27 November	Won	**2**	**1**	7 May	Lost	**0**	**2**	4th	3rd
1994-95	Prem'ship	18 September	Lost	**2**	**3**	19 March	Lost	**0**	**1**	12th	6th
1995-96	Prem'ship	23 March	Won	**2**	**0**	2 January	Lost	**0**	**2**	5th	2nd
1996-97	Prem'ship	3 May	Lost	**0**	**1**	30 November	Won	**2**	**1**	3rd	2nd
1997-98	Prem'ship	11 April	Won	**3**	**1**	6 December	Won	**1**	**0**	1st	13th
1998-99	Prem'ship	4 October	Won	**3**	**0**	28 February	Drew	**1**	**1**	2nd	13th
1999-00	Prem'ship	30 October	Drew	**0**	**0**	14 May	Lost	**2**	**4**	2nd	11th
2000-01	Prem'ship	9 December	Won	**5**	**0**	15 May	Drew	**0**	**0**	2nd	11th
2001-02	Prem'ship	18 December	Lost	**1**	**3**	2 March	Won	**2**	**0**	1st	4th
2002-03	Prem'ship	9 November	Won	**1**	**0**	9 February	Drew	**1**	**1**	2nd	3rd
2003-04	Prem'ship	26 September	Won	**3**	**2**	11 April	Drew	**0**	**0**	1st	5th

FA Cup

										Division	
1901-02	Round 1	25 January	Lost	**0**	**2**					Div 2	Div 1
1905-06	Semi Final	31 March				Victoria Ground, Stoke	Lost	**0**	**2**	Div 1	Div 1
1931-32	Final	23 April				Wembley	Lost	**1**	**2**	Div 1	Div 1
1935-36	Round 5	19 February	Won	**3**	**0**	15 February	Drew	**3**	**3**	Div 1	Div 2
1951-52	Final	3 May				Wembley	Lost	**0**	**1**	Div 1	Div 1
1997-98	Final	16 May				Wembley	Won	**2**	**0**	Prem	Prem
2001-02	Round 5	23 March	Won	**3**	**0**	9 March	Drew	**1**	**1**	Prem	Prem

League Cup

1971-72	Round 3	6 October	Won	**4**	**0**					Div 1	Div 1
1995-96	Q'ter Final	10 January	Won	**2**	**0**					Prem	Prem

Summary	P	W	D	L	F	A
Arsenal's home league record:	71	34	16	21	115	79
Arsenal's away league record:	71	17	15	39	80	135
Arsenal's cup record:	11	5	2	4	19	11
TOTAL	**153**	**56**	**33**	**64**	**214**	**214**

FACT FILE

- **Arsenal's first-ever league fixture was against Newcastle. Walter Shaw scored Arsenal's first league goal as Arsenal went 2-0 up, but a late Newcastle equaliser salvaged a draw.**
- **Arsenal have played Newcastle in three FA Cup finals. Arsenal were unlucky to lose the first two. In 1932, they took the lead but Newcastle equalised when the ball was cut back from a position clearly over the goal-line, and Arsenal never recovered. In 1952, Arsenal right-back Wally Barnes went off injured after only 20 minutes, and they did well to hold out until the 84th minute. In 1998, however, they completely outplayed Newcastle to clinch the second of their three league and cup doubles.**
- **Arsenal won once in 22 visits to Tyneside between 1950 and 1972.**
- **Arsenal lost one in 15 at home between 1966 and 1985.**
- **Arsenal won six games in a row from 1976 to 1984.**

Arsenal's top scorers vs Newcastle

Joe Hulme, Ian Wright 7
Don Roper 6
Nicolas Anelka, George Graham 5
Dennis Bergkamp, Thierry Henry, David Herd, Ray Kennedy, Doug Lishman, Malcolm Macdonald, Paddy O'Brien 4

Arsenal hat-tricks vs Newcastle

29 Oct 1949 Don Roper
15 Apr 1950 Peter Goring
4 Dec 1976 Malcolm Macdonald
9 Dec 2000 Ray Parlour

Played for both clubs

Alex Caie	Arsenal 1896-97	Newcastle United 1901-03
Jimmy Jackson	Newcastle United 1897-99	Arsenal 1899-1904-05
James Laidlaw	Newcastle United 1900-01	Arsenal 1901-02
Bob Benson	Newcastle United 1902-03	Arsenal 1913-15
Bobby Templeton	Newcastle United 1902-05	Arsenal 1904-06
Wally Hardinge	Newcastle United 1905-06	Arsenal 1913-20
Charles Randall	Newcastle United 1908-11	Arsenal 1911-14
Jock Rutherford	Newcastle United 1901-13	Arsenal 1913-26
George Jobey	Newcastle United 1906-13	Arsenal 1913-14
Harry Woods	Newcastle United 1921-23	Arsenal 1923-26
Ralph Birkett	Arsenal 1933-35	Newcastle United 1938-40
Tim Rogers	Arsenal 1934-36	Newcastle United 1936-39
Ray Bowden	Arsenal 1932-38	Newcastle United 1937-40
George Eastham	Newcastle United 1956-60	Arsenal 1960-66
Malcolm Macdonald	Newcastle United 1971-76	Arsenal 1976-79
Pat Howard	Newcastle United 1971-77	Arsenal 1976-77
Alex Cropley	Arsenal 1974-77	Newcastle United 1979-80
Kenny Sansom	Arsenal 1980-88	Newcastle United 1988-89
Andy Cole	Arsenal 1990-91	Newcastle United 1992-95

v. Newport County

FA Cup	Date	Result	Away Arsenal	Away Newport	Division Arsenal	Division Newport
1956-57 Round 4	26 January	Won	**2**	**0**	Div 1	Div 3S

Summary	P	W	D	L	F	A
Arsenal's cup record:	1	1	0	0	2	0
TOTAL	**1**	**1**	**0**	**0**	**2**	**0**

FACT FILE

- **Derek Tapscott and David Herd scored the goals.**

Played for both clubs

Eddie Carr	Arsenal 1937-39	Newport County 1946-50
Brian Walsh	Arsenal 1953-56	Newport County 1961-63
Derek Tapscott	Arsenal 1953-58	Newport County 1965-66
David Jenkins	Arsenal 1967-69	Newport County 1973-74
George Johnston	Arsenal 1967-69	Newport County 1973-74

Derek Tapscott gets in his shot despite the close attention of Spurs goalkeeper Ted Ditchburn at White Hart Lane in September 1955. That season the Gunners finished fifth in the first division and again reached the quarter-finals of the FA Cup before going out to Birmingham. Tapscott later spent a season at Newport County.

v. Northampton Town

		Home					Away			Final Positions	
Season	League	Date	Result	Arsenal	North'ton	Date	Result	Arsenal	North'ton	Arsenal	North'ton
1965-66	Division 1	28 September	Drew	**1**	**1**	25 August	Drew	**1**	**1**	14th	21stR

FA Cup										Division	
1950-51	Round 4	27 January	Won	**3**	**2**					Div 1	Div 3S
1957-58	Round 3					4 January	Lost	**1**	**3**	Div 1	Div 3S

Summary	P	W	D	L	F	A
Arsenal's home league record:	1	0	1	0	1	1
Arsenal's away league record:	1	0	1	0	1	1
Arsenal's cup record:	2	1	0	1	4	5
TOTAL	4	1	2	1	6	7

FACT FILE

- **Arsenal have not won in their last three matches against the Cobblers.**

Arsenal's top scorers vs Northampton

Reg Lewis 2

Played for both clubs

George Jobey	Arsenal 1913-14	Northampton Town 1920-22
Alex Mackie	Arsenal 1922-26	Northampton Town 1935-37
Ted Bowen	Arsenal 1926-27	Northampton Town 1927-32
Dave Bowen	Northampton Town 1947-49/59-60	Arsenal 1950-59
Jim Fotheringham	Arsenal 1954-59	Northampton Town 1959-60
Cliff Holton	Arsenal 1950-59	Northampton Town 1961-63
Peter Kane	Northampton Town 1959-60/63-64	Arsenal 1960-61
Dennis Clapton	Arsenal 1959-61	Northampton Town 1961-62
Mike Everitt	Arsenal 1959-61	Northampton Town 1960-67
Laurie Brown	Northampton Town 1960-61	Arsenal 1961-64
John Roberts	Northampton Town 1967-69	Arsenal 1969-73
Mark Heeley	Arsenal 1977-79	Northampton Town 1979-83
Danny O'Shea	Arsenal 1982-83	Northampton Town 1994-97
Colin Hill	Arsenal 1982-85	Northampton Town 1997-99
Eddie McGoldrick	Northampton Town 1986-89	Arsenal 1993-96
Lee Harper	Arsenal 1996-97	Northampton Town 2002-04

v. Northwich Victoria

		Home						Away			Final Positions	
Season	League	Date	Result	Arsenal	Northwich	Date	Result	Arsenal	Northwich		Arsenal	Northwich
1893-94	Division 2	23 March	Won	**6**	**0**	9 December	Drew	**2**	**2**		9th	15thF

Summary	P	W	D	L	F	A
Arsenal's home league record:	1	1	0	0	6	0
Arsenal's away league record:	1	0	1	0	2	2
TOTAL	**2**	**1**	**1**	**0**	**8**	**2**

FACT FILE

- **This was Northwich's only season of league football.**

Arsenal's top scorers vs Northwich

James Henderson, G.H. Jaques 2

v. Norwich City

		Home					Away			Final Positions	
Season	League	Date	Result	Arsenal	Norwich	Date	Result	Arsenal	Norwich	Arsenal	Norwich
1972-73	Division 1	26 December	Won	2	0	23 September	Lost	2	3	2nd	20th
1973-74	Division 1	12 January	Won	2	0	15 September	Won	4	0	10th	22ndR
1975-76	Division 1	26 August	Won	2	1	7 February	Lost	1	3	17th	10th
1976-77	Division 1	15 January	Won	1	0	25 August	Won	3	1	8th	16th
1977-78	Division 1	28 February	Drew	0	0	24 September	Lost	0	1	5th	13th
1978-79	Division 1	28 April	Drew	1	1	9 December	Drew	0	0	3rd	16th
1979-80	Division 1	21 December	Drew	1	1	2 April	Lost	1	2	4th	12th
1980-81	Division 1	21 October	Won	3	1	21 March	Drew	1	1	3rd	20thR
1982-83	Division 1	31 August	Drew	1	1	20 April	Lost	1	3	10th	14th
1983-84	Division 1	24 September	Won	3	0	2 January	Drew	1	1	6th	14th
1984-85	Division 1	6 April	Won	2	0	26 December	Lost	0	1	7th	20thR
1986-87	Division 1	9 May	Lost	1	2	13 December	Drew	1	1	4th	5th
1987-88	Division 1	4 April	Won	2	0	14 November	Won	4	2	6th	14th
1988-89	Division 1	1 May	Won	5	0	10 December	Drew	0	0	1st	4th
1989-90	Division 1	4 November	Won	4	3	5 May	Drew	2	2	4th	10th
1990-91	Division 1	6 October	Won	2	0	23 March	Drew	0	0	1st	15th
1991-92	Division 1	11 February	Drew	1	1	8 April	Won	3	1	4th	18th
1992-93	Prem'ship	15 August	Lost	2	4	3 March	Drew	1	1	10th	3rd
1993-94	Prem'ship	30 October	Drew	0	0	13 February	Drew	1	1	4th	12th
1994-95	Prem'ship	1 April	Won	5	1	10 September	Drew	0	0	12th	20thR

FA Cup										Division	
1951-52	Round 3					12 January	Won	5	0	Div 1	Div 3S
1953-54	Round 4	30 January	Lost	1	2					Div 1	Div 3S
1973-74	Round 3					5 January	Won	1	0	Div 1	Div 1

Laurie Brown, in his first season with the Gunners, also played for Norwich City. He is in this team photo of Arsenal, 1961-62. Standing (left to right): Ted Magill, Mel Charles, Laurie Brown, Jack Kelsey, John McClelland, Alan Skirton, Allan Young, Terry Neill. Seated: George Swindon (manager), Danny Clapton, John Snedden, Jackie Henderson, George Eastham, Vic Groves, Billy McCulloch, Geoff Strong, Dave Bacuzzi, Bertie Mee (physiotherapist). On ground: John McLeod, Gerry Ward, Len Wills, John Petts.

League Cup		Home Date	Result	Arsenal	Norwich	Away Date	Result	Arsenal	Norwich	Division Arsenal	Norwich
1972-73	Q'ter Final	21 November	Lost	0	3					Div 1	Div 1
1981-82	Round 3	10 November	Won	1	0					Div 1	Div 2
1993-94	Round 3	26 October	Drew	1	1	10 November	Won	3	0	Prem	Prem

Summary	P	W	D	L	F	A
Arsenal's home league record:	20	12	6	2	40	16
Arsenal's away league record:	20	4	10	6	26	24
Arsenal's cup record:	7	4	1	2	12	6
TOTAL	**47**	**20**	**17**	**10**	**78**	**46**

FACT FILE

- **Arsenal were undefeated in their first 11 home league games.**
- **Arsenal have won just two of their last 16 away league games.**
- **Arsenal's first ever Premiership game was at home against Norwich. They were 2-0 up at half-time, but ended up losing 4-2. The result was particularly surprising given that Arsenal had ended the previous season with a 17-game unbeaten run.**

Arsenal's top scorers vs Norwich

Ian Wright 6
Alan Ball, Alan Smith 5
Paul Merson 4
Kevin Campbell, Paul Davis, Lee Dixon, David Rocastle 3

Played for both clubs

Joe North	Arsenal 1919-22	Norwich City 1924-26
Tim Williamson	Arsenal 1919-23	Norwich City 1923-25
Tim Coleman	Arsenal 1931-34	Norwich City 1936-39
Alf Kirchen	Norwich City 1933-35	Arsenal 1934-40
Paddy Sloan	Arsenal 1946-48	Norwich City 1951-52
Bryn Jones	Arsenal 1938-49	Norwich City 1949-50
Laurie Brown	Arsenal 1961-64	Norwich City 1966-69
Terry Anderson	Arsenal 1962-65	Norwich City 1964-74
Steve Walford	Arsenal 1977-81	Norwich City 1980-83
Willie Young	Arsenal 1976-82	Norwich City 1983-84
John Devine	Arsenal 1977-83	Norwich City 1983-85
Andy Linighan	Norwich City 1987-90	Arsenal 1990-97
David Rocastle	Arsenal 1985-1992	Norwich City 1996-97
Brian McGovern	Arsenal 1999-2000	Norwich City 2000-02

Bryn Jones was another Arsenal player who went on to play for Norwich City.

v. Nottingham Forest

		Home				Away					Final Positions	
Season	*League*	*Date*	*Result*	Arsenal	Forest	*Date*	*Result*	Arsenal	Forest		Arsenal	Forest
1904-05	Division 1	22 October	Lost	**0**	**3**	27 December	Won	**3**	**0**		10th	16th
1905-06	Division 1	2 April	Won	**3**	**1**	25 November	Lost	**1**	**3**		12th	19thR
1907-08	Division 1	16 November	Won	**3**	**1**	14 March	Lost	**0**	**1**		14th=	9th
1908-09	Division 1	20 March	Lost	**1**	**2**	14 November	Won	**1**	**0**		6th	14th
1909-10	Division 1	9 October	Lost	**0**	**1**	2 March	Drew	**1**	**1**		18th	14th
1910-11	Division 1	25 February	Won	**3**	**2**	22 October	Won	**3**	**2**		10th	20thR
1913-14	Division 2	1 November	Won	**3**	**2**	7 March	Drew	**0**	**0**		3rd	20th
1914-15	Division 2	24 April	Won	**7**	**0**	18 November	Drew	**1**	**1**		5thP	18th
1922-23	Division 1	10 February	Won	**2**	**0**	3 February	Lost	**1**	**2**		11th	20th
1923-24	Division 1	22 March	Won	**1**	**0**	15 March	Lost	**1**	**2**		19th	20th
1924-25	Division 1	27 December	Won	**2**	**1**	30 August	Won	**2**	**0**		20th	22ndR
1957-58	Division 1	21 April	Drew	**1**	**1**	9 November	Lost	**0**	**4**		12th	10th
1958-59	Division 1	15 November	Won	**3**	**1**	4 April	Drew	**1**	**1**		3rd	13th
1959-60	Division 1	1 September	Drew	**1**	**1**	26 August	Won	**3**	**0**		13th	20th
1960-61	Division 1	27 August	Won	**3**	**0**	31 December	Won	**5**	**3**		11th	14th
1961-62	Division 1	18 November	Won	**2**	**1**	7 April	Won	**1**	**0**		10th	19th
1962-63	Division 1	6 April	Drew	**0**	**0**	17 November	Lost	**0**	**3**		7th	9th
1963-64	Division 1	26 October	Won	**4**	**2**	7 March	Lost	**0**	**2**		8th	13th
1964-65	Division 1	6 October	Lost	**0**	**3**	13 March	Lost	**0**	**3**		13th	5th
1965-66	Division 1	14 September	Won	**1**	**0**	7 September	Won	**1**	**0**		14th	18th
1966-67	Division 1	22 April	Drew	**1**	**1**	26 November	Lost	**1**	**2**		7th	2nd
1967-68	Division 1	23 December	Won	**3**	**0**	26 August	Lost	**0**	**2**		9th	11th
1968-69	Division 1	1 February	Drew	**1**	**1**	16 November	Won	**2**	**0**		4th	18th
1969-70	Division 1	23 August	Won	**2**	**1**	26 December	Drew	**1**	**1**		12th	15th
1970-71	Division 1	3 October	Won	**4**	**0**	13 April	Won	**3**	**0**		1st	16th
1971-72	Division 1	1 April	Won	**3**	**0**	27 December	Drew	**1**	**1**		5th	21stR
1977-78	Division 1	3 September	Won	**3**	**0**	21 January	Lost	**0**	**2**		5th	1st
1978-79	Division 1	13 January	Won	**2**	**1**	9 September	Lost	**1**	**2**		7th	2nd
1979-80	Division 1	5 May	Drew	**0**	**0**	1 December	Drew	**1**	**1**		4th	5th
1980-81	Division 1	27 September	Won	**1**	**0**	21 February	Lost	**1**	**3**		3rd	7th
1981-82	Division 1	17 April	Won	**2**	**0**	21 November	Won	**2**	**1**		5th	12th
1982-83	Division 1	5 March	Drew	**0**	**0**	23 October	Lost	**0**	**3**		10th	5th
1983-84	Division 1	22 October	Won	**4**	**1**	25 February	Won	**1**	**0**		6th	3rd
1984-85	Division 1	13 April	Drew	**1**	**1**	29 August	Lost	**0**	**2**		7th	9th
1985-86	Division 1	8 April	Drew	**1**	**1**	26 October	Lost	**2**	**3**		7th	8th
1986-87	Division 1	17 March	Drew	**0**	**0**	27 September	Lost	**0**	**1**		4th	8th
1987-88	Division 1	26 December	Lost	**0**	**2**	12 September	Won	**1**	**0**		6th	3rd
1988-89	Division 1	11 March	Lost	**1**	**3**	6 November	Won	**4**	**1**		1st	3rd
1989-90	Division 1	7 March	Won	**3**	**0**	16 September	Won	**2**	**1**		4th	9th
1990-91	Division 1	20 March	Drew	**1**	**1**	22 September	Won	**2**	**0**		1st	8th
1991-92	Division 1	31 March	Drew	**3**	**3**	8 December	Lost	**2**	**3**		4th	8th
1992-93	Prem'ship	21 April	Drew	**1**	**1**	17 October	Won	**1**	**0**		10th	22ndR
1994-95	Prem'ship	21 February	Won	**1**	**0**	3 December	Drew	**2**	**2**		12th	3rd
1995-96	Prem'ship	29 August	Drew	**1**	**1**	10 February	Won	**1**	**0**		5th	9th

			Home					Away		Final Positions	
Season	*League*	*Date*	*Result*	Arsenal	Forest	*Date*	*Result*	Arsenal	Forest	Arsenal	Forest
1996-97	Prem'ship	8 March	Won	**2**	**0**	21 December	Lost	**1**	**2**	3rd	20thR
1998-99	Prem'ship	17 August	Won	**2**	**1**	16 January	Won	**1**	**0**	2nd	20thR

FA Cup										*Division*	
1978-79	Round 5					26 February	Won	**1**	**0**	Div 1	Div 1
1987-88	Q'ter Final	12 March	Lost	**1**	**2**					Div 1	Div 1
1992-93	Round 5	13 February	Won	**2**	**0**					Prem	Prem

League Cup											
1986-87	Q'ter Final	21 January	Won	**2**	**0**					Div 1	Div 1
1992-93	Q'ter Final	12 January	Won	**2**	**0**					Prem	Prem

Summary	P	W	D	L	F	A
Arsenal's home league record:	46	26	14	6	83	41
Arsenal's away league record:	46	19	8	19	58	61
Arsenal's cup record:	5	4	0	1	8	2
TOTAL	**97**	**49**	**22**	**26**	**149**	**104**

FACT FILE

- **In 1915, Arsenal beat Forest 7-0 on the last day of the season to finish fifth in Division Two. The league was then suspended for four years due to World War One, but on its resumption Arsenal were controversially elected to Division One, and have stayed in the top flight ever since. Thus the 7-0 win was Arsenal's last Division Two match to date.**
- **Arsenal have lost one of their last 13 matches against Forest.**
- **Arsenal lost only once in 32 home games between 1911 and 1987.**
- **Arsenal are undefeated in their last 10 home games.**
- **Their longest run without a win at the City Ground was four matches (1914-24).**

Doug Lishman, seen here with Spurs goalkeeper Ted Ditchburn diving bravely at his feet, was a class player and, for five seasons in succession, he was Arsenal's leading scorer. Indeed, until the advent of John Radford he was Arsenal's most prolific post-war scorer. He continued scoring goals after he left Arsenal to join Forest in 1955.

Arsenal's top scorers vs Forest

Frank Stapleton, Ian Wright 6
George Graham , David Herd, Ray Kennedy, Alan Smith 5
Harry King, Geoff Strong 4

Arsenal hat-tricks vs Forest

24 Apr 1915 Harry King (4)
26 Aug 1959 Danny Clapton
31 Dec 1960 David Herd
3 Oct 1970 Ray Kennedy

Played for both clubs

Gordon Coles	Nottingham Forest 1899-1900	Arsenal 1900-04
George Wolfe	Arsenal 1900-03	Nottingham Forest 1905-11
Tim Coleman	Arsenal 1902-08	Nottingham Forest 1914-15
Charlie Jones	Nottingham Forest 1925-28	Arsenal 1928-34
Reg Trim	Arsenal 1934-35	Nottingham Forest 1937-40
Noel Kelly	Arsenal 1949-50	Nottingham Forest 1951-55
Doug Lishman	Arsenal 1948-56	Nottingham Forest 1955-57
Len Julians	Arsenal 1958-60	Nottingham Forest 1960-64
John Barnwell	Arsenal 1956-64	Nottingham Forest 1963-70
Joe Baker	Arsenal 1962-66	Nottingham Forest 1965-69
Colin Addison	Nottingham Forest 1960-67	Arsenal 1966-68
Charlie George	Arsenal 1969-75	Nottingham Forest 1979-80
Tony Woodcock	Nottingham Forest 1973-80	Arsenal 1982-86
Willie Young	Arsenal 1976-82	Nottingham Forest 1981-83
Viv Anderson	Nottingham Forest 1974-84	Arsenal 1984-87
Lee Chapman	Arsenal 1982-84	Nottingham Forest 1988-90
Kevin Campbell	Arsenal 1987-95	Nottingham Forest 1995-98
Ian Wright	Arsenal 1991-98	Nottingham Forest 1999-1900
David Platt	Arsenal 1995-98	Nottingham Forest 1999-2001
Matthew Upson	Arsenal 1997-2002	Nottingham Forest 2000-01

Arsenal in 1964-65. Back row (left to right): Geoff Strong, Gordon Ferry, Alan Skirton, Don Howe, Bob Wilson, Jim Furnell, John Snedden, Ian Ure, Peter Simpson and Terry Neill. Front row: Jim Magill, Terry Anderson, Freddie Clarke, Joe Baker, George Eastham, David Court, Billy McCullough, George Armstrong and John Sammels. Joe Baker was to transfer at the end of the season to Nottingham Forest.

v. Notts County

				Home				Away		Final Positions	
Season	League	Date	Result	Arsenal	Notts C	Date	Result	Arsenal	Notts C	Arsenal	Notts C
1893-94	Division 2	24 March	Lost	**1**	**2**	9 September	Lost	**2**	**3**	9th	3rd
1894-95	Division 2	3 November	Won	**2**	**1**	27 October	Drew	**2**	**2**	8th	2nd
1895-96	Division 2	7 March	Won	**2**	**0**	2 November	Won	**4**	**3**	7th	10th
1896-97	Division 2	26 September	Lost	**2**	**3**	7 November	Lost	**4**	**7**	10th	1stP
1904-05	Division 1	15 April	Lost	**1**	**2**	17 December	Won	**5**	**1**	10th	18th
1905-06	Division 1	16 September	Drew	**1**	**1**	20 January	Lost	**0**	**1**	12th	16th
1906-07	Division 1	20 October	Won	**1**	**0**	17 April	Lost	**1**	**4**	7th	18th
1907-08	Division 1	2 September	Drew	**1**	**1**	14 September	Lost	**0**	**2**	14th=	18th
1908-09	Division 1	2 January	Won	**1**	**0**	5 September	Lost	**1**	**2**	6th	15th
1909-10	Division 1	18 December	Lost	**1**	**2**	7 October	Lost	**1**	**5**	18th	9th
1910-11	Division 1	24 December	Won	**2**	**1**	29 April	Won	**2**	**0**	10th	11th
1911-12	Division 1	27 April	Lost	**0**	**3**	23 December	Lost	**1**	**3**	10th	16th
1912-13	Division 1	25 December	Drew	**0**	**0**	26 December	Lost	**1**	**2**	20thR	19thR
1913-14	Division 2	15 September	Won	**3**	**0**	1 January	Lost	**0**	**1**	3rd	1stP
1919-20	Division 1	22 November	Won	**3**	**1**	29 November	Drew	**2**	**2**	10th	21stR
1923-24	Division 1	27 December	Drew	**0**	**0**	26 December	Won	**2**	**1**	19th	10th
1924-25	Division 1	8 November	Lost	**0**	**1**	14 March	Lost	**1**	**2**	20th	9th
1925-26	Division 1	25 December	Won	**3**	**0**	26 December	Lost	**1**	**4**	2nd	22ndR
1981-82	Division 1	13 February	Won	**1**	**0**	3 October	Lost	**1**	**2**	5th	15th
1982-83	Division 1	18 September	Won	**2**	**0**	22 January	Lost	**0**	**1**	10th	15th
1983-84	Division 1	21 January	Drew	**1**	**1**	17 September	Won	**4**	**0**	6th	21stR
1991-92	Division 1	26 October	Won	**2**	**0**	8 February	Won	**1**	**0**	4th	21stR

FA Cup										*Division*	
1976-77	Round 3					8 January	Won	**1**	**0**	Div 1	Div 2
1978-79	Round 4	27 January	Won	**2**	**0**					Div 1	Div 2

Summary	P	W	D	L	F	A
Arsenal's home league record:	22	11	5	6	30	19
Arsenal's away league record:	22	6	2	14	36	48
Arsenal's cup record:	2	2	0	0	3	0
TOTAL	**46**	**19**	**7**	**20**	**69**	**67**

FACT FILE

- **Only four sides have met Arsenal more than 20 times and won more than they've lost. Not surprisingly, three of these are Liverpool, Manchester United and Newcastle. More surprisingly, Notts County are the other.**
- **Notts County won 12 out of 15 home league games between 1906 and 1983.**
- **Arsenal are undefeated in their last five home games.**

Arsenal's top scorers vs Notts County

Tom Fitchie 4
Fred Pagnam 3
Henry Boyd, Alf Common, Robert Gordon, Adam Haywood, Gordon Hoare, David Neave, Paddy O'Brien, Graham Rix, Charlie Satterthwaite, Alan Smith, Stephen Stonley, Brian Talbot 2

Arsenal hat-tricks vs Notts County

17 Dec 1904 Tom Fitchie

Played for both clubs

Gordon Coles	Notts County 1895-96	Arsenal 1900-04
Richard Hannigan	Notts County 1898-99	Arsenal 1899-1900
Paddy Logan	Notts County 1898-99	Arsenal 1899-1902
Reginald Boreham	Notts County 1920-21	Arsenal 1921-24
Donald Cock	Notts County 1922-25	Arsenal 1924-26
Horace Cope	Notts County 1920-27	Arsenal 1926-33
Samson Haden	Arsenal 1923-27	Notts County 1927-36
Horace Cumner	Arsenal 1938-40	Notts County 1946-48
Bill Dickson	Notts County 1946-48	Arsenal 1953-56
Ian McPherson	Arsenal 1946-51	Notts County 1951-53
Tommy Lawton	Notts County 1947-52	Arsenal 1953-56
Jeff Blockley	Arsenal 1972-75	Notts County 1978-80
Eddie Kelly	Arsenal 1969-76	Notts County 1980-81

Tommy Lawton, one of the finest post-war strikers, who spent three seasons at Notts County.

Later to play for Notts County, Eddie Kelly scores a hugely important goal against Stoke at Highbury on 1 May 1971. It proved to be the winner and took Arsenal to within touching distance of the league championship.

v. Oldham Athletic

Season	League	Home Date	Home Result	Arsenal	Oldham	Away Date	Away Result	Arsenal	Oldham	Final Positions Arsenal	Oldham
1910-11	Division 1	1 October	Drew	**0**	**0**	6 March	Lost	**0**	**3**	10th	7th
1911-12	Division 1	30 September	Drew	**1**	**1**	9 March	Drew	**0**	**0**	10th	18th
1912-13	Division 1	8 February	Drew	**0**	**0**	5 October	Drew	**0**	**0**	20thR	9th
1919-20	Division 1	7 February	Won	**3**	**2**	14 February	Lost	**0**	**3**	10th	17th
1920-21	Division 1	19 February	Drew	**2**	**2**	12 February	Drew	**1**	**1**	9th	19th
1921-22	Division 1	24 December	Lost	**0**	**1**	17 December	Lost	**1**	**2**	17th	19th
1922-23	Division 1	17 March	Won	**2**	**0**	24 March	Drew	**0**	**0**	11th	22ndR
1991-92	Division 1	10 March	Won	**2**	**1**	16 November	Drew	**1**	**1**	4th	17th
1992-93	Prem'ship	26 August	Won	**2**	**0**	20 February	Won	**1**	**0**	10th	19thR
1993-94	Prem'ship	22 January	Drew	**1**	**1**	23 October	Drew	**0**	**0**	4th	21stR

League Cup

Season	Round	Home Date	Home Result	Arsenal	Oldham	Away Date	Away Result	Arsenal	Oldham	Arsenal	Oldham
1989-90	Round 4					22 November	Lost	**1**	**3**	Div 1	Div 2
1994-95	Round 3	9 November	Won	**2**	**0**	26 October	Drew	**0**	**0**	Prem	Div 1

Summary	P	W	D	L	F	A
Arsenal's home league record:	10	4	5	1	13	8
Arsenal's away league record:	10	1	6	3	4	10
Arsenal's cup record:	3	1	1	1	3	3
TOTAL	**23**	**6**	**12**	**5**	**20**	**21**

FACT FILE

- **Arsenal have never scored more than once in an away match against Oldham.**
- **Neither side has managed an average of a goal a game in an uninspiring series dominated by draws.**
- **Oldham last won at Highbury in 1921.**

Arsenal's top scorers vs Oldham

Ian Wright 4

Billy Blyth, Paul Dickov, Alec Graham 2

Played for both clubs

Hugh McDonald	Arsenal 1905-10/12-13	Oldham Athletic 1910-12
Charlie Jones	Oldham Athletic 1922-25	Arsenal 1928-34
Bill Johnstone	Arsenal 1929-31	Oldham Athletic 1930-33
Frank Moss	Oldham Athletic 1929-32	Arsenal 1931-36
Andy Linighan	Oldham Athletic 1985-88	Arsenal 1990-97

v. Oxford United

		Home					Away			Final Positions	
Season	League	Date	Result	Arsenal	Oxford	Date	Result	Arsenal	Oxford	Arsenal	Oxford
1985-86	Division 1	16 November	Won	**2**	**1**	5 May	Lost	**0**	**3**	7th	18th
1986-87	Division 1	20 September	Drew	**0**	**0**	25 February	Drew	**0**	**0**	4th	18th
1987-88	Division 1	10 October	Won	**2**	**0**	30 March	Drew	**0**	**0**	6th	21stR

FA Cup										Division	
1962-63	Round 3	30 January	Won	**5**	**1**					Div 1	Div 4
2002-03	Round 3	4 January	Won	**2**	**0**					Prem	Div 3

League Cup											
1984-85	Round 3					31 October	Lost	**2**	**3**	Div 1	Div 2

Summary	P	W	D	L	F	A
Arsenal's home league record:	3	2	1	0	4	1
Arsenal's away league record:	3	0	2	1	0	3
Arsenal's cup record:	3	2	0	1	9	4
TOTAL	**9**	**4**	**3**	**2**	**13**	**8**

FACT FILE

- **Neither side has won away in the nine meetings of the sides.**
- **Arsenal have not conceded a goal in the last five encounters.**

Arsenal's top scorers vs Oxford

Joe Baker, Paul Davis, Geoff Strong 2

Played for both clubs

Rod Smithson	Arsenal 1962-63	Oxford United 1965-75
Brian McDermott	Arsenal 1978-84	Oxford United 1984-87
Chris Whyte	Arsenal 1981-86	Oxford United 1996-97
Tommy Caton	Arsenal 1983-86	Oxford United 1986-88
Jimmy Carter	Arsenal 1991-95	Oxford United 1993-95
Andy Linighan	Arsenal 1990-97	Oxford United 2000-01

Tommy Caton joined Oxford United after he left Arsenal in 1986.

v. Peterborough United

FA Cup		Date	Result	Away Arsenal	Away Pet'borough	Division Arsenal	Division Pet'borough
1964-65	Round 4	30 January	Lost	1	2	Div 1	Div 3

Summary	P	W	D	L	F	A
Arsenal's cup record:	1	0	0	1	1	2
TOTAL	**1**	**0**	**0**	**1**	**1**	**2**

FACT FILE

- **John Radford's goal was not enough to prevent one of Arsenal's more embarrassing cup exits.**

Played for both clubs

Eddie Clamp	Arsenal 1961-63	Peterborough United 1964-65
Mark Heeley	Peterborough United 1975-77	Arsenal 1977-79
David Price	Arsenal 1972-81	Peterborough United 1974-75
David Seaman	Peterborough United 1982-85	Arsenal 1990-2003
Steve Morrow	Arsenal 1991-97	Peterborough United 2000-01
Paul Shaw	Arsenal 1994-97	Peterborough United 1995-96
Brian McGovern	Arsenal 1999-2000	Peterborough United 2002-03
Stuart Taylor	Peterborough United 2000-01	Arsenal 2001-03

An ex-Posh, David Seaman has just put Arsenal through to the 1995 European Cup-winners' Cup Final with a magnificent display in the shoot out.

v. Plymouth Argyle

FA Cup		Date	Result	Home Arsenal	Home Plymouth					Division Arsenal	Division Plymouth
1931-32	Round 4	23 January	Won	**4**	**2**					Div 1	Div 2
1986-87	Round 4	31 January	Won	**6**	**1**					Div 1	Div 2
League Cup											
1983-84	Round 2	25 October	Won	**1**	**0**	4 October	Drew	**1**	**1**	Div 1	Div 3
1989-90	Round 2	19 September	Won	**2**	**0**	3 October	Won	**6**	**1**	Div 1	Div 2

Summary	P	W	D	L	F	A
Arsenal's cup record:	6	5	1	0	20	5
TOTAL	**6**	**5**	**1**	**0**	**20**	**5**

FACT FILE

- **Plymouth have not beaten Arsenal in six meetings.**

Arsenal's top scorers vs Plymouth

Michael Thomas 3

Viv Anderson, Jack Lambert, Alan Smith 2

Arsenal hat-tricks vs Plymouth

3 Oct 1989 Michael Thomas (cup)

Played for both clubs

David Jack	Plymouth Argyle 1920-21	Arsenal 1928-34
Bill Harper	Arsenal 1925-27/30-32	Plymouth Argyle 1931-39
Ray Bowden	Plymouth Argyle 1926-33	Arsenal 1932-38
Jimmy Bloomfield	Arsenal 1954-61	Plymouth Argyle 1966-68
Mike Everitt	Arsenal 1959-61	Plymouth Argyle 1966-68
Tony Burns	Arsenal 1964-66	Plymouth Argyle 1978-79
Jim Furnell	Arsenal 1963-68	Plymouth Argyle 1970-76
Paul Mariner	Plymouth Argyle 1973-77	Arsenal 1983-86
John Matthews	Arsenal 1974-78	Plymouth Argyle 1985-89
Paul Barron	Plymouth Argyle 1976-78	Arsenal 1978-80
Lee Chapman	Plymouth Argyle 1978-79	Arsenal 1982-84
Raphael Meade	Arsenal 1981-85	Plymouth Argyle 1990-91
Rhys Wilmot	Arsenal 1985-87	Plymouth Argyle 1988-92
Alan Miller	Plymouth Argyle 1988-89	Arsenal 1992-94
Kwame Ampadu	Arsenal 1989-90	Plymouth Argyle 1990-91
Neil Heaney	Arsenal 1991-94	Plymouth Argyle 2001-02

v. Port Vale

Season	League	Date	Result	Home Arsenal	Home Port Vale	Date	Result	Away Arsenal	Away Port Vale	Final Positions Arsenal	Final Positions Port Vale
1893-94	Division 2	25 December	Won	**4**	**1**	6 January	Lost	**1**	**2**	9th	7th
1894-95	Division 2	25 December	Won	**7**	**0**	19 January	Won	**1**	**0**	8th	15th
1895-96	Division 2	25 December	Won	**2**	**1**	15 February	Won	**2**	**0**	7th	14thF
1898-99	Division 2	25 February	Won	**1**	**0**	5 September	Lost	**0**	**3**	7th	9th
1899-00	Division 2	16 September	Won	**1**	**0**	13 January	Drew	**1**	**1**	8th	11th
1900-01	Division 2	8 December	Won	**3**	**0**	13 April	Lost	**0**	**1**	7th	9th
1901-02	Division 2	26 December	Won	**3**	**1**	28 September	Lost	**0**	**1**	4th	12th
1902-03	Division 2	13 September	Won	**3**	**0**	10 January	Drew	**1**	**1**	3rd	9th
1903-04	Division 2	25 April	Drew	**0**	**0**	24 October	Won	**3**	**2**	2ndP	13th

FA Cup										*Division*	
1926-27	Round 4	2 February	Won	**1**	**0**	29 January	Drew	**2**	**2**	Div 1	Div 2
1997-98	Round 3	3 January	Drew	**0**	**0**	14 January	Drew*	**1**	**1**	Prem	Div 1
							won 4-3 pens				

Summary	P	W	D	L	F	A	
Arsenal's home league record:	9	8	1	0	24	3	
Arsenal's away league record:	9	3	2	4	9	11	
Arsenal's cup record:	4	1	3	0	4	3	
TOTAL	**22**	**12**	**6**	**4**	**37**	**17**	(+one penalty shoot-out victory)

FACT FILE

- **Port Vale have avoided defeat away to Arsenal twice in 11 matches.**
- **Arsenal are unbeaten in the last nine matches.**

Arsenal's top scorers vs Port Vale

Tommy Briercliffe 4
Paddy O'Brien 3
Charlie Buchan, Bob Buchanan, Gavin Crawford, Bill Gooing, James Henderson, Walter Place 2

Arsenal hat-tricks vs Port Vale

25 Dec 1894 Paddy O'Brien

Played for both clubs

John Wilkinson	Arsenal 1954-55	Port Vale 1957-60
Mel Charles	Arsenal 1959-62	Port Vale 1966-67

v. Portsmouth

		Home					Away			Final Positions	
Season	League	Date	Result	Arsenal	Portsmouth	Date	Result	Arsenal	Portsmouth	Arsenal	Portsmouth
1927-28	Division 1	28 March	Lost	**0**	**2**	8 October	Won	**3**	**2**	10th	20th
1928-29	Division 1	19 January	Won	**4**	**0**	8 September	Lost	**0**	**2**	9th	20th
1929-30	Division 1	26 December	Lost	**1**	**2**	25 December	Won	**1**	**0**	14th	13th
1930-31	Division 1	6 April	Drew	**1**	**1**	3 April	Drew	**1**	**1**	1st	4th
1931-32	Division 1	9 September	Drew	**3**	**3**	16 September	Won	**3**	**0**	2nd	8th
1932-33	Division 1	15 April	Won	**2**	**0**	3 December	Won	**3**	**1**	1st	9th
1933-34	Division 1	4 November	Drew	**1**	**1**	18 April	Lost	**0**	**1**	1st	10th
1934-35	Division 1	29 December	Drew	**1**	**1**	25 August	Drew	**3**	**3**	1st	9th
1935-36	Division 1	22 February	Lost	**2**	**3**	19 October	Lost	**1**	**2**	6th	10th
1936-37	Division 1	17 April	Won	**4**	**0**	12 December	Won	**5**	**1**	3rd	9th
1937-38	Division 1	16 October	Drew	**1**	**1**	26 February	Drew	**0**	**0**	1st	19th
1938-39	Division 1	27 August	Won	**2**	**0**	24 December	Drew	**0**	**0**	5th	17th
1946-47	Division 1	25 December	Won	**2**	**1**	26 December	Won	**2**	**0**	13th	12th
1947-48	Division 1	4 October	Drew	**0**	**0**	21 April	Drew	**0**	**0**	1st	8th
1948-49	Division 1	4 May	Won	**3**	**2**	27 November	Lost	**1**	**4**	5th	1st
1949-50	Division 1	3 May	Won	**2**	**0**	10 December	Lost	**1**	**2**	6th	1st
1950-51	Division 1	23 March	Lost	**0**	**1**	26 March	Drew	**1**	**1**	5th	7th
1951-52	Division 1	25 December	Won	**4**	**1**	26 December	Drew	**1**	**1**	3rd	4th
1952-53	Division 1	10 September	Won	**3**	**1**	17 September	Drew	**2**	**2**	1st	15th
1953-54	Division 1	16 April	Won	**3**	**0**	19 April	Drew	**1**	**1**	12th	14th
1954-55	Division 1	16 October	Lost	**0**	**1**	30 April	Lost	**1**	**2**	9th	3rd
1955-56	Division 1	17 September	Lost	**1**	**3**	1 January	Lost	**2**	**5**	5th	12th
1956-57	Division 1	12 January	Drew	**1**	**1**	8 September	Won	**3**	**2**	5th	19th
1957-58	Division 1	16 November	Won	**3**	**2**	29 March	Lost	**4**	**5**	12th	20th
1958-59	Division 1	25 April	Won	**5**	**2**	6 December	Won	**1**	**0**	3rd	22ndR
1987-88	Division 1	29 August	Won	**6**	**0**	1 January	Drew	**1**	**1**	6th	19thR
2003-04	Prem'ship	13 September	Drew	**1**	**1**	4 May	Drew	**1**	**1**	1st	13th

FA Cup										Division	
1931-32	Round 5					13 February	Won	**2**	**0**	Div 1	Div 1
1970-71	Round 4	1 February	Won	**3**	**2**	23 January	Drew	**1**	**1**	Div 1	Div 2
2003-04	Q'ter Final					6 March	Won	**5**	**1**	Prem	Prem

Summary	P	W	D	L	F	A
Arsenal's home league record:	27	13	8	6	56	30
Arsenal's away league record:	27	8	11	8	42	40
Arsenal's cup record:	4	3	1	0	11	4
TOTAL	**58**	**24**	**20**	**14**	**109**	**74**

Arsenal's top scorers vs Portsmouth

Cliff Bastin 10

Peter Goring 5

Bobby Davidson, David Herd, Alan Smith, Derek Tapscott 4

Arsenal hat-tricks vs Portsmouth

12 Dec 1936 Bobby Davidson (4)

25 Apr 1959 Vic Groves

29 Aug 1987 Alan Smith

Played for both clubs

Alex Mackie	Arsenal 1922-26	Portsmouth 1928-35
Ted Platt	Arsenal 1946-53	Portsmouth 1953-55
Jackie Henderson	Portsmouth 1951-58	Arsenal 1958-62
Jim Standen	Arsenal 1957-61	Portsmouth 1970-72
Roy Pack	Arsenal 1965-66	Portsmouth 1966-69
Roger Davidson	Arsenal 1967-68	Portsmouth 1969-70
George Graham	Arsenal 1966-73	Portsmouth 1974-77
Peter Marinello	Arsenal 1969-73	Portsmouth 1973-76
Alex Cropley	Arsenal 1974-77	Portsmouth 1981-82
Trevor Ross	Arsenal 1974-78	Portsmouth 1982-83
Lee Chapman	Arsenal 1982-84	Portsmouth 1993-94
Paul Mariner	Arsenal 1983-86	Portsmouth 1986-88
Michael Thomas	Portsmouth 1986-87	Arsenal 1986-92
Jimmy Carter	Arsenal 1991-95	Portsmouth 1995-98
Paul Merson	Arsenal 1986-97	Portsmouth 2002-03
David Hillier	Arsenal 1990-97	Portsmouth 1996-99
Paulo Vernazza	Arsenal 1997-2001	Portsmouth 1999-2000
Stathis Tavlaridis	Arsenal 2002-03	Portsmouth 2002-03

Pompey's Jackie Henderson transferred to Arsenal in 1958.

FACT FILE

- **Arsenal are unbeaten in their last nine matches against Pompey.**
- **Portsmouth were undefeated in nine home matches from 1948 to 1956.**
- **Portsmouth won four in a row from 1954 to 1956.**
- **Arsenal were undefeated in 10 matches from 1936 to 1948.**

Never quite living up to his 'next George Best' tag, Peter Marinello takes the ball away from Liverpool's Steve Heighway at Highbury in September 1972. The result was a goalless draw and Arsenal finished runners-up, three points behind champions Liverpool, that season. After four seasons at Highbury, Marinello transferred to Portsmouth.

v. Preston North End

		Home					Away			Final Positions	
Season	*League*	*Date*	*Result*	Arsenal	Preston NE	*Date*	*Result*	Arsenal	Preston NE	Arsenal	Preston NE
1901-02	Division 2	11 January	Drew	**0**	**0**	14 September	Lost	**0**	**2**	4th	3rd
1902-03	Division 2	3 January	Won	**3**	**1**	6 September	Drew	**2**	**2**	3rd	7th
1903-04	Division 2	9 April	Drew	**0**	**0**	1 April	Drew	**0**	**0**	2ndP	1stP
1904-05	Division 1	10 September	Drew	**0**	**0**	7 January	Lost	**0**	**3**	10th	8th
1905-06	Division 1	18 September	Drew	**2**	**2**	23 December	Drew	**2**	**2**	12th	2nd
1906-07	Division 1	19 January	Won	**1**	**0**	15 September	Won	**3**	**0**	7th	14th
1907-08	Division 1	25 January	Drew	**1**	**1**	28 September	Lost	**0**	**3**	14th=	12th
1908-09	Division 1	26 September	Won	**1**	**0**	30 January	Drew	**0**	**0**	6th	10th
1909-10	Division 1	23 April	Lost	**1**	**3**	11 December	Won	**4**	**3**	18th	12th
1910-11	Division 1	22 April	Won	**2**	**0**	17 December	Lost	**1**	**4**	10th	14th
1911-12	Division 1	8 April	Won	**4**	**1**	21 October	Won	**1**	**0**	10th	19thR
1914-15	Division 2	12 December	Lost	**1**	**2**	17 April	Lost	**0**	**3**	5thP	2ndP
1919-20	Division 1	24 April	Drew	**0**	**0**	17 April	Drew	**1**	**1**	10th	19th
1920-21	Division 1	25 April	Won	**2**	**1**	26 February	Won	**1**	**0**	9th	16th
1921-22	Division 1	5 September	Won	**1**	**0**	29 August	Lost	**2**	**3**	17th	16th
1922-23	Division 1	14 April	Drew	**1**	**1**	21 April	Won	**2**	**1**	11th	16th
1923-24	Division 1	3 May	Lost	**1**	**2**	26 April	Won	**2**	**0**	19th	18th
1924-25	Division 1	6 December	Won	**4**	**0**	11 April	Lost	**0**	**2**	20th	21stR
1934-35	Division 1	25 December	Won	**5**	**3**	26 December	Lost	**1**	**2**	1st	11th
1935-36	Division 1	26 October	Won	**2**	**1**	14 March	Lost	**0**	**1**	6th	7th
1936-37	Division 1	25 December	Won	**4**	**1**	28 December	Won	**3**	**1**	3rd	14th
1937-38	Division 1	11 December	Won	**2**	**0**	23 April	Won	**3**	**1**	1st	3rd
1938-39	Division 1	22 October	Won	**1**	**0**	25 February	Lost	**1**	**2**	5th	9th
1946-47	Division 1	15 March	Won	**4**	**1**	9 November	Lost	**0**	**2**	13th	7th
1947-48	Division 1	31 January	Won	**3**	**0**	13 September	Drew	**0**	**0**	1st	7th
1948-49	Division 1	12 March	Drew	**0**	**0**	16 October	Drew	**1**	**1**	5th	21stR
1951-52	Division 1	16 February	Drew	**3**	**3**	6 October	Lost	**0**	**2**	3rd	7th
1952-53	Division 1	19 March	Drew	**1**	**1**	25 April	Lost	**0**	**2**	1st	2nd

John Barnwell is just too late to prevent Preston North End's 16-year-old goalkeeper John Barton collecting the ball at Highbury in December 1958. Barton was making his league debut after playing mostly for Preston's fourth team that season and he helped his side to a 2-1 win. Arsenal, though, had a good season and finished third in the table.

Season	League	Home Date	Home Result	Home Arsenal	Home Preston NE	Away Date	Away Result	Away Arsenal	Away Preston NE	Final Positions Arsenal	Final Positions Preston NE
1953-54	Division 1	3 October	Won	3	2	24 February	Won	1	0	12th	11th
1954-55	Division 1	5 February	Won	2	0	18 September	Lost	1	3	9th	14th
1955-56	Division 1	6 March	Won	3	2	19 November	Won	1	0	5th	19th
1956-57	Division 1	4 September	Lost	1	2	10 September	Lost	0	3	5th	3rd
1957-58	Division 1	14 December	Won	4	2	26 April	Lost	0	3	12th	2nd
1958-59	Division 1	20 December	Lost	1	2	23 August	Lost	1	2	3rd	12th
1959-60	Division 1	17 October	Lost	0	3	5 March	Won	3	0	13th	9th
1960-61	Division 1	23 August	Won	1	0	30 August	Lost	0	2	11th	22ndR

FA Cup

Season	Round	Home Date	Home Result	Arsenal	Preston NE	Away Date	Away Result	Arsenal	Preston NE	Division	
1921-22	Q'ter Final	4 March	Drew	1	1	8 March	Lost*	1	2	Div 1	Div 1
1937-38	Round 5	12 February	Lost	0	1					Div 1	Div 1
1956-57	Round 5	19 February	Won	2	1	16 February	Drew	3	3	Div 1	Div 1
1998-99	Round 3					4 January	Won	4	2	Prem	Div 2

League Cup

Season	Round	Home Date	Home Result	Arsenal	Preston NE	Away Date	Away Result	Arsenal	Preston NE	Division	
1999-00	Round 3	12 October	Won	2	1					Prem	Div 2

Summary	P	W	D	L	F	A
Arsenal's home league record:	36	20	10	6	65	37
Arsenal's away league record:	36	11	7	18	37	56
Arsenal's cup record:	7	3	2	2	13	11
TOTAL	**79**	**34**	**19**	**26**	**115**	**104**

FACT FILE

- **Arsenal recovered from two goals down to beat Preston in the 1999 FA Cup.**
- **Between 1924 and 1956, Arsenal were unbeaten in 14 home league games, a run which started with eight straight wins.**
- **Preston's longest unbeaten run at home is six matches (1939-53).**

Arsenal's top scorers vs Preston

Reg Lewis 8
Bert White 6
Cliff Bastin, Jimmy Bloomfield 4
Alf Common, David Neav, Don Roper 4

Arsenal hat-tricks vs Preston

6 Dec 1924 Harry Woods
15 Mar 1947 Reg Lewis

Played for both clubs

Moses Sanders	Preston North End 1891-99	Arsenal 1899-1900
Tom Pratt	Preston North End 1896-99/1900-03	Arsenal 1903-04
Alf Common	Arsenal 1910-13	Preston North End 1912-14
Alex James	Preston North End 1925-29	Arsenal 1929-37
Frank Moss	Preston North End 1927-29	Arsenal 1931-36
Alf Calverley	Arsenal 1946-47	Preston North End 1947-48
Tommy Docherty	Preston North End 1949-58	Arsenal 1958-61
John Kay	Arsenal 1982-84	Preston North End 1996-97

v. Queen's Park Rangers

Season	League	Home Date	Home Result	Home Arsenal	Home QPR	Away Date	Away Result	Away Arsenal	Away QPR	Final Positions Arsenal	Final Positions QPR
1968-69	Division 1	31 August	Won	2	1	22 March	Won	1	0	4th	22ndR
1973-74	Division 1	30 April	Drew	1	1	27 October	Lost	0	2	10th	8th
1974-75	Division 1	12 October	Drew	2	2	19 April	Drew	0	0	16th	11th
1975-76	Division 1	27 December	Won	2	0	19 April	Lost	1	2	17th	2nd
1976-77	Division 1	2 October	Won	3	2	12 March	Lost	1	2	8th	14th
1977-78	Division 1	15 October	Won	1	0	11 April	Lost	1	2	5th	19th
1978-79	Division 1	2 September	Won	5	1	13 February	Won	2	1	7th	20thR
1983-84	Division 1	4 February	Lost	0	2	1 October	Lost	0	2	6th	5th
1984-85	Division 1	17 November	Won	1	0	20 April	Lost	0	1	7th	19th
1985-86	Division 1	28 December	Won	3	1	3 September	Won	1	0	7th	13th
1986-87	Division 1	6 December	Won	3	1	4 May	Won	4	1	4th	16th
1987-88	Division 1	2 January	Drew	0	0	22 August	Lost	0	2	6th	5th
1988-89	Division 1	22 October	Won	2	1	18 February	Drew	0	0	1st	9th
1989-90	Division 1	18 November	Won	3	0	3 March	Lost	0	2	4th	11th
1990-91	Division 1	23 April	Won	2	0	24 November	Won	3	1	1st	12th
1991-92	Division 1	17 August	Drew	1	1	18 January	Drew	0	0	4th	11th
1992-93	Prem'ship	4 May	Drew	0	0	2 September	Drew	0	0	10th	5th
1993-94	Prem'ship	3 January	Drew	0	0	27 April	Drew	1	1	4th	9th
1994-95	Prem'ship	31 December	Lost	1	3	8 April	Lost	1	3	12th	8th
1995-96	Prem'ship	26 December	Won	3	0	2 March	Drew	1	1	5th	19thR

FA Cup										Division	
1920-21	Round 1					8 January	Lost	0	2	Div 1	Div 3
1921-22	Round 1	7 January	Drew	0	0	11 January	Won	2	1	Div 1	Div 3S
1989-90	Round 4	27 January	Drew	0	0	31 January	Lost	0	2	Div 1	Div 1
2000-01	Round 4					27 January	Won	6	0	Prem	Div 1

A better day: Pat Rice is congratulated by Liam Brady and Malcolm Macdonald after scoring against QPR at Highbury in October 1976. The Gunners went on to win 3-2 and finished the season in eighth place.

League Cup	Date	Result	Away Arsenal	Away QPR	Final Positions Arsenal	Final Positions QPR
1976-77 Q'ter Final	1 December	Lost	**1**	**2**	Div 1	Div 1

Summary	P	W	D	L	F	A
Arsenal's home league record:	20	12	6	2	35	16
Arsenal's away league record:	20	5	6	9	17	23
Arsenal's cup record:	7	2	2	3	9	7
TOTAL	**47**	**19**	**14**	**14**	**61**	**46**

FACT FILE

- **There were six consecutive draws between 1991 and 1994. The run ended when, despite John Jensen's first and only goal for Arsenal, they lost 3-1 at Highbury.**
- **Arsenal lost one home game out of 20 between 1968 and 1994.**
- **Arsenal have not won in their last five away league games, although they did win 6-0 in the FA Cup in 2001.**

Arsenal's top scorers vs QPR

Paul Merson 7
Liam Brady, Graham Rix 5
Frank Stapleton 4
Martin Hayes, Brian Kidd, Alan Smith 3

Played for both clubs

George Grant	Arsenal 1911-15	Queen's Park Rangers 1920-22
Dick Burgess	Arsenal 1919-22	Queen's Park Rangers 1925-27
Andy Neil	Arsenal 1923-26	Queen's Park Rangers 1927-30
Dave Nelson	Arsenal 1936-47	Queen's Park Rangers 1949-51
Frank McLintock	Arsenal 1964-73	Queen's Park Rangers 1973-77
Terry Mancini	Queen's Park Rangers 1971-75	Arsenal 1974-76
Eddie Kelly	Arsenal 1969-76	Queen's Park Rangers 1976-77
John Hollins	Queen's Park Rangers 1975-79	Arsenal 1979-83
Paul Barron	Arsenal 1978-80	Queen's Park Rangers 1985-87
Kenny Sansom	Arsenal 1980-88	Queen's Park Rangers 1989-91
Gus Caesar	Arsenal 1985-90	Queen's Park Rangers 1990-91
David Seaman	Queen's Park Rangers 1986-90	Arsenal 1990-2003
Chris Kiwomya	Arsenal 1994-95	Queen's Park Rangers 1998-2001
Andy Linighan	Arsenal 1990-97	Queen's Park Rangers 1998-99
Steve Morrow	Arsenal 1991-97	Queen's Park Rangers 1996-2001
Matthew Rose	Arsenal 1995-97	Queen's Park Rangers 1997-2004
Lee Harper	Arsenal 1996-97	Queen's Park Rangers 1997-2001
Brian McGovern	Arsenal 1999-2000	Queen's Park Rangers 1999-2000

v. Reading

FA Cup		Date	Result	Away Arsenal	Away Reading	Division Arsenal	Division Reading
1934-35	Round 4	16 February	Won	**1**	**0**	1	Div 3S
1971-72	Round 4	5 February	Won	**2**	**1**	Div 1	Div 4
1986-87	Round 3	10 January	Won	**3**	**1**	Div 1	Div 2

League Cup						Division Arsenal	Division Reading
1967-68	Round 3	11 October	Won	**1**	**0**	Div 1	Div 3

Summary	P	W	D	L	F	A
Arsenal's cup record:	4	4	0	0	7	2
TOTAL	**4**	**4**	**0**	**0**	**7**	**2**

FACT FILE

- **Only Hartlepool have played as many games against Arsenal without avoiding defeat.**

Arsenal's top scorers vs Reading

Charlie Nicholas 2

Played for both clubs

Sidney Crawford	Arsenal 1911-13	Reading 1920-22
Joe North	Arsenal 1919-22	Reading 1922-23
Bill Johnstone	Reading 1926-29	Arsenal 1929-31
Charlie Barley	Arsenal 1926-29	Reading 1929-37
George Marks	Arsenal 1938-40	Reading 1948-53
John Petts	Arsenal 1957-62	Reading 1962-65
Dave Bacuzzi	Arsenal 1960-64	Reading 1966-70
Paul Barron	Arsenal 1978-80	Reading 1986-87
David Madden	Arsenal 1983-84	Reading 1987-88
Steve Morrow	Reading 1990-92	Arsenal 1991-97
Matthew Upson	Arsenal 1997-2002	Reading 2002-03

v. Rochdale

FA Cup		Date	Result	Away Arsenal	Away Rochdale	Division Arsenal	Division Rochdale
1919-20	Round 1	10 January	Won	**4**	**2**	Div 1	Non L

Summary	P	W	D	L	F	A
Arsenal's cup record:	1	1	0	0	4	2
TOTAL	**1**	**1**	**0**	**0**	**4**	**2**

FACT FILE

- **The goalscorers for the Gunners were Rutherford, Groves, Graham and Pagnam.**

Played for both clubs

Bert Humpish	Arsenal 1929-30	Rochdale 1934-35

v. Rotherham Town

		Home					Away			Final Positions	
Season	*League*	*Date*	*Result*	Arsenal	Rotherham	*Date*	*Result*	Arsenal	Rotherham	Arsenal	Rotherham
1893-94	Division 2	13 November	Won	**3**	**0**	6 February	Drew	**1**	**1**	9th	14th
1894-95	Division 2	9 February	Drew	**1**	**1**	20 October	Won	**2**	**1**	8th	12th
1895-96	Division 2	5 October	Won	**5**	**0**	26 October	Lost	**0**	**3**	7th	15thF

Summary	P	W	D	L	F	A
Arsenal's home league record:	3	2	1	0	9	1
Arsenal's away league record:	3	1	1	1	3	5
TOTAL	**6**	**3**	**2**	**1**	**12**	**6**

FACT FILE

- **Arsenal were unbeaten in their first five games.**
- **In 1925, Rotherham Town merged with Rotherham County to form Rotherham United.**

Arsenal's top scorers vs Town

Walter Shaw 2

v. Rotherham United

FA Cup		Home Date	Result	Arsenal	Rotherham	Away Date	Result	Arsenal	Rotherham	Final Positions Arsenal	Rotherham
1959-60	Round 3	13 January	Drew*	1	1	9 January	Drew	2	2	Div 1	Div 2
		18 January		Hillsborough (2nd replay)			Lost	0	2		
1985-86	Round 4	25 January	Won	5	1					Div 1	Div 3

League Cup		Home Date	Result	Arsenal	Rotherham	Away Date	Result	Arsenal	Rotherham	Arsenal	Rotherham
1972-73	Round 3	3 October	Won	5	0					Div 1	Div 3
1978-79	Round 2					29 August	Lost	1	3	Div 1	Div 3
2003-04	Round 3	28 October	Drew*	1	1					Prem	Div 1
			won 9-8 pens								

Summary	P	W	D	L	F	A	
Arsenal's cup record:	7	2	3	2	15	10	
TOTAL	**7**	**2**	**3**	**2**	**15**	**10**	(+ one penalty shoot-out victory)

FACT FILE

- **The 1978-79 league cup tie was the last second round tie that Arsenal lost.**

Arsenal's top scorers vs Rotherham

Ian Allinson, John Radford 2

Played for both clubs

Archie Roe	Arsenal 1922-23	Rotherham County 1924-25
Jack Lambert	Rotherham County 1922-23	Arsenal 1926-34
Joey Williams	Rotherham County 1921-24	Arsenal 1929-32
Jim Furnell	Arsenal 1963-68	Rotherham United 1968-70
Adrian Clarke	Arsenal 1994-97	Rotherham United 1996-97
Scott Marshall	Arsenal 1992-98	Rotherham United 1993-94

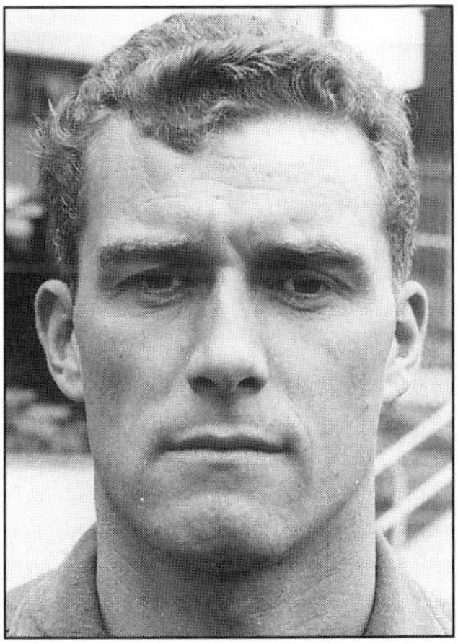

Goalkeeper Jim Furnell left the Gunners to join Rotherham in 1968.

v. St Albans

FA Cup		Date	Result	Home Arsenal	Home St Albans	Division Arsenal	Division St Albans
1897-98	3rd Qual	30 October	Won	**9**	**0**	Div 2	Non L

Summary	P	W	D	L	F	A
Arsenal's cup record:	1	1	0	0	9	0
TOTAL	**1**	**1**	**0**	**0**	**9**	**0**

Arsenal's top scorers vs St Albans

Fergus Hunt 3

Arsenal hat-tricks vs St Albans

30 Oct 1897 Fergus Hunt (cup)

v. Scarborough

League Cup		Date	Result	Away Arsenal	Away Scar'brgh	Final Positions Arsenal	Final Positions Scar'brgh
1992-93	Round 4	6 January	Won	1	0	Prem	Div 3

Summary	P	W	D	L	F	A
Arsenal's cup record:	1	1	0	0	1	0
TOTAL	**1**	**1**	**0**	**0**	**1**	**0**

FACT FILE

- **Nigel Winterburn scored as Arsenal continued on their way to the final against Sheffield Wednesday.**

Played for both clubs

John Kay	Arsenal 1982-84	Scarborough 1996-99

Having met only once, in the League Cup, left-back Nigel Winterburn was the only scorer at the McCain Stadium 1-0 victory in January 1993.

v. 2nd Scots Guards

FA Cup		Date	Result	Away Arsenal	Away 2nd Scots	Final Positions Arsenal	Final Positions 2nd Scots
1893-94	4th Qual	16 December	Won*	2	1	Div 2	Non L

Summary	P	W	D	L	F	A
Arsenal's cup record:	1	1	0	0	2	1
TOTAL	**1**	**1**	**0**	**0**	**2**	**1**

Arsenal's top scorers vs the Guards

James Henderson 2

v. Scunthorpe United

League Cup		Date	Result	Away Arsenal	Away Scunthorpe	Final Positions Arsenal	Final Positions Scunthorpe
1968-69	Round 3	25 September	Won	6	1	Div 1	Div 4

Summary	P	W	D	L	F	A
Arsenal's cup record:	1	1	0	0	6	1
TOTAL	**1**	**1**	**0**	**0**	**6**	**1**

Arsenal's top scorers vs Scunthorpe

David Jenkins 3

Arsenal hat-tricks vs Scunthorpe

25 Sep 1968 David Jenkins (cup)

Played for both clubs

Horace Cumner	Arsenal 1938-40	Scunthorpe United 1950-53
Terry Anderson	Arsenal 1962-65	Scunthorpe United 1974-75
John Hawley	Arsenal 1981-83	Scunthorpe United 1985-86
David Cork	Arsenal 1983-84	Scunthorpe United 1988-89

When war broke out in September 1939 the Football League programme was abandoned after only three matches. Eventually, properly structured regional competitions were arranged, but in the early weeks, only friendly games were allowed. On 23 September 1939, Arsenal lost such a match, 3-0 at Brentford. Here Arsenal's Horace Cumner gets the ball across as the Bees' centre-half Joe James tries to get in a tackle. During the war, Cumner received severe burns in service but continued playing when football resumed.

v. Sheffield United

		Home					Away			Final Positions	
Season	*League*	*Date*	*Result*	Arsenal	Sheff Utd	*Date*	*Result*	Arsenal	Sheff Utd	Arsenal	Sheff Utd
1904-05	Division 1	24 December	Won	**1**	**0**	28 December	Lost	**0**	**4**	10th	6th
1905-06	Division 1	6 January	Won	**5**	**1**	9 September	Lost	**1**	**3**	12th	13th
1906-07	Division 1	2 March	Lost	**0**	**1**	27 October	Lost	**2**	**4**	7th	4th
1907-08	Division 1	2 November	Won	**5**	**1**	29 February	Drew	**2**	**2**	14th=	17th
1908-09	Division 1	1 April	Won	**1**	**0**	31 October	Drew	**1**	**1**	6th	12th
1909-10	Division 1	4 September	Drew	**0**	**0**	8 January	Lost	**0**	**2**	18th	6th
1910-11	Division 1	10 September	Drew	**0**	**0**	7 January	Lost	**2**	**3**	10th	9th
1911-12	Division 1	27 January	Won	**3**	**1**	23 September	Lost	**1**	**2**	10th	14th
1912-13	Division 1	18 January	Lost	**1**	**3**	21 September	Won	**3**	**1**	20thR	15th
1919-20	Division 1	13 March	Won	**3**	**0**	6 March	Lost	**0**	**2**	10th	14th
1920-21	Division 1	26 March	Lost	**2**	**6**	2 April	Drew	**1**	**1**	9th	20th
1921-22	Division 1	27 August	Lost	**1**	**2**	3 September	Lost	**1**	**4**	17th	11th
1922-23	Division 1	28 April	Won	**2**	**0**	2 October	Lost	**1**	**2**	11th	10th
1923-24	Division 1	25 February	Lost	**1**	**3**	9 February	Lost	**1**	**3**	19th	5th
1924-25	Division 1	20 September	Won	**2**	**0**	24 January	Lost	**1**	**2**	20th	14th
1925-26	Division 1	17 March	Won	**4**	**0**	24 October	Lost	**0**	**4**	2nd	5th
1926-27	Division 1	22 January	Drew	**1**	**1**	4 September	Lost	**0**	**4**	11th	8th
1927-28	Division 1	3 September	Won	**6**	**1**	7 January	Lost	**4**	**6**	10th	13th
1928-29	Division 1	10 November	Won	**2**	**0**	23 March	Drew	**2**	**2**	9th	11th
1929-30	Division 1	12 April	Won	**8**	**1**	16 December	Lost	**1**	**4**	14th	20th
1930-31	Division 1	4 October	Drew	**1**	**1**	7 February	Drew	**1**	**1**	1st	15th
1931-32	Division 1	26 December	Lost	**0**	**2**	25 December	Lost	**1**	**4**	2nd	7th
1932-33	Division 1	24 December	Won	**9**	**2**	6 May	Lost	**1**	**3**	1st	10th
1933-34	Division 1	5 May	Won	**2**	**0**	23 December	Won	**3**	**1**	1st	22ndR
1946-47	Division 1	2 November	Lost	**2**	**3**	7 June	Lost	**1**	**2**	13th	6th
1947-48	Division 1	3 January	Won	**3**	**2**	30 August	Won	**2**	**1**	1st	12th
1948-49	Division 1	15 January	Won	**5**	**3**	4 September	Drew	**1**	**1**	5th	22ndR
1953-54	Division 1	1 September	Drew	**1**	**1**	24 August	Lost	**0**	**1**	12th	20th
1954-55	Division 1	11 September	Won	**4**	**0**	18 April	Drew	**1**	**1**	9th	13th
1955-56	Division 1	12 November	Won	**2**	**1**	24 March	Won	**2**	**0**	5th	22ndR
1961-62	Division 1	28 April	Won	**2**	**0**	9 December	Lost	**1**	**2**	10th	5th
1962-63	Division 1	10 November	Won	**1**	**0**	13 April	Drew	**3**	**3**	7th	10th
1963-64	Division 1	28 March	Lost	**1**	**3**	2 November	Drew	**2**	**2**	8th	12th
1964-65	Division 1	6 March	Drew	**1**	**1**	24 October	Lost	**0**	**4**	13th	19th
1965-66	Division 1	6 November	Won	**6**	**2**	25 April	Lost	**0**	**3**	14th	9th
1966-67	Division 1	25 March	Won	**2**	**0**	10 December	Drew	**1**	**1**	7th	10th
1967-68	Division 1	13 January	Drew	**1**	**1**	9 September	Won	**4**	**2**	9th	21stR
1971-72	Division 1	24 August	Lost	**0**	**1**	29 January	Won	**5**	**0**	5th	10th
1972-73	Division 1	3 March	Won	**3**	**2**	7 October	Lost	**0**	**1**	2nd	14th
1973-74	Division 1	11 September	Won	**1**	**0**	4 September	Lost	**0**	**5**	10th	13th
1974-75	Division 1	31 March	Won	**1**	**0**	28 December	Drew	**1**	**1**	16th	6th
1975-76	Division 1	31 January	Won	**1**	**0**	19 August	Won	**3**	**1**	17th	22ndR
1990-91	Division 1	29 December	Won	**4**	**1**	6 April	Won	**2**	**0**	1st	13th
1991-92	Division 1	21 September	Won	**5**	**2**	18 April	Drew	**1**	**1**	4th	9th

			Home					Away		Final Positions	
Season	League	Date	Result	Arsenal	Sheff Utd	Date	Result	Arsenal	Sheff Utd	Arsenal	Sheff Utd
1992-93	Prem'ship	9 January	Drew	**1**	**1**	19 September	Drew	**1**	**1**	10th	14th
1993-94	Prem'ship	29 December	Won	**3**	**0**	4 April	Drew	**1**	**1**	4th	20thR

FA Cup										Division	
1902-03	Round 1	7 February	Lost	**1**	**3**					Div 2	Div 1
1926-27	Round 3					8 January	Won	**3**	**2**	Div 1	Div 1
1935-36	Final	25 April		Wembley			Won	**1**	**0**	Div 1	Div 2
1958-59	Round 5	14 February	Drew	**2**	**2**	18 February	Lost	**0**	**3**	Div 1	Div 2
1977-78	Round 3					7 January	Won	**5**	**0**	Div 1	Div 2
1995-96	Round 3	6 January	Drew	**1**	**1**	17 January	Lost	**0**	**1**	Prem	Div 1
1998-99	Round 5	23 February	Won	**2**	**1**					Prem	Div 1
2002-03	Semi Final	13 April		Old Trafford			Won	**1**	**0**	Prem	Div 1

League Cup											
1971-72	Round 4	26 October	Drew	**0**	**0**	8 November	Lost	**0**	**2**	Div 1	Div 1
1972-73	Round 4					31 October	Won	**2**	**1**	Div 1	Div 1
1981-82	Round 2	27 October	Won	**2**	**0**	6 October	Lost	**0**	**1**	Div 1	Div 4

Summary	P	W	D	L	F	A
Arsenal's home league record:	46	29	8	9	110	50
Arsenal's away league record:	46	8	14	24	62	99
Arsenal's cup record:	15	7	3	5	20	17
TOTAL	**107**	**44**	**25**	**38**	**192**	**166**

FACT FILE

- **The FA Cup tie of 1999 was originally played at Highbury on 13 February. Arsenal won 2-1, but their winning goal was highly controversial as United had kicked the ball out of play for a player to receive treatment. Rather than give the ball back, however, recent signing Kanu crossed for Overmars to score. In an unprecedented move, Arsenal offered a rematch which the Blades accepted. Ten days later, the same scoreline ensued.**
- **The winning goal in the 2003 tie was not without controversy either, but David Seaman's fantastic late save from Paul Peschisolido secured Arsenal's third consecutive FA Cup Final appearance.**
- **Sheffield United were the last lower division team to beat Arsenal, in an FA Cup tie in 1996.**
- **Arsenal have not lost in their last 12 home games (13 if you include the first 1999 match), a sequence stretching back to 1971.**
- **Arsenal won only once in their first 23 league visits to Bramall Lane.**
- **Arsenal twice scored eight in a game against United.**

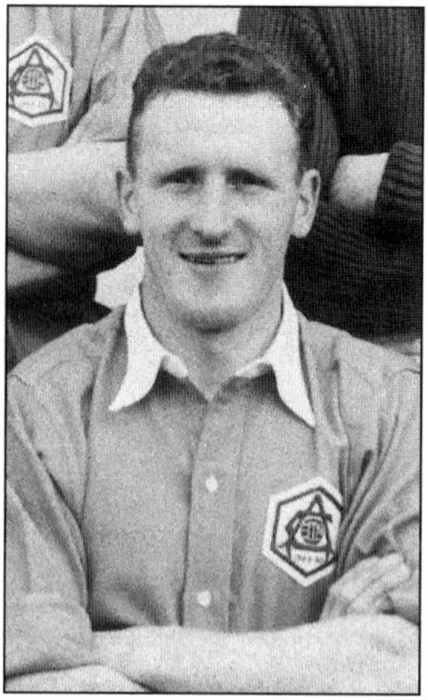

Alf Common (left) and Alex Forbes (right) were two great players to have played for both Sheffield United and Arsenal.

Arsenal's top scorers vs United

Jack Lambert 9
Jimmy Brain, Kevin Campbell, Charlie George, Joe Hulme 6
Charlie Buchan, George Graham 5
Joe Baker, Cliff Bastin, Billy Blyth, Ronnie Rooke, Don Roper, Alan Smith, Geoff Strong 4

Arsenal hat-tricks vs United

12 Apr 1930 Jack Lambert
24 Dec 1932 Jack Lambert (5)
24 Dec 1932 Cliff Bastin

Played for both clubs

Ralph Gaudie	Sheffield United 1897-98	Arsenal 1899-1901
Walter Anderson	Sheffield United 1899-1902	Arsenal 1901-03
Alf Common	Sheffield United 1901-04	Arsenal 1910-13
Edward Anderson	Arsenal 1903-04	Sheffield United 1905-06
Joe Fidler	Sheffield United 1903-05	Arsenal 1912-14
Peter Kyle	Arsenal 1906-08	Sheffield United 1908-09
Joe Lievesley	Sheffield United 1904-13	Arsenal 1913-15
Wally Hardinge	Sheffield United 1907-13	Arsenal 1913-20
Bob Benson	Sheffield United 1905-14	Arsenal 1913-15
Jimmy Dunne	Sheffield United 1926-34	Arsenal 1933-36
Alex Forbes	Sheffield United 1946-48	Arsenal 1947-56
Paddy Sloan	Arsenal 1946-48	Sheffield United 1947-48
John Wilkinson	Arsenal 1954-55	Sheffield United 1955-57
John Barnwell	Arsenal 1956-64	Sheffield United 1970-71
Colin Addison	Arsenal 1966-68	Sheffield United 1967-71
Wilf Rostron	Arsenal 1974-77	Sheffield United 1989-91
John Matthews	Arsenal 1974-78	Sheffield United 1978-82
Trevor Ross	Arsenal 1974-78	Sheffield United 1982-84
Colin Hill	Arsenal 1982-85	Sheffield United 1989-92
Brian Marwood	Arsenal 1987-90	Sheffield United 1990-92
Scott Marshall	Arsenal 1992-98	Sheffield United 1994-95
Paul Shaw	Arsenal 1994-97	Sheffield United 2003-04

v. Sheffield Wednesday

		Home				Away				Final Positions	
Season	League	Date	Result	Arsenal	Sheff W	Date	Result	Arsenal	Sheff W	Arsenal	Sheff W
1899-00	Division 2	11 November	Lost	**1**	**2**	17 March	Lost	**1**	**3**	8th	1stP
1904-05	Division 1	25 February	Won	**3**	**0**	29 October	Won	**3**	**0**	10th	9th
1905-06	Division 1	18 November	Lost	**0**	**2**	24 March	Lost	**2**	**4**	12th	3th
1906-07	Division 1	29 March	Won	**1**	**0**	1 January	Drew	**1**	**1**	7th	13th
1907-08	Division 1	20 April	Drew	**1**	**1**	31 December	Lost	**0**	**6**	14th=	5th
1908-09	Division 1	12 April	Won	**2**	**0**	28 December	Lost	**2**	**6**	6th	5th
1909-10	Division 1	26 March	Lost	**0**	**1**	13 November	Drew	**1**	**1**	18th	11th
1910-11	Division 1	12 November	Won	**1**	**0**	18 March	Drew	**0**	**0**	10th	6th
1911-12	Division 1	2 December	Lost	**0**	**2**	6 April	Lost	**0**	**3**	10th	5th
1912-13	Division 1	29 March	Lost	**2**	**5**	23 November	Lost	**0**	**2**	20thR	3rd
1919-20	Division 1	20 December	Won	**3**	**1**	27 December	Won	**2**	**1**	10th	22ndR
1926-27	Division 1	23 October	Won	**6**	**2**	12 March	Lost	**2**	**4**	11th	16th
1927-28	Division 1	2 May	Drew	**1**	**1**	22 October	Drew	**1**	**1**	10th	14th
1928-29	Division 1	29 December	Drew	**2**	**2**	25 August	Lost	**2**	**3**	9th	1st
1929-30	Division 1	4 January	Lost	**2**	**3**	7 September	Won	**2**	**0**	14th	1st
1930-31	Division 1	21 March	Won	**2**	**0**	15 November	Won	**2**	**1**	1st	3rd
1931-32	Division 1	16 April	Won	**3**	**1**	5 December	Won	**3**	**1**	2nd	3rd
1932-33	Division 1	14 April	Won	**4**	**2**	2 January	Lost	**2**	**3**	1st	3rd
1933-34	Division 1	6 January	Drew	**1**	**1**	2 September	Won	**2**	**1**	1st	11th
1934-35	Division 1	2 February	Won	**4**	**1**	22 September	Drew	**0**	**0**	1st	3rd
1935-36	Division 1	14 September	Drew	**2**	**2**	18 January	Lost	**2**	**3**	6th	20th
1936-37	Division 1	10 October	Drew	**1**	**1**	13 February	Drew	**0**	**0**	3rd	22ndR
1950-51	Division 1	2 September	Won	**3**	**0**	30 December	Won	**2**	**0**	5th	21stR
1952-53	Division 1	11 October	Drew	**2**	**2**	2 March	Won	**4**	**1**	1st	18th
1953-54	Division 1	31 October	Won	**4**	**1**	20 March	Lost	**1**	**2**	12th	19th
1954-55	Division 1	26 February	Won	**3**	**2**	9 October	Won	**2**	**1**	9th	22ndR
1956-57	Division 1	2 February	Won	**6**	**3**	22 September	Won	**4**	**2**	5th	14th
1957-58	Division 1	22 March	Won	**1**	**0**	23 November	Lost	**0**	**2**	12th	22ndR
1959-60	Division 1	22 August	Lost	**0**	**1**	19 December	Lost	**1**	**5**	13th	5th
1960-61	Division 1	26 December	Drew	**1**	**1**	23 December	Drew	**1**	**1**	11th	2nd
1961-62	Division 1	14 November	Won	**1**	**0**	20 September	Drew	**1**	**1**	10th	6th
1962-63	Division 1	8 September	Lost	**1**	**2**	18 May	Won	**3**	**2**	7th	6th
1963-64	Division 1	24 March	Drew	**1**	**1**	30 March	Won	**4**	**0**	8th	6th
1964-65	Division 1	25 August	Drew	**1**	**1**	2 September	Lost	**1**	**2**	13th	8th
1965-66	Division 1	28 December	Won	**5**	**2**	27 December	Lost	**0**	**4**	14th	17th
1966-67	Division 1	6 September	Drew	**1**	**1**	13 May	Drew	**1**	**1**	7th	11th
1967-68	Division 1	30 April	Won	**3**	**2**	4 May	Won	**2**	**1**	9th	19th
1968-69	Division 1	11 January	Won	**2**	**0**	1 March	Won	**5**	**0**	4th	15th
1969-70	Division 1	6 September	Drew	**0**	**0**	20 December	Drew	**1**	**1**	12th	22ndR
1984-85	Division 1	27 April	Won	**1**	**0**	25 November	Lost	**1**	**2**	7th	8th
1985-86	Division 1	14 September	Won	**1**	**0**	16 April	Lost	**0**	**2**	7th	5th
1986-87	Division 1	2 September	Won	**2**	**0**	14 February	Drew	**1**	**1**	4th	13th
1987-88	Division 1	5 December	Won	**3**	**1**	30 April	Drew	**3**	**3**	6th	11th
1988-89	Division 1	21 January	Drew	**1**	**1**	24 September	Lost	**1**	**2**	1st	15th

Season	League	Home Date	Home Result	Home Arsenal	Home Sheff W	Away Date	Away Result	Away Arsenal	Away Sheff W	Final Positions Arsenal	Final Positions Sheff W
1989-90	Division 1	9 September	Won	**5**	**0**	17 February	Lost	**0**	**1**	4th	18thR
1991-92	Division 1	15 February	Won	**7**	**1**	23 November	Drew	**1**	**1**	4th	3rd
1992-93	Prem'ship	29 August	Won	**2**	**1**	6 May	Lost	**0**	**1**	10th	7th
1993-94	Prem'ship	12 December	Won	**1**	**0**	21 August	Won	**1**	**0**	4th	7th
1994-95	Prem'ship	6 November	Drew	**0**	**0**	4 February	Lost	**1**	**3**	12th	13th
1995-96	Prem'ship	21 November	Won	**4**	**2**	8 April	Lost	**0**	**1**	5th	15th
1996-97	Prem'ship	16 September	Won	**4**	**1**	26 December	Drew	**0**	**0**	3rd	7th
1997-98	Prem'ship	28 March	Won	**1**	**0**	22 November	Lost	**0**	**2**	1st	16th
1998-99	Prem'ship	9 March	Won	**3**	**0**	27 September	Lost	**0**	**1**	2nd	12th
1999-00	Prem'ship	9 May	Drew	**3**	**3**	3 January	Drew	**1**	**1**	2nd	19thR

FA Cup

Season	Round	Home Date	Home Result	Home Arsenal	Home Sheff W	Away Date	Away Result	Away Arsenal	Away Sheff W	Division Arsenal	Division Sheff W
1893-94	Round 1	27 January	Lost	**1**	**2**					Div 2	Div 1
1906-07	Semi Final	23 March				St Andrew's	Lost	**1**	**3**	Div 1	Div 1
1934-35	Round 5					2 March	Lost	**1**	**2**	Div 1	Div 1
1949-50	Round 3	7 January	Won	**1**	**0**					Div 1	Div 2
1962-63	Round 4	12 March	Won	**2**	**0**					Div 1	Div 1
1978-79	Round 3	9 January	Drew	**1**	**1**	6 January	Drew*	**1**	**1**	Div 1	Div 3
		15 January				Filbert Street (2nd replay)	Drew*	**2**	**2**		
		17 January				Filbert Street (3rd replay)	Drew*	**3**	**3**		
		22 January				Filbert Street (4th replay)	Won	**2**	**0**		
1992-93	Final	15 May				Wembley	Drew*	**1**	**1**	Prem	Prem
		20 May				Wembley	Won*	**2**	**1**		

League Cup

Season	Round	Home Date	Home Result	Home Arsenal	Home Sheff W	Away Date	Away Result	Away Arsenal	Away Sheff W	Division Arsenal	Division Sheff W
1982-83	Q'ter Final	18 January	Won	**1**	**0**					Div 1	Div 2
1987-88	Q'ter Final					20 January	Won	**1**	**0**	Div 1	Div 1
1992-93	Final	18 April				Wembley	Won	**2**	**1**	Prem	Prem
1994-95	Round 4	30 November	Won	**2**	**0**					Prem	Prem
1995-96	Round 4	29 November	Won	**2**	**1**					Prem	Prem

Summary	P	W	D	L	F	A
Arsenal's home league record:	54	31	15	8	115	59
Arsenal's away league record:	54	15	15	24	73	91
Arsenal's cup record:	17	9	5	3	26	18
TOTAL	**125**	**55**	**35**	**35**	**214**	**168**

FACT FILE

- **Arsenal and Sheffield Wednesday are the only teams ever to meet each other in both domestic cup finals in the same season. Arsenal won them both with unlikely heroes. Steve Morrow, who only ever scored three goals for Arsenal, scored the winner in the League Cup final, while Andy Linighan (eight goals for Arsenal), scored the winner in the FA Cup Final – in the last minute of extra-time in the replay. It is the closest the FA Cup Final has ever got to a penalty shoot-out.**

FACT FILE

- **Arsenal have won one of their last 16 league matches at Hillsborough.**
- **Arsenal have not lost in their last 27 home games, since Wednesday last won there in 1962.**
- **Wednesday won the first three cup ties between the sides, but Arsenal have won the last nine. They needed four replays against third division Wednesday in 1979, but once they were past that hurdle, they went on to win the cup.**
- **The match at Highbury in January 1934 took place just 12 hours after the sudden death of Arsenal's manager, the legendary Herbert Chapman.**

Arsenal's top scorers vs Wednesday

Ian Wright 10
Jimmy Brain, Paul Merson 8
Cliff Bastin, Cliff Holton, David Jack 7
John Radford, Derek Tapscott 6
Jimmy Logie 5

Arsenal hat-tricks vs Wednesday

23 Oct 1926 Jimmy Brain (4)
2 Feb 1935 Alex James
2 Mar 1953 Cliff Holton (4)
26 Feb 1955 Derek Tapscott
2 Feb 1957 David Herd
30 Mar 1964 Alan Skirton
1 Mar 1969 John Radford
16 Sep 1996 Ian Wright

Played for both clubs

Bill Gooing	Sheffield Wednesday 1895-96	Arsenal 1901-05
James Maxwell	Sheffield Wednesday 1906-08	Arsenal 1908-09
Frank Bradshaw	Sheffield Wednesday 1905-10	Arsenal 1914-23
George Drury	Sheffield Wednesday 1936-38	Arsenal 1937-40
George Hunt	Arsenal 1937-38	Sheffield Wednesday 1946-48
Brian Hornsby	Arsenal 1972-76	Sheffield Wednesday 1977-82
Wilf Rostron	Arsenal 1974-77	Sheffield Wednesday 1988-89
Lee Chapman	Arsenal 1982-84	Sheffield Wednesday 1984-88
Viv Anderson	Arsenal 1984-87	Sheffield Wednesday 1990-93
Brian Marwood	Sheffield Wednesday 1984-88	Arsenal 1987-90
Siggi Jonsson	Sheffield Wednesday 1984-89	Arsenal 1989-91

George Eastham sees his penalty saved by Sheffield Wednesday goalkeeper Dave McLaren at Highbury in March 1964 in front of only 18,000 spectators. Arsenal drew 1-1 that night but six days later won 4-0 at Hillsborough.

v. Sheppey United

FA Cup		Date	Result	Home Arsenal	Home Sheppey	Division Arsenal	Division Sheppey
1897-98	4thQual	20 November	Won	**3**	**0**	Div 2	Non L

Summary	P	W	D	L	F	A
Arsenal's cup record:	1	1	0	0	3	0
TOTAL	**1**	**1**	**0**	**0**	**3**	**0**

FACT FILE

- **Crawford, Haywood and Brock scored the goals.**

v. Shrewsbury Town

FA Cup		Home Date	Home Result	Arsenal	Shrewsbury	Away Date	Away Result	Arsenal	Shrewsbury	Division Arsenal	Division Shrewsbury
1967-68	Round 3	30 January	Won	**2**	**0**	27 January	Drew	**1**	**1**	Div 1	Div 3
1990-91	Round 5					27 February	Won	**1**	**0**	Div 1	Div 3

Summary	P	W	D	L	F	A
Arsenal's cup record:	3	2	1	0	4	1
TOTAL	**3**	**2**	**1**	**0**	**4**	**1**

Played for both clubs

David Jenkins	Arsenal 1967-69	Shrewsbury Town 1974-75
Brian Hornsby	Arsenal 1972-76	Shrewsbury Town 1976-78
Paul Gorman	Arsenal 1981-84	Shrewsbury Town 1989-92
John Kay	Arsenal 1982-84	Shrewsbury Town 1995-96

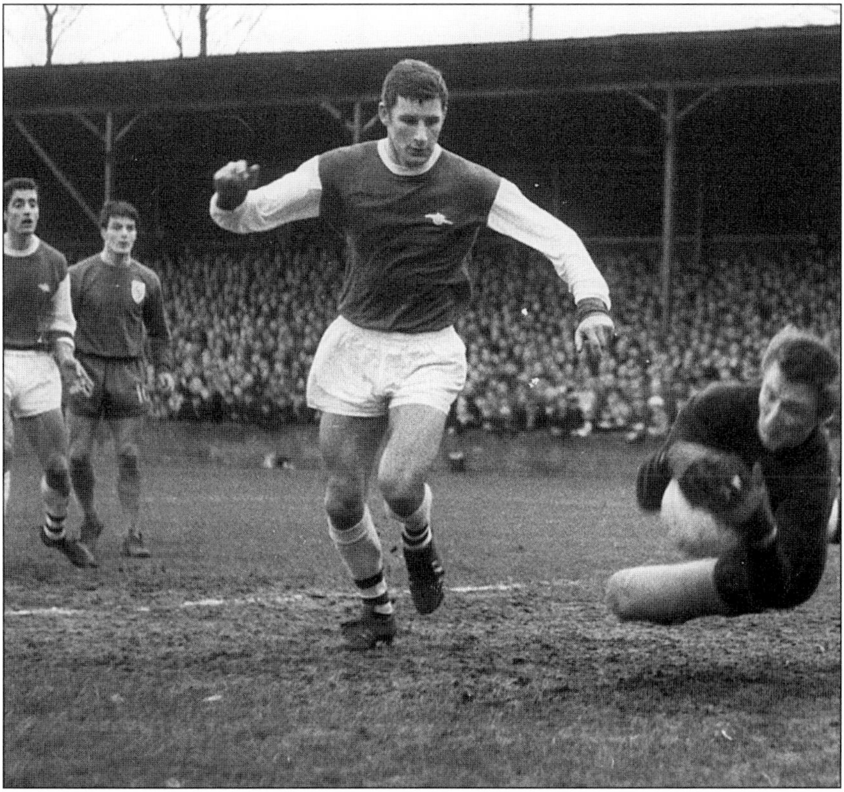

Terry Neill, who came on as a substitute for the injured John Radford, in action at Gay Meadow in January 1968, when Arsenal drew 1-1 with Shrewsbury Town in the third round of the FA Cup. The Gunners won the replay 2-0. They eventually reached the fifth round, where they lost a replay at Birmingham.

v. Southampton

Season	League	Home Date	Home Result	Home Arsenal	Home South'ton	Away Date	Away Result	Away Arsenal	Away South'ton	Final Positions Arsenal	Final Positions South'ton
1966-67	Division 1	26 December	Won	**4**	**1**	27 December	Lost	**1**	**2**	7th	19th
1967-68	Division 1	15 April	Lost	**0**	**3**	10 April	Lost	**0**	**2**	9th	16th
1968-69	Division 1	29 March	Drew	**0**	**0**	7 September	Won	**2**	**1**	4th	7th
1969-70	Division 1	6 December	Drew	**2**	**2**	21 March	Won	**2**	**0**	12th	19th
1970-71	Division 1	27 December	Drew	**0**	**0**	10 April	Won	**2**	**1**	1st	7th
1971-72	Division 1	28 March	Won	**1**	**0**	2 October	Won	**1**	**0**	5th	19th
1972-73	Division 1	30 September	Won	**1**	**0**	23 April	Drew	**2**	**2**	2nd	13th
1973-74	Division 1	2 March	Won	**1**	**0**	26 December	Drew	**1**	**1**	10th	20thR
1978-79	Division 1	21 October	Won	**1**	**0**	23 March	Lost	**0**	**2**	7th	14th
1979-80	Division 1	5 April	Drew	**1**	**1**	1 January	Won	**1**	**0**	4th	8th
1980-81	Division 1	19 August	Drew	**1**	**1**	11 November	Lost	**1**	**3**	3rd	6th
1981-82	Division 1	15 May	Won	**4**	**1**	23 January	Lost	**1**	**3**	5th	7th
1982-83	Division 1	2 April	Drew	**0**	**0**	28 February	Drew	**2**	**2**	10th	12th
1983-84	Division 1	31 December	Drew	**2**	**2**	3 September	Lost	**0**	**1**	6th	2nd
1984-85	Division 1	6 May	Won	**1**	**0**	8 December	Lost	**0**	**1**	7th	5th
1985-86	Division 1	20 August	Won	**3**	**2**	7 December	Lost	**0**	**3**	7th	14th
1986-87	Division 1	27 December	Won	**1**	**0**	15 November	Won	**4**	**0**	4th	12th
1987-88	Division 1	21 November	Lost	**0**	**1**	9 April	Lost	**2**	**4**	6th	12th
1988-89	Division 1	17 September	Drew	**2**	**2**	25 March	Won	**3**	**1**	1st	13th
1989-90	Division 1	2 May	Won	**2**	**1**	26 December	Lost	**0**	**1**	4th	7th
1990-91	Division 1	17 November	Won	**4**	**0**	9 April	Drew	**1**	**1**	1st	14th
1991-92	Division 1	2 May	Won	**5**	**1**	28 September	Won	**4**	**0**	4th	16th
1992-93	Prem'ship	20 March	Won	**4**	**3**	5 December	Lost	**0**	**2**	10th	18th
1993-94	Prem'ship	25 September	Won	**1**	**0**	19 March	Won	**4**	**0**	4th	18th
1994-95	Prem'ship	24 January	Drew	**1**	**1**	19 November	Lost	**0**	**1**	12th	10th
1995-96	Prem'ship	23 September	Won	**4**	**2**	9 December	Drew	**0**	**0**	5th	17th
1996-97	Prem'ship	4 December	Won	**3**	**1**	15 March	Won	**2**	**0**	3rd	16th
1997-98	Prem'ship	31 January	Won	**3**	**0**	23 August	Won	**3**	**1**	1st	12th
1998-99	Prem'ship	17 October	Drew	**1**	**1**	3 April	Drew	**0**	**0**	2nd	17th
1999-00	Prem'ship	26 February	Won	**3**	**1**	18 September	Won	**1**	**0**	2nd	15th
2000-01	Prem'ship	2 December	Won	**1**	**0**	19 May	Lost	**2**	**3**	2nd	10th
2001-02	Prem'ship	2 February	Drew	**1**	**1**	13 October	Won	**2**	**0**	1st	11th
2002-03	Prem'ship	7 May	Won	**6**	**1**	23 November	Lost	**2**	**3**	2nd	8th
2003-04	Prem'ship	10 February	Won	**2**	**0**	29 December	Won	**1**	**0**	1st	12th

FA Cup

Season	Round	Home Date	Home Result	Home Arsenal	Home South'ton	Away Date	Away Result	Away Arsenal	Away South'ton	Division Arsenal	Division South'ton
1926-27	Semi Final	26 March				Stamford Bridge	Won	**2**	**1**	Div 1	Div 2
1978-79	Q'ter Final	21 March	Won	**2**	**0**	19 March	Drew	**1**	**1**	Div 1	Div 1
2002-03	Final	17 May				Millennium Stadium	Won	**1**	**0**	Prem	Prem

League Cup

Season	Round	Home Date	Home Result	Home Arsenal	Home South'ton	Away Date	Away Result	Away Arsenal	Away South'ton	Division Arsenal	Division South'ton
1969-70	Round 2	4 September	Won	**2**	**0**	2 September	Drew	**1**	**1**	Div 1	Div 1
1977-78	Round 3	25 October	Won	**2**	**0**					Div 1	Div 2
1979-80	Round 3	25 September	Won	**2**	**1**					Div 1	Div 1
1985-86	Round 4	19 November	Drew	**0**	**0**	26 November	Won	**3**	**1**	Div 1	Div 1

Summary	P	W	D	L	F	A
Arsenal's home league record:	34	21	11	2	66	29
Arsenal's away league record:	34	14	6	14	47	41
Arsenal's cup record:	10	7	3	0	16	5
TOTAL	**78**	**42**	**20**	**16**	**129**	**75**

FACT FILE

- **In 2003, Arsenal became the first side to reach three consecutive FA Cup Finals twice (they also did it from 1978 to 1980). Robert Pires's goal saw them become the first side to retain the cup for 21 years.**
- **Arsenal have lost one of their last 37 home matches, and none of their last 16, since Southampton's win in 1987.**
- **All-time leading Arsenal goalscorer Ian Wright is the only Gunner to score three hat-tricks against the same opposition.**
- **Southampton were undefeated in six home matches from 1980 to 1985.**
- **In February 2002, Southampton were the last team to take a league point off Arsenal that season, as Arsenal stormed to the double in style.**

Arsenal's top scorers vs Southampton

Ian Wright 11
Dennis Bergkamp, Robert Pires, John Radford 7
Paul Merson 5
Thierry Henry, Alan Smith 4

Arsenal hat-tricks vs Southampton

28 Sep 1991 Ian Wright
2 May 1992 Ian Wright
19 Mar 1994 Ian Wright
7 May 2003 Robert Pires
7 May 2003 Jermaine Pennant

Played for both clubs

Bill Henderson	Arsenal 1921-23	Southampton 1923-28
Tom Parker	Southampton 1920-26	Arsenal 1925-33
Peter Dougal	Southampton 1929-32	Arsenal 1933-36
Ted Drake	Southampton 1931-34	Arsenal 1933-40
Ray Parkin	Arsenal 1928-36	Southampton 1037-39
Frank Hill	Arsenal 1932-36	Southampton 1937-39
Jimmy Dunne	Arsenal 1933-36	Southampton 1936-37
George Curtis	Arsenal 1938-47	Southampton 1947-52
Tom Rudkin	Arsenal 1946-47	Southampton 1947-49
Don Roper	Southampton 1946-47/56-59	Arsenal 1947-57
Charlie George	Arsenal 1969-75	Southampton 1978-81
Alan Ball	Arsenal 1971-77	Southampton 1976-83
Steve Williams	Southampton 1975-85	Arsenal 1984-88
Kevin Richardson	Arsenal 1987-90	Southampton 1997-98
Perry Groves	Arsenal 1986-92	Southampton 1992-93
Neil Heaney	Arsenal 1991-94	Southampton 1993-97
Scott Marshall	Arsenal 1992-98	Southampton 1998-99
Luis Boa Morte	Arsenal 1997-2000	Southampton 1999-2000

v. Stockport County

		Home					Away			Final Positions	
Season	League	Date	Result	Arsenal	Stockport	Date	Result	Arsenal	Stockport	Arsenal	Stockport
1900-01	Division 2	13 October	Won	**2**	**0**	16 February	Lost	**1**	**3**	7th	17th
1901-02	Division 2	8 March	Won	**3**	**0**	9 November	Drew	**0**	**0**	4th	17th
1902-03	Division 2	28 February	Won	**3**	**1**	1 January	Won	**1**	**0**	3rd	17th
1903-04	Division 2	12 March	Won	**5**	**2**	1 January	Drew	**0**	**0**	2ndP	16thF
1913-14	Division 2	13 April	Won	**4**	**0**	10 April	Lost	**0**	**2**	3rd	12th
1914-15	Division 2	23 January	Won	**3**	**1**	19 September	Drew	**1**	**1**	5thP	14th

League Cup

1980-81	Round 3					22 September	Won	**3**	**1**	Div 1	Div 4

Summary	P	W	D	L	F	A
Arsenal's home league record:	6	6	0	0	20	4
Arsenal's away league record:	6	1	3	2	3	6
rsenal's cup record:	1	1	0	0	3	1
TOTAL	**13**	**8**	**3**	**2**	**26**	**11**

FACT FILE

- **Only Gainsborough have been to Arsenal more times without picking up a point.**

Arsenal's top scorers vs Stockport

Pat Flanagan 4

Tim Coleman, Bill Gooing 3

Walter Anderson, Bill Linward 2

Played for both clubs

Ernest Cottrell	Arsenal 1898-1901	Stockport County 1903-04
Andrew Swann	Arsenal 1901-02	Stockport County 1901-02
Jimmy Blair	Arsenal 1905-07	Stockport County 1912-13
Charlie Jones	Stockport County 1921-23	Arsenal 1928-34
Bert Humpish	Arsenal 1929-30	Stockport County 1932-34
David Herd	Stockport County 1950-54	Arsenal 1954-61
George Armstrong	Arsenal 1961-77	Stockport County 1978-79
Eddie McGoldrick	Arsenal 1993-96	Stockport County 1997-98

v. Stoke City

Season	League	Home Date	Home Result	Arsenal	Stoke City	Away Date	Away Result	Arsenal	Stoke City	Final Positions Arsenal	Final Positions Stoke City
1904-05	Division 1	12 November	Won	**2**	**1**	11 March	Lost	**0**	**2**	10th	12th
1905-06	Division 1	27 January	Lost	**1**	**2**	23 September	Lost	**1**	**2**	12th	10th
1906-07	Division 1	17 November	Won	**2**	**1**	15 April	Lost	**0**	**2**	7th	20thR
1922-23	Division 1	30 December	Won	**3**	**0**	6 January	Lost	**0**	**1**	11th	21stR
1933-34	Division 1	18 November	Won	**3**	**0**	31 March	Drew	**1**	**1**	1st	12th
1934-35	Division 1	20 February	Won	**2**	**0**	6 October	Drew	**2**	**2**	1st	10th
1935-36	Division 1	1 February	Won	**1**	**0**	28 September	Won	**3**	**0**	6th	4th
1936-37	Division 1	26 March	Drew	**0**	**0**	29 March	Drew	**0**	**0**	3rd	10th
1937-38	Division 1	5 March	Won	**4**	**0**	23 October	Drew	**1**	**1**	1st	17th
1938-39	Division 1	17 December	Won	**4**	**1**	22 April	Lost	**0**	**1**	5th	7th
1946-47	Division 1	19 October	Won	**1**	**0**	22 February	Lost	**1**	**3**	13th	4th
1947-48	Division 1	20 September	Won	**3**	**0**	7 February	Drew	**0**	**0**	1st	15th
1948-49	Division 1	25 August	Won	**3**	**0**	30 August	Lost	**0**	**1**	5th	11th
1949-50	Division 1	10 April	Won	**6**	**0**	6 May	Won	**5**	**2**	6th	19th
1950-51	Division 1	25 December	Lost	**0**	**3**	26 December	Lost	**0**	**1**	5th	13th
1951-52	Division 1	19 April	Won	**4**	**1**	1 December	Lost	**1**	**2**	3rd	20th
1952-53	Division 1	18 April	Won	**3**	**1**	29 November	Drew	**1**	**1**	1st	21stR
1963-64	Division 1	29 February	Drew	**1**	**1**	9 October	Won	**2**	**1**	8th	17th
1964-65	Division 1	26 December	Won	**3**	**2**	28 December	Lost	**1**	**4**	13th	11th
1965-66	Division 1	21 August	Won	**2**	**1**	29 January	Won	**3**	**1**	14th	10th
1966-67	Division 1	6 May	Won	**3**	**1**	1 April	Drew	**2**	**2**	7th	12th
1967-68	Division 1	19 August	Won	**2**	**0**	16 December	Won	**1**	**0**	9th	18th
1968-69	Division 1	14 September	Won	**1**	**0**	19 April	Won	**3**	**1**	4th	19th
1969-70	Division 1	7 February	Drew	**0**	**0**	11 October	Drew	**0**	**0**	12th	9th
1970-71	Division 1	1 May	Won	**1**	**0**	26 September	Lost	**0**	**5**	1st	13th
1971-72	Division 1	28 August	Lost	**0**	**1**	8 January	Drew	**0**	**0**	5th	17th
1972-73	Division 1	19 August	Won	**2**	**0**	30 December	Drew	**0**	**0**	2nd	15th
1973-74	Division 1	22 September	Won	**2**	**1**	30 March	Drew	**0**	**0**	10th	5th
1974-75	Division 1	29 March	Drew	**1**	**1**	21 December	Won	**2**	**0**	16th	5th
1975-76	Division 1	23 August	Lost	**0**	**1**	13 December	Lost	**1**	**2**	17th	12th
1976-77	Division 1	16 October	Won	**2**	**0**	23 March	Drew	**1**	**1**	8th	21stR
1979-80	Division 1	20 October	Drew	**0**	**0**	1 March	Won	**3**	**2**	4th	18th
1980-81	Division 1	13 September	Won	**2**	**0**	7 February	Drew	**1**	**1**	3rd	11th
1981-82	Division 1	29 August	Lost	**0**	**1**	20 January	Won	**1**	**0**	5th	18th
1982-83	Division 1	15 January	Won	**3**	**0**	28 August	Lost	**1**	**2**	10th	13th
1983-84	Division 1	7 April	Won	**3**	**1**	28 January	Lost	**0**	**1**	6th	18th
1984-85	Division 1	22 September	Won	**4**	**0**	30 March	Lost	**0**	**2**	7th	22ndR

FA Cup

Season	Round	Date	Result	Arsenal	Stoke City	Venue	Result	Arsenal	Stoke City	Division Arsenal	Division Stoke City
1927-28	Q'ter Final	3 March	Won	**4**	**1**					Div 1	Div 2
1928-29	Round 3	12 January	Won	**2**	**1**					Div 1	Div 2
1956-57	Round 3	5 January	Won	**4**	**2**					Div 1	Div 2
1970-71	Semi Final	27 March				Hillsborough	Drew	**2**	**2**	Div 1	Div 1
		31 March				Villa Park (replay)	Won	**2**	**0**		

			Home			Away			Final Positions	
FA Cup cont		*Date*			*Date*	*Result*	Arsenal	Stoke City	Arsenal	Stoke City
1971-72	Semi Final	15 April	Villa Park			Drew	**1**	**1**	Div 1	Div 1
		19 April	Goodison Pk (replay)			Won	**2**	**1**		
1989-90	Round 3				6 January	Won	**1**	**0**	Div 1	Div 2

League Cup

1987-88	Round 4	17 November	Won	**3**	**0**						Div 1	Div 2
1996-97	Round 3	13 November	Won	**5**	**2**	23 October	Drew	**1**	**1**		Prem	Div 1

Summary	P	W	D	L	F	A
Arsenal's home league record:	37	27	5	5	74	21
Arsenal's away league record:	37	9	13	15	38	47
Arsenal's cup record:	11	8	3	0	27	11
TOTAL	**85**	**44**	**21**	**20**	**139**	**79**

FACT FILE

- **Between 1906 and 1971, Arsenal lost just once in 26 home games.**
- **In the 11 home league games from 1922 to 1950, Arsenal conceded only one goal.**
- **Arsenal failed to score in five visits to Stoke from 1969 to 1974.**
- **Arsenal have won all eight cup ties between the sides.**
- **The last six league games all resulted in home wins.**

Arsenal's top scorers vs Stoke

Doug Lishman 9
Joe Baker, Cliff Bastin 6
George Graham, John Radford 5
Reg Lewis 4

Arsenal hat-tricks vs Stoke

6 May 1950 Doug Lishman
18 Apr 1953 Doug Lishman

Played for both clubs

Joe Murphy	Stoke City 1897-99	Arsenal 1899-1900
Dick Roose	Stoke City 1901-04/05-08	Arsenal 1911-12
Jackie Chalmers	Stoke City 1905-08	Arsenal 1910-12
Joey Williams	Stoke City 1925-29	Arsenal 1929-32
David Herd	Arsenal 1954-61	Stoke City 1968-70
Eddie Clamp	Arsenal 1961-63	Stoke City 1962-64
George Eastham	Arsenal 1960-66	Stoke City 1966-74
Jimmy Robertson	Arsenal 1968-70	Stoke City 1972-77
Alan Hudson	Stoke City 1973-77/83-86	Arsenal 1976-78
Paul Barron	Arsenal 1978-80	Stoke City 1984-85
Lee Chapman	Stoke City 1979-82	Arsenal 1982-84
John Devine	Arsenal 1977-83	Stoke City 1985-86
Brian Talbot	Arsenal 1978-85	Stoke City 1986-88
Ian Allinson	Arsenal 1983-87	Stoke City 1987-88
Steve Bould	Stoke City 1981-88	Arsenal 1988-99
Lee Dixon	Stoke City 1986-88	Arsenal 1987-2002

v. Sunderland

		Home				Away				Final Positions	
Season	League	Date	Result	Arsenal	Sunderland	Date	Result	Arsenal	Sunderland	Arsenal	Sunderland
1904-05	Division 1	5 November	Drew	0	0	4 March	Drew	1	1	10th	5th
1905-06	Division 1	21 October	Won	2	0	25 April	Drew	2	2	12th	14th
1906-07	Division 1	1 December	Lost	0	1	6 April	Won	3	2	7th	10th
1907-08	Division 1	28 December	Won	4	0	1 January	Lost	2	5	14th=	16th
1908-09	Division 1	21 November	Lost	0	4	27 March	Lost	0	1	6th	3rd
1909-10	Division 1	26 February	Lost	1	2	16 October	Lost	2	6	18th	8th
1910-11	Division 1	24 September	Drew	0	0	28 January	Drew	2	2	10th	3rd
1911-12	Division 1	18 November	Won	3	0	23 March	Lost	0	1	10th	8th
1912-13	Division 1	19 October	Lost	1	3	1 January	Lost	1	4	20thR	1st
1919-20	Division 1	20 September	Won	3	2	13 September	Drew	1	1	10th	5th
1920-21	Division 1	29 January	Lost	1	2	5 February	Lost	1	5	9th	12th
1921-22	Division 1	15 October	Lost	1	2	8 October	Lost	0	1	17th	12th
1922-23	Division 1	25 November	Lost	2	3	18 November	Drew	3	3	11th	2nd
1923-24	Division 1	12 April	Won	2	0	19 April	Drew	1	1	19th	3rd
1924-25	Division 1	22 November	Drew	0	0	28 March	Lost	0	2	20th	7th
1925-26	Division 1	28 November	Won	2	0	10 April	Lost	1	2	2nd	3rd
1926-27	Division 1	20 November	Lost	2	3	9 April	Lost	1	5	11th	3rd
1927-28	Division 1	17 September	Won	2	1	14 March	Lost	1	5	10th	15th
1928-29	Division 1	26 December	Drew	1	1	1 January	Lost	1	5	9th	4th
1929-30	Division 1	28 April	Lost	0	1	21 September	Won	1	0	14th	9th
1930-31	Division 1	17 January	Lost	1	3	13 September	Won	4	1	1st	11th
1931-32	Division 1	12 September	Won	2	0	6 April	Lost	0	2	2nd	13th
1932-33	Division 1	3 September	Won	6	1	7 January	Lost	2	3	1st	12th
1933-34	Division 1	21 April	Won	2	1	9 December	Lost	0	3	1st	6th
1934-35	Division 1	9 March	Drew	0	0	27 October	Lost	1	2	1st	2nd
1935-36	Division 1	31 August	Won	3	1	28 December	Lost	4	5	6th	1st
1936-37	Division 1	12 September	Won	4	1	9 January	Drew	1	1	3rd	8th
1937-38	Division 1	18 September	Won	4	1	29 January	Drew	1	1	1st	8th
1938-39	Division 1	24 February	Won	2	0	1 October	Drew	0	0	5th	16th
1939-40	Division 1	2 September	Won	5	2						
1946-47	Division 1	7 September	Drew	2	2	4 January	Won	4	1	13th	9th
1947-48	Division 1	23 August	Won	3	1	20 December	Drew	1	1	1st	20th
1948-49	Division 1	5 February	Won	5	0	18 September	Drew	1	1	5th	8th
1949-50	Division 1	24 December	Won	5	0	27 August	Lost	2	4	6th	3rd
1950-51	Division 1	11 November	Won	5	1	31 March	Won	2	0	5th	12th
1951-52	Division 1	1 September	Won	3	0	29 December	Lost	1	4	3rd	12th
1952-53	Division 1	30 August	Lost	1	2	3 January	Lost	1	3	1st	9th
1953-54	Division 1	23 January	Lost	1	4	12 September	Lost	1	7	12th	18th
1954-55	Division 1	30 October	Lost	1	3	19 March	Won	1	0	9th	4th
1955-56	Division 1	4 February	Won	3	1	24 September	Lost	1	3	5th	9th
1956-57	Division 1	1 December	Drew	1	1	13 April	Lost	0	1	5th	20th
1957-58	Division 1	21 December	Won	3	0	24 August	Won	1	0	12th	21stR
1964-65	Division 1	12 September	Won	3	1	16 January	Won	2	0	13th	15th
1965-66	Division 1	23 April	Drew	1	1	20 April	Won	2	0	14th	19th

		Home				Away				Final Positions	
Season	*League*	*Date*	*Result*	Arsenal	Sunderland	*Date*	*Result*	Arsenal	Sunderland	Arsenal	Sunderland
1966-67	Division 1	17 December	Won	**2**	**0**	20 August	Won	**3**	**1**	7th	17th
1967-68	Division 1	14 October	Won	**2**	**1**	20 April	Lost	**0**	**2**	9th	15th
1968-69	Division 1	28 September	Drew	**0**	**0**	5 April	Drew	**0**	**0**	4th	17th
1969-70	Division 1	28 February	Won	**3**	**1**	18 October	Drew	**1**	**1**	12th	21stR
1976-77	Division 1	5 February	Drew	**0**	**0**	28 August	Drew	**2**	**2**	17th	20thR
1980-81	Division 1	18 October	Drew	**2**	**2**	13 December	Lost	**0**	**2**	3rd	17th
1981-82	Division 1	12 September	Drew	**1**	**1**	6 February	Drew	**0**	**0**	5th	19th
1982-83	Division 1	7 May	Lost	**0**	**1**	18 December	Lost	**0**	**3**	10th	16th
1983-84	Division 1	5 November	Lost	**1**	**2**	3 March	Drew	**2**	**2**	6th	13th
1984-85	Division 1	20 October	Won	**3**	**2**	9 March	Drew	**0**	**0**	7th	21stR
1990-91	Division 1	27 October	Won	**1**	**0**	4 May	Drew	**0**	**0**	1st	19thR
1996-97	Prem'ship	28 September	Won	**2**	**0**	11 January	Lost	**0**	**1**	3rd	18thR
1999-00	Prem'ship	15 January	Won	**4**	**1**	14 August	Drew	**0**	**0**	2nd	7th
2000-01	Prem'ship	30 December	Drew	**2**	**2**	19 August	Lost	**0**	**1**	2nd	7th
2001-02	Prem'ship	30 March	Won	**3**	**0**	27 October	Drew	**1**	**1**	1st	17th
2002-03	Prem'ship	6 October	Won	**3**	**1**	11 May	Won	**4**	**0**	2nd	20thR

FA Cup

										Division	
1893	Round 1					21 January	Lost	**0**	**6**	Non L	Div 1
1905-06	Round 3	24 February	Won	**5**	**0**					Div 1	Div 1
1960-61	Round 3					7 January	Lost	**1**	**2**	Div 1	Div 2
1972-73	Semi Final	7 April		Hillsborough			Lost	**1**	**2**	Div 1	Div 2
1990-91	Round 3	5 January	Won	**2**	**1**					Div 1	Div 1
1996-97	Round 3	4 January	Drew	**1**	**1**	15 January	Won	**2**	**0**	Prem	Prem

League Cup

1968-69	Round 2	4 September	Won	**1**	**0**					Div 1	Div 1
2002-03	Round 3	6 November	Lost	**2**	**3**					Prem	Prem

Summary	P	W	D	L	F	A
Arsenal's home league record:	60	32	13	15	122	66
Arsenal's away league record:	59	11	20	28	70	113
Arsenal's cup record:	9	4	1	4	15	15
TOTAL	**128**	**47**	**34**	**47**	**207**	**194**

Arsenal's top scorers vs Sunderland

Doug Lishman 12

Ted Drake 10

Joe Hulme, Jack Lambert, Reg Lewis 7

Cliff Bastin, David Herd 5

Charlie Lewis, Jon Sammels, Bert White 4

Arsenal hat-tricks vs Sunderland

18 Nov 1911 Charles Randall

20 Sep 1919 Bert White

13 Sep 1930 Jack Lambert

3 Sep 1932 Joe Hulme

2 Sep 1939 Ted Drake (4)

11 Nov 1950 Doug Lishman (4)

1 Sep 1951 Doug Lishman

11 May 2003 Freddie Ljungberg

FACT FILE

- **Arsenal's victory in Sunderland in 2003 was their first since 1966.**
- **Arsenal's nine game unbeaten home run came to an end in the 2002-03 league cup. Their last home league defeat was in 1983.**
- **Arsenal were unbeaten in 15 home games from 1931 to 1951.**
- **Between 1908 and 1929, Arsenal failed to win in 16 games at Roker Park. They conceded five or more on six occasions in this run.**
- **Eighteen games passed without a home win for either side from 1931 to 1946.**

Played for both clubs

David Hannah	Sunderland 1890-94	Arsenal 1897-99
Alf Common	Sunderland 1900-02/04-05	Arsenal 1910-13
Tim Coleman	Arsenal 1902-08	Sunderland 1910-11
Jackie Mordue	Arsenal 1906-08	Sunderland 1908-20
Sam Raybould	Sunderland 1907-08	Arsenal 1908-09
Harry Logan	Sunderland 1909-10	Arsenal 1910-11
Dick Roose	Sunderland 1907-11	Arsenal 1911-12
George Payne	Sunderland 1911-12	Arsenal 1912-13
Charlie Buchan	Sunderland 1910-25	Arsenal 1925-28
Dave Halliday	Sunderland 1925-30	Arsenal 1929-30
Ray Daniel	Arsenal 1948-53	Sunderland 1953-57
Joe Baker	Arsenal 1962-66	Sunderland 1969-71
Brian Chambers	Sunderland 1970-73	Arsenal 1973-74
Wilf Rostron	Arsenal 1974-77	Sunderland 1977-80
John Hawley	Sunderland 1979-81	Arsenal 1981-83
Lee Chapman	Arsenal 1982-84	Sunderland 1983-84
John Kay	Arsenal 1982-84	Sunderland 1987-94
Niall Quinn	Arsenal 1985-90	Sunderland 1996-2003
Steve Bould	Arsenal 1988-99	Sunderland 1999-2001

Footballing legend Charlie Buchan was with Sunderland for 15 years before joining Arsenal in 1925.

v. Swansea City

		Home					Away			Final Positions	
Season	*League*	*Date*	*Result*	Arsenal	Swansea	*Date*	*Result*	Arsenal	Swansea	Arsenal	Swansea
1981-82	Division 1	27 February	Lost	**0**	**2**	10 October	Lost	**0**	**2**	5th	6th
1982-83	Division 1	1 January	Won	**2**	**1**	20 November	Won	**2**	**1**	10th	21stR

FA Cup										*Division*	
1925-26	Q'ter Final					6 March	Lost	**1**	**2**	Div 1	Div 2
1949-50	Round 4	28 January	Won	**2**	**1**					Div 1	Div 2
1967-68	Round 4					17 February	Won	**1**	**0**	Div 1	Div 4

League Cup											
1980-81	Round 2	2 September	Won	**3**	**1**	26 August	Drew	**1**	**1**	Div 1	Div 2

Summary	P	W	D	L	F	A
Arsenal's home league record:	2	1	0	1	2	3
Arsenal's away league record:	2	1	0	1	2	3
Arsenal's cup record:	5	3	1	1	8	5
TOTAL	**9**	**5**	**1**	**3**	**12**	**11**

FACT FILE

- **The longest unbeaten run for either side is four matches (by Arsenal between 1950 and 1980).**

Arsenal's top scorers vs Swansea

Alan Sunderland, Tony Woodcock 2

Played for both clubs

Len Thompson	Swansea City 1922-28	Arsenal 1927-32
Tim Rogers	Arsenal 1934-36	Swansea City 1939-40
Les Jones	Arsenal 1937-40	Swansea City 1946-47
Ray Daniel	Arsenal 1948-53	Swansea City 1957-60
Mel Charles	Swansea City 1952-59	Arsenal 1959-62
John Roberts	Swansea City 1965-68	Arsenal 1969-73
Ray Kennedy	Arsenal 1969-74	Swansea City 1981-84
Jimmy Rimmer	Swansea City 1973-74 /83-86	Arsenal 1973-77
Lee Chapman	Arsenal 1982-84	Swansea City 1995-96
Rhys Wilmot	Arsenal 1985-87	Swansea City 1988-89
Martin Hayes	Arsenal 1985-90	Swansea City 1992-95
Kwame Ampadu	Arsenal 1989-90	Swansea City 1993-98

v. Swifts

				Home		Final Positions	
Season	*League*	*Date*	*Result*	Arsenal	Swifts	Arsenal	Swifts
1889-90	4th Qual	7 December	Lost	**1**	**5**	Non L	Non L

Summary	P	W	D	L	F	A
Arsenal's cup record:	1	0	0	1	1	5
TOTAL	**1**	**0**	**0**	**1**	**1**	**5**

FACT FILE

- **This was Arsenal's first FA Cup defeat.**
- **The Swifts were based in Slough.**

v. Swindon Town

Season	League	Date	Result	Home Arsenal	Home Swindon	Date	Result	Away Arsenal	Away Swindon	Final Positions Arsenal	Final Positions Swindon
1993-94	Prem'ship	2 April	Drew	1	1	27 December	Won	4	0	4th	22ndR

FA Cup

										Division	
1910-11	Round 2					4 February	Lost	0	1	Div 1	Non L
1928-29	Round 5	20 February	Won	1	0	16 February	Drew	0	0	Div 1	Div 3S
1971-72	Round 3					15 January	Won	2	0	Div 1	Div 2

League Cup

1968-69	Final	15 March				Wembley	Lost*	1	3	Div 1	Div 3
1979-80	Q'ter Final	4 December	Drew	1	1	11 December	Lost*	3	4	Div 1	Div 3

Summary	P	W	D	L	F	A
Arsenal's home league record:	1	0	1	0	1	1
Arsenal's away league record:	1	1	0	0	4	0
Arsenal's cup record:	7	2	2	3	8	9
TOTAL	**9**	**3**	**3**	**3**	**13**	**10**

FACT FILE

- **Third division Swindon stunned Arsenal – and everybody else – by winning the 1969 League Cup. Fortunately for Arsenal, however, Swindon's lower league status precluded them from European competition. Arsenal thus took their place, and won the Fairs Cup.**
- **The 1911 FA Cup defeat was Arsenal's last by a non-league side.**

Arsenal's top scorers vs Swindon

Kevin Campbell 3

Liam Brady 2

Arsenal hat-tricks vs Swindon

27 Dec 1993 Kevin Campbell

Played for both clubs

Reg Trim	Arsenal 1934-35	Swindon Town 1946-47
Frank Boulton	Arsenal 1936-38	Swindon Town 1946-50
Brian Marwood	Arsenal 1987-90	Swindon Town 1992-93

v. Thorpe

FA Cup		Date	Result	Away Arsenal	Away Thorpe	Division Arsenal	Division Thorpe
1889-90	2nd Qual	26 October	Drew*	2	2	Non L	Non L

Summary	P	W	D	L	F	A
Arsenal's cup record:	1	0	1	0	2	2
TOTAL	**1**	**0**	**1**	**0**	**2**	**2**

FACT FILE

- **Following this draw, Thorpe withdrew from the competition, and Arsenal progressed.**

v. Tottenham Hotspur

Season	League	Home Date	Home Result	Home Arsenal	Home Tottenham	Away Date	Away Result	Away Arsenal	Away Tottenham	Final Positions Arsenal	Final Positions Tottenham
1909-10	Division 1	4 December	Won	1	0	16 April	Drew	1	1	18th	15th
1910-11	Division 1	8 April	Won	2	0	3 December	Lost	1	3	10th	15th
1911-12	Division 1	26 December	Won	3	1	25 December	Lost	0	5	10th	12th
1912-13	Division 1	14 December	Lost	0	3	19 April	Drew	1	1	20thR	17th
1920-21	Division 1	22 January	Won	3	2	15 January	Lost	1	2	9th	6th
1921-22	Division 1	22 April	Won	1	0	15 April	Lost	0	2	17th	2nd
1922-23	Division 1	30 September	Lost	0	2	23 September	Won	2	1	11th	12th
1923-24	Division 1	17 November	Drew	1	1	24 November	Lost	0	3	19th	15th
1924-25	Division 1	25 October	Won	1	0	28 February	Lost	0	2	20th	12th
1925-26	Division 1	29 August	Lost	0	1	2 January	Drew	1	1	2nd	15th
1926-27	Division 1	18 December	Lost	2	4	7 May	Won	4	0	11th	13th
1927-28	Division 1	2 January	Drew	1	1	7 April	Lost	0	2	10th	21stR
1933-34	Division 1	31 January	Lost	1	3	16 September	Drew	1	1	1st	3rd
1934-35	Division 1	20 October	Won	5	1	6 March	Won	6	0	1st	22ndR
1950-51	Division 1	26 August	Drew	2	2	23 December	Lost	0	1	5th	1st
1951-52	Division 1	29 September	Drew	1	1	9 February	Won	2	1	3rd	2nd
1952-53	Division 1	7 February	Won	4	0	20 September	Won	3	1	1st	10th
1953-54	Division 1	27 February	Lost	0	3	10 October	Won	4	1	12th	16th
1954-55	Division 1	4 September	Won	2	0	15 January	Won	1	0	9th	16th
1955-56	Division 1	14 January	Lost	0	1	10 September	Lost	1	3	5th	18th
1956-57	Division 1	20 October	Won	3	1	13 March	Won	3	1	5th	2nd
1957-58	Division 1	22 February	Drew	4	4	12 October	Lost	1	3	12th	3rd
1958-59	Division 1	13 September	Won	3	1	31 January	Won	4	1	3rd	18th
1959-60	Division 1	5 September	Drew	1	1	16 January	Lost	0	3	13th	3rd
1960-61	Division 1	10 September	Lost	2	3	21 January	Lost	2	4	11th	1st
1961-62	Division 1	23 December	Won	2	1	26 August	Lost	3	4	10th	3rd
1962-63	Division 1	23 February	Lost	2	3	6 October	Drew	4	4	7th	2nd
1963-64	Division 1	15 October	Drew	4	4	22 February	Lost	1	3	8th	4th
1964-65	Division 1	23 February	Won	3	1	10 October	Lost	1	3	13th	6th
1965-66	Division 1	8 March	Drew	1	1	11 September	Drew	2	2	14th	8th
1966-67	Division 1	7 January	Lost	0	2	3 September	Lost	1	3	7th	3rd
1967-68	Division 1	16 September	Won	4	0	20 January	Lost	0	1	9th	7th
1968-69	Division 1	24 March	Won	1	0	10 August	Won	2	1	4th	6th
1969-70	Division 1	16 September	Lost	2	3	2 May	Lost	0	1	12th	11th
1970-71	Division 1	5 September	Won	2	0	3 May	Won	1	0	1st	3rd
1971-72	Division 1	11 May	Lost	0	2	24 November	Drew	1	1	5th	6th
1972-73	Division 1	14 April	Drew	1	1	9 December	Won	2	1	2nd	8th
1973-74	Division 1	16 February	Lost	0	1	13 October	Lost	0	2	10th	11th
1974-75	Division 1	26 April	Won	1	0	19 October	Lost	0	2	16th	19th
1975-76	Division 1	3 April	Lost	0	2	27 September	Drew	0	0	17th	9th
1976-77	Division 1	11 April	Won	1	0	27 December	Drew	2	2	8th	22ndR
1978-79	Division 1	10 April	Won	1	0	23 December	Won	5	0	7th	11th
1979-80	Division 1	26 December	Won	1	0	7 April	Won	2	1	4th	14th
1980-81	Division 1	30 August	Won	2	0	17 January	Lost	0	2	3rd	10th

Season	League	Home Date	Home Result	Arsenal	Tottenham	Away Date	Away Result	Arsenal	Tottenham	Final Positions Arsenal	Final Positions Tottenham
1981-82	Division 1	12 April	Lost	1	3	29 March	Drew	2	2	5th	4th
1982-83	Division 1	27 December	Won	2	0	4 April	Lost	0	5	10th	4th
1983-84	Division 1	21 April	Won	3	2	26 December	Won	4	2	6th	8th
1984-85	Division 1	1 January	Lost	1	2	17 April	Won	2	0	7th	3rd
1985-86	Division 1	1 January	Drew	0	0	29 March	Lost	0	1	7th	10th
1986-87	Division 1	6 September	Drew	0	0	4 January	Won	2	1	4th	3rd
1987-88	Division 1	6 March	Won	2	1	18 October	Won	2	1	6th	13th
1988-89	Division 1	2 January	Won	2	0	10 September	Won	3	2	1st	6th
1989-90	Division 1	20 January	Won	1	0	18 October	Lost	1	2	4th	3rd
1990-91	Division 1	1 September	Drew	0	0	12 January	Drew	0	0	1st	10th
1991-92	Division 1	1 December	Won	2	0	22 February	Drew	1	1	4th	15th
1992-93	Prem'ship	11 May	Lost	1	3	12 December	Lost	0	1	10th	8th
1993-94	Prem'ship	6 December	Drew	1	1	16 August	Won	1	0	4th	15th
1994-95	Prem'ship	29 April	Drew	1	1	2 January	Lost	0	1	12th	7th
1995-96	Prem'ship	15 April	Drew	0	0	18 November	Lost	1	2	5th	8th
1996-97	Prem'ship	24 November	Won	3	1	15 February	Drew	0	0	3rd	10th
1997-98	Prem'ship	30 August	Drew	0	0	28 December	Drew	1	1	1st	14th
1998-99	Prem'ship	14 November	Drew	0	0	5 May	Won	3	1	2nd	11th
1999-00	Prem'ship	19 March	Won	2	1	7 November	Lost	1	2	2nd	10th
2000-01	Prem'ship	31 March	Won	2	0	18 December	Drew	1	1	2nd	12th
2001-02	Prem'ship	6 April	Won	2	1	17 November	Drew	1	1	1st	9th
2002-03	Prem'ship	16 November	Won	3	0	15 December	Drew	1	1	2nd	10th
2003-04	Prem'ship	8 November	Won	2	1	25 April	Drew	2	2	1st	14th

FA Cup										Division	
1948-49	Round 3	8 January	Won	3	0					Div 1	Div 2
1981-82	Round 3					2 January	Lost	0	1	Div 1	Div 1
1990-91	Semi Final	14 April		Wembley			Lost	1	3	Div 1	Div 1
1992-93	Semi Final	4 April		Wembley			Won	1	0	Prem	Prem
2000-01	Semi Final	8 April		Old Trafford			Won	2	1	Prem	Prem

TV pundit Bob Wilson, veteran of some 300 senior games for Arsenal, was always in the thick of the action. Here, he is going in where it hurts against Tottenham's 20-year-old debutant Jimmy Pearce at White Hart Lane on the opening day of the 1968-69 season.

League Cup		Date	Result	Home Arsenal	Home Tottenham	Date	Result	Away Arsenal	Away Tottenham	Final Positions Arsenal	Final Positions Tottenham
1968-69	Semi Final	20 November	Won	**1**	**0**	4 December	Drew	**1**	**1**	Div 1	Div 1
1980-81	Round 4					4 November	Lost	**0**	**1**	Div 1	Div 1
1983-84	Round 3					9 November	Won	**2**	**1**	Div 1	Div 1
1986-87	Semi Final	8 February	Lost	**0**	**1**	1 March	Won*	**2**	**1**	Div 1	Div 1
			(2nd replay)			4 March	Won	**2**	**1**		

Summary	P	W	D	L	F	A
Arsenal's home league record:	67	33	17	17	102	74
Arsenal's away league record:	67	21	18	28	95	106
Arsenal's cup record:	12	7	1	4	15	11
TOTAL	**146**	**61**	**36**	**49**	**212**	**191**

FACT FILE

- **Walter Lawrence was Arsenal's first goalscorer against their big rivals.**
- **The current score in terms of league wins is 54-45 in Arsenal's favour. Arsenal have led the series since January 1987. Their current lead of nine is the largest enjoyed by either side.**
- **Spurs have won only one of the last 19 at Highbury, in May 1993.**
- **Arsenal have completed 12 league doubles, the last in 1989.**
- **Spurs have completed six league doubles.**
- **Tottenham have won one of the last 18 in all competitions.**
- **Since the war, both sides have won 5-0, Arsenal in 1978 and Spurs in 1983.**
- **Between 1959 and 1967, Arsenal won twice in 16 matches. Spurs also finished higher in the league every season throughout this period.**
- **The last four cup ties between the sides have been semi-finals. Arsenal have won three of them, with David Rocastle, Tony Adams and Robert Pires all scoring winning goals. The 1987 League cup tie was particularly dramatic, with Arsenal losing the first game at home, going a goal down in the return, scoring a late goal to take the tie to extra-time, losing the toss for home advantage in the replay, going a goal down again, and scoring twice in the last 10 minutes to win the tie.**
- **Neither team has won more than five in a row in the series.**

Arsenal's top scorers vs Tottenham

Alan Sunderland 8
David Herd , John Radford 7
Joe Baker, Robert Pires, Ian Wright 6
Ted Drake, Jimmy Logie, Charlie Nicholas 5

Arsenal hat-tricks vs Tottenham

20 Oct 1934 Ted Drake
23 Dec 1978 Alan Sunderland

Cliff Holton does battle with the Tottenham defence at Highbury in September 1951. The sides drew 1-1 before a crowd of 68,164.

FACT FILE

- **Arsenal's title success of 1970-71 was made all the sweeter by being achieved at White Hart Lane. With Leeds having finished their programme, Arsenal knew what they had to do. A win or a 0-0 draw would suffice, but due to the vagaries of goal average, a score draw would hand the title to Leeds. Ray Kennedy broke the deadlock in the 87th minute, and Spurs spent the rest of the match attacking frantically, but the Gunners held out for glory.**
- **History repeated itself 33 years later, as a fine first half performance by Arsenal proved sufficient for the one point they needed for the league title. Arsene Wenger became the first Arsenal manager to win the league three times.**

Played for both clubs

Jimmy Brain	Arsenal 1924-31	Tottenham Hotspur 1931-35
George Hunt	Tottenham Hotspur 1930-37	Arsenal 1937-38
Freddie Cox	Tottenham Hotspur 1938-49	Arsenal 1949-53
Vic Groves	Tottenham Hotspur 1952-54	Arsenal 1955-64
Laurie Brown	Arsenal 1961-64	Tottenham Hotspur 1963-66
Jimmy Robertson	Tottenham Hotspur 1963-69	Arsenal 1968-70
David Jenkins	Arsenal 1967-69	Tottenham Hotspur 1968-70
Steve Walford	Tottenham Hotspur 1975-76	Arsenal 1977-81
Pat Jennings	Tottenham Hotspur 1964-77	Arsenal 1977-85
Willie Young	Tottenham Hotspur 1975-77	Arsenal 1976-82
Sol Campbell	Tottenham Hotspur 1992-2001	Arsenal 2001-04

Jubilant Arsenal players at the final whistle against Spurs at White Hart Lane on 3 May 1971. Their 1-0 victory gave them the league championship and left them on the brink of the Double.

v. Tranmere Rovers

FA Cup		Date	Home Result	Arsenal	Tranmere	Date	Away Result	Arsenal	Tranmere	Division Arsenal	Division Tranmere
1973-74	Round 2	2 October	Lost	**0**	**1**					Div 1	Div 3

Summary	P	W	D	L	F	A
Arsenal's cup record:	1	0	0	1	0	1
TOTAL	**1**	**0**	**0**	**1**	**0**	**1**

FACT FILE

- **Of all Arsenal's 116 opponents, Tranmere are the only ones against whom they have never scored.**

Played for both clubs

Andy Kennedy	Arsenal 1922-28	Tranmere Rovers 1930-31
Archie Clark	Arsenal 1927-28	Tranmere Rovers 1935-39
Noel Kelly	Arsenal 1949-50	Tranmere Rovers 1955-57
Jimmy Harvey	Arsenal 1977-79	Tranmere Rovers 1987-92

v. Walsall

		Home					Away		Final Positions	
Season	*League*	*Date*	*Result*	Arsenal	Walsall	*Date*	*Result*	Arsenal	Walsall	Arsenal	Walsall
1893-94	Division 2	11 September	Won	**4**	**0**	12 February	Won	**2**	**1**	9th	10th
1894-95	Division 2	12 April	Won	**6**	**1**	10 November	Lost	**1**	**4**	8th	14thF
1896-97	Division 2	12 September	Drew	**1**	**1**	17 October	Lost	**3**	**5**	10th	12th
1897-98	Division 2	13 November	Won	**4**	**0**	6 November	Lost	**2**	**3**	5th	10th
1898-99	Division 2	11 February	Drew	**0**	**0**	15 October	Lost	**1**	**4**	7th	6th
1899-00	Division 2	20 January	Won	**3**	**1**	23 September	Lost	**0**	**2**	8th	12th
1900-01	Division 2	8 September	Drew	**1**	**1**	24 December	Lost	**0**	**1**	7th	16thF

FA Cup

										Division	
1932-33	Round 3					14 January	Lost	**0**	**2**	Div 1	Div 3N
1977-78	Round 5	18 February	Won	**4**	**1**					Div 1	Div 3

League Cup

1983-84	Round 4	29 November	Lost	**1**	**2**					Div 1	Div 3

Summary	P	W	D	L	F	A
Arsenal's home league record:	7	4	3	0	19	4
Arsenal's away league record:	7	1	0	6	9	20
Arsenal's cup record:	3	1	0	2	5	5
TOTAL	**17**	**6**	**3**	**8**	**33**	**29**

Long-serving Woolwich Arsenal half-back John Dick won his only major honour with the club when they were promoted to the First Division in 1904. Dick featured in both matches against Walsall in 1900-01.

FACT FILE

- **Many historians view the 1933 FA Cup defeat as the biggest shock in FA Cup history. Arsenal were on their way to the league title; Walsall were on poor form in Division Three North. Arsenal under-estimated the opposition and rested several first team regulars, and were made to pay as Alsop and Sheppard scored for Walsall.**
- **Fifty-one years later, lightning struck twice as Arsenal lost at home to third division Walsall in the League Cup.**
- **This was Walsall's first win at Highbury in nine attempts.**
- **Arsenal have lost their last seven away games to Walsall.**

Arsenal's top scorers vs Walsall

Billy Heath, Archie McGeoch 3
Henry Boyd, Gavin Crawford,Charlie Hare,
Adam Haywood, Paddy Logan, Peter Mortimer,
Frank Stapleton 2

Arsenal hat-tricks vs Walsall

11 Sep 1893 Billy Heath
13 Nov 1897 Archie McGeoch

Played for both clubs

Caesar Jenkyns	Arsenal 1895-96	Walsall 1897-1901
Jack Aston	Walsall 1896-99	Arsenal 1899-1900
Jock Dailly	Arsenal 1898-99	Walsall 1899-1900
Joe Connor	Walsall 1899-1901	Arsenal 1902-03
Bert White	Arsenal 1919-23	Walsall 1925-28
Wilf Walsh	Arsenal 1938-39	Walsall 1946-48
Stan Morgan	Arsenal 1946-47	Walsall 1948-49
Doug Lishman	Walsall 1946-48	Arsenal 1948-56
George Johnston	Arsenal 1967-69	Walsall 1970-71
Jimmy Robertson	Arsenal 1968-70	Walsall 1977-78
Lee Harper	Arsenal 1996-97	Walsall 2001-02
Paul Merson	Arsenal 1986-97	Walsall 2003-04

v. Watford

Season	League	Home Date	Home Result	Home Arsenal	Home Watford	Away Date	Away Result	Away Arsenal	Away Watford	Final Positions Arsenal	Final Positions Watford
1982-83	Division 1	27 November	Lost	**2**	**4**	30 April	Lost	**1**	**2**	10th	2nd
1983-84	Division 1	17 December	Won	**3**	**1**	12 May	Lost	**1**	**2**	6th	11th
1984-85	Division 1	22 December	Drew	**1**	**1**	1 September	Won	**4**	**3**	7th	11th
1985-86	Division 1	31 March	Lost	**0**	**2**	1 April	Lost	**0**	**3**	7th	12th
1986-87	Division 1	11 October	Won	**3**	**1**	21 March	Lost	**0**	**2**	4th	9th
1987-88	Division 1	15 April	Lost	**0**	**1**	28 November	Lost	**0**	**2**	6th	20thR
1999-00	Prem'ship	25 September	Won	**1**	**0**	23 April	Won	**3**	**2**	2nd	20thR

FA Cup

Season	Round	Home Date	Home Result	Arsenal	Watford	Away Date	Away Result	Arsenal	Watford	Division Arsenal	Division Watford
1905-06	Round 2	3 February	Won	**3**	**0**					Div 1	Non L
1909-10	1	15 January	Won	**3**	**0**					Div 1	Non L
1979-80	Q'ter Final					8 March	Won	**2**	**1**	Div 1	Div 2
1986-87	Q'ter Final	14 March	Lost	**1**	**3**					Div 1	Div 1
2001-02	Round 3					5 January	Won	**4**	**2**	Prem	Div 1

Summary	P	W	D	L	F	A
Arsenal's home league record:	7	3	1	3	10	10
Arsenal's away league record:	7	2	0	5	9	16
Arsenal's cup record:	5	4	0	1	13	6
TOTAL	**19**	**9**	**1**	**9**	**32**	**32**

FACT FILE

- **Arsenal have won their last three matches (having lost their previous four).**
- **Watford won six games out of seven between 1986 and 1988.**
- **The two league matches of 1986-87 took place on consecutive days.**

Former Watford player Terry Mancini was a £20,000 signing from Queen's Park Rangers and left on a free transfer to Aldershot in 1976.

Arsenal's top scorers vs Watford

Thierry Henry, Raphael Meade 3
Ian Allinson, Nwankwo Kanu, Charlie Lewis, Charlie Nicholas, Stewart Robson, Frank Stapleton, Brian Talbot 2

Arsenal hat-tricks vs Watford

17 Dec 1983 Raphael Meade

Played for both clubs

Fred Pagnam	Arsenal 1919-21	Watford 1921-27
Joe North	Arsenal 1919-22	Watford 1926-27
Ernie Wallington	Watford 1920-23	Arsenal 1923-24
George Drury	Arsenal 1937-40	Watford 1948-50
Horace Cumner	Arsenal 1938-40	Watford 1948-51
Lionel Smith	Arsenal 1947-54	Watford 1954-55
Arthur Shaw	Arsenal 1949-55	Watford 1955-56
Brian Marden	Arsenal 1950-55	Watford 1955-57
Cliff Holton	Arsenal 1950-59	Watford 1958-62/65-66
Peter Goy	Arsenal 1958-59	Watford 1964-65
Pat Jennings	Watford 1962-64	Arsenal 1977-85
Terry Mancini	Watford 1961-66	Arsenal 1974-76
Tom Walley	Arsenal 1965-67	Watford 1966-72/76-77
Wilf Rostron	Arsenal 1974-77	Watford 1979-89
Pat Rice	Arsenal 1967-81	Watford 1980-84
Peter Nicholas	Arsenal 1980-83	Watford 1990-92
Brian Talbot	Arsenal 1978-85	Watford 1985-87
Kevin Richardson	Watford 1986-87	Arsenal 1987-90
Steve Morrow	Watford 1991-92	Arsenal 1991-97
Stephen Hughes	Arsenal 1994-2000	Watford 2001-02
Paulo Vernazza	Arsenal 1997-2001	Watford 2000-04
Jermaine Pennant	Watford 2001-03	Arsenal 2002-03

Now assisting Arsene Wenger, Pat Rice spent several years at Watford before returning home to Highbury.

Towards the end of his career Brian Talbot joined Watford after he joined the Gunners from Ipswich. Here he scores Arsenal's first goal of the 1979 FA Cup Final against Manchester United, getting between Martin Buchan and Steve Coppell and past Jimmy Nichol (2). The other Arsenal player is Alan Sunderland.

v. West Bromwich Albion

Season	League	Home Date	Home Result	Home Arsenal	Home WBA	Away Date	Away Result	Away Arsenal	Away WBA	Final Positions Arsenal	Final Positions WBA
1901-02	Division 2	31 March	Won	2	1	12 April	Lost	1	2	4th	1stP
1911-12	Division 1	16 March	Lost	0	2	11 November	Drew	1	1	10th	9th
1912-13	Division 1	15 March	Won	1	0	9 November	Lost	1	2	20thR	10th
1919-20	Division 1	5 April	Won	1	0	6 April	Lost	0	1	10th	1st
1920-21	Division 1	28 March	Won	2	1	29 March	Won	4	3	9th	14th
1921-22	Division 1	18 April	Drew	2	2	17 April	Won	3	0	17th	13th
1922-23	Division 1	7 October	Won	3	1	14 October	Lost	0	7	11th	7th
1923-24	Division 1	15 September	Won	1	0	8 September	Lost	0	4	19th	16th
1924-25	Division 1	14 April	Won	2	0	13 April	Lost	0	2	20th	2nd
1925-26	Division 1	12 December	Won	1	0	24 April	Lost	1	2	2nd	13th
1926-27	Division 1	16 April	Won	4	1	27 November	Won	3	1	11th	22ndR
1931-32	Division 1	29 April	Lost	0	1	2 January	Lost	0	1	2nd	6th
1932-33	Division 1	31 August	Lost	1	2	14 September	Drew	1	1	1st	4th
1933-34	Division 1	6 September	Won	3	1	13 September	Lost	0	1	1st	7th
1934-35	Division 1	15 September	Won	4	3	30 January	Won	3	0	1st	9th
1935-36	Division 1	10 April	Won	4	0	13 April	Lost	0	1	6th	18th
1936-37	Division 1	3 April	Won	2	0	28 November	Won	4	2	3rd	16th
1937-38	Division 1	13 November	Drew	1	1	26 March	Drew	0	0	1st	22ndR
1949-50	Division 1	14 September	Won	4	1	7 September	Won	2	1	6th	14th
1950-51	Division 1	30 September	Won	3	0	17 February	Lost	0	2	5th	16th
1951-52	Division 1	10 November	Won	6	3	21 April	Lost	1	3	3rd	13th
1952-53	Division 1	21 March	Drew	2	2	1 November	Lost	0	2	1st	4th
1953-54	Division 1	12 December	Drew	2	2	19 August	Lost	0	2	12th	2nd
1954-55	Division 1	1 January	Drew	2	2	28 August	Lost	1	3	9th	17th
1955-56	Division 1	10 December	Won	2	0	21 April	Lost	1	2	5th	13th
1956-57	Division 1	1 September	Won	4	1	29 December	Won	2	0	5th	11th
1957-58	Division 1	27 August	Drew	2	2	4 September	Won	2	1	12th	4th
1958-59	Division 1	4 October	Won	4	3	21 February	Drew	1	1	3rd	5th
1959-60	Division 1	28 November	Lost	2	4	30 April	Lost	0	1	13th	4th
1960-61	Division 1	1 October	Won	1	0	18 February	Won	3	2	11th	10th
1961-62	Division 1	3 February	Lost	0	1	16 September	Lost	0	4	10th	9th
1962-63	Division 1	12 April	Won	3	2	15 April	Won	2	1	7th	14th
1963-64	Division 1	27 August	Won	3	2	4 September	Lost	0	4	8th	10th
1964-65	Division 1	3 April	Drew	1	1	21 November	Drew	0	0	13th	14th
1965-66	Division 1	5 April	Drew	1	1	11 April	Drew	4	4	14th	6th
1966-67	Division 1	22 October	Lost	2	3	18 March	Won	1	0	7th	13th
1967-68	Division 1	11 May	Won	2	1	6 September	Won	3	1	9th	8th
1968-69	Division 1	21 December	Won	2	0	19 October	Lost	0	1	4th	10th
1969-70	Division 1	7 October	Drew	1	1	16 August	Won	1	0	12th	16th
1970-71	Division 1	19 September	Won	6	2	24 April	Drew	2	2	1st	17th
1971-72	Division 1	18 December	Won	2	0	4 September	Won	1	0	5th	16th
1972-73	Division 1	16 December	Won	2	1	28 February	Lost	0	1	2nd	22ndR
1976-77	Division 1	8 March	Lost	1	2	9 April	Won	2	0	8th	7th
1977-78	Division 1	25 March	Won	4	0	27 December	Won	3	1	5th	6th

Season	League	Home Date	Result	Arsenal	WBA	Away Date	Result	Arsenal	WBA	Final Positions Arsenal	WBA
1978-79	Division 1	26 December	Lost	**1**	**2**	14 April	Drew	**1**	**1**	7th	3rd
1979-80	Division 1	26 April	Drew	**1**	**1**	15 December	Drew	**2**	**2**	4th	10th
1980-81	Division 1	15 November	Drew	**2**	**2**	16 August	Won	**1**	**0**	3rd	4th
1981-82	Division 1	16 March	Drew	**2**	**2**	2 September	Won	**2**	**0**	5th	17th
1982-83	Division 1	16 October	Won	**2**	**0**	26 February	Drew	**0**	**0**	10th	11th
1983-84	Division 1	3 December	Lost	**0**	**1**	5 May	Won	**3**	**1**	6th	17th
1984-85	Division 1	15 December	Won	**4**	**0**	11 May	Drew	**2**	**2**	7th	12th
1985-86	Division 1	26 April	Drew	**2**	**2**	23 November	Drew	**0**	**0**	7th	22ndR
2002-03	Prem'ship	27 August	Won	**5**	**2**	26 December	Won	**2**	**1**	2nd	19thR

FA Cup

Season	Round	Home Date	Result	Arsenal	WBA	Away Date	Result	Arsenal	WBA	Division Arsenal	WBA
1900-01	Round 2	23 February	Lost	**0**	**1**					Div 2	Div 1
1927-28	Round 3	14 January	Won	**2**	**0**					Div 1	Div 2
1936-37	Q'ter Final					6 March	Lost	**1**	**3**	Div 1	Div 1
1956-57	Q'ter Final	5 March	Lost	**1**	**2**	2 March	Drew	**2**	**2**	Div 1	Div 1
1963-64	Round 4	29 January	Won	**2**	**0**	25 January	Drew	**3**	**3**	Div 1	Div 1
1968-69	Round 5					12 February	Lost	**0**	**1**	Div 1	Div 1

League Cup

Season	Round	Home Date	Result	Arsenal	WBA	Away Date	Result	Arsenal	WBA	Arsenal	WBA
2003-04	Q'ter Final					16 December	Won	**2**	**0**	Prem	Div 1

Summary	P	W	D	L	F	A
Arsenal's home league record:	53	31	13	9	117	65
Arsenal's away league record:	53	20	12	21	67	77
Arsenal's cup record:	9	3	2	4	13	12
TOTAL	**115**	**54**	**27**	**34**	**197**	**154**

West Brom's goalkeeper George Ashmore dives on the ball but eventually Brain and Hulme put Arsenal through to the next round in the third round FA Cup tie at Highbury in January 1928. The Gunners won 2-0.

FACT FILE

- **Between 1933 and 1958, Arsenal were unbeaten in 15 home league games.**
- **Arsenal lost six in a row at the Hawthorns from 1951 to 1956.**
- **Arsenal are unbeaten in their last eight matches in the series.**
- **Arsenal are unbeaten in their last 12 visits to the Hawthorns.**
- **The fixture saw eight consecutive home wins from 1922 to 1926.**

Arsenal's top scorers vs West Brom

Doug Lishman 10
George Armstrong 7
Malcolm Macdonald 6
Joe Baker, Cliff Bastin, David Herd,
Alan Sunderland, Derek Tapscott 5

Arsenal hat-tricks vs West Brom

10 Nov 1951 Doug Lishman
25 Mar 1978 Malcolm Macdonald

Played for both clubs

Henry Boyd	West Bromwich Albion 1892-93	Arsenal 1894-97
Adam Haywood	Arsenal 1895-99	West Bromwich Albion 1905-08
Joe Connor	West Bromwich Albion 1897-99	Arsenal 1902-03
George Drury	Arsenal 1937-40	West Bromwich Albion 1946-48
Freddie Cox	Arsenal 1949-53	West Bromwich Albion 1953-54
Don Howe	West Bromwich Albion 1955-64	Arsenal 1964-67
Bobby Gould	Arsenal 1967-70	West Bromwich Albion 1971-73
Brendan Batson	Arsenal 1971-74	West Bromwich Albion 1977-83
Paul Barron	Arsenal 1978-80	West Bromwich Albion 1982-85
Steve Walford	Arsenal 1977-81	West Bromwich Albion 1988-89
David Cork	Arsenal 1983-84	West Bromwich Albion 1988-89
Brian Talbot	Arsenal 1978-85	West Bromwich Albion 1987-90
Chris Whyte	Arsenal 1981-86	West Bromwich Albion 1988-90
Kwame Ampadu	Arsenal 1990-91	West Bromwich Albion 1990-94
Alan Miller	West Bromwich Albion 1991-92/96-2000	Arsenal 1992-94

One of football's greatest coaches, Don Howe was signed from West Bromwich Albion and later returned to the Hawthorns as manager.

Cliff Holton watches his shot go narrowly wide against West Brom at Highbury in March 1953. Holton and Roper scored in the 2-2 draw as Arsenal moved on their way to the League title.

v. West Ham United

		Home					Away				Final Positions	
Season	League	Date	Result	Arsenal	WHU	Date	Result	Arsenal	WHU	Arsenal	WHU
1923-24	Division 1	10 September	Won	4	1	27 August	Lost	0	1	19th	13th
1924-25	Division 1	23 March	Lost	1	2	27 September	Lost	0	1	20th	18th
1925-26	Division 1	21 September	Won	3	2	5 October	Won	4	0	2nd	18th
1926-27	Division 1	16 October	Drew	2	2	7 March	Lost	0	7	11th	6th
1927-28	Division 1	1 October	Drew	2	2	11 February	Drew	2	2	10th	17th
1928-29	Division 1	13 October	Lost	2	3	23 February	Won	4	3	9th	17th
1929-30	Division 1	2 November	Lost	0	1	8 March	Lost	2	3	14th	7th
1930-31	Division 1	25 October	Drew	1	1	28 February	Won	4	2	1st	18th
1931-32	Division 1	14 November	Won	4	1	26 March	Drew	1	1	2nd	22ndR
1958-59	Division 1	28 March	Lost	1	2	8 November	Drew	0	0	3rd	6th
1959-60	Division 1	14 November	Lost	1	3	2 April	Drew	0	0	13th	14th
1960-61	Division 1	25 March	Drew	0	0	5 November	Lost	0	6	11th	16th
1961-62	Division 1	2 December	Drew	2	2	21 April	Drew	3	3	10th	8th
1962-63	Division 1	13 October	Drew	1	1	2 March	Won	4	0	7th	12th
1963-64	Division 1	9 November	Drew	3	3	21 March	Drew	1	1	8th	14th
1964-65	Division 1	14 November	Lost	0	3	27 March	Lost	1	2	13th	9th
1965-66	Division 1	20 November	Won	3	2	16 April	Lost	1	2	14th	12th
1966-67	Division 1	23 August	Won	2	1	29 August	Drew	2	2	7th	16th
1967-68	Division 1	25 November	Drew	0	0	29 March	Drew	1	1	9th	12th
1968-69	Division 1	26 October	Drew	0	0	21 April	Won	2	1	4th	8th
1969-70	Division 1	4 April	Won	2	1	25 August	Drew	1	1	12th	17th
1970-71	Division 1	9 January	Won	2	0	17 August	Drew	0	0	1st	20th
1971-72	Division 1	22 April	Won	2	1	4 December	Drew	0	0	5th	14th
1972-73	Division 1	29 August	Won	1	0	28 April	Won	2	1	2nd	6th
1973-74	Division 1	6 April	Drew	0	0	24 November	Won	3	1	10th	18th
1974-75	Division 1	26 October	Won	3	0	28 April	Lost	0	1	16th	13th
1975-76	Division 1	20 March	Won	6	1	29 November	Lost	0	1	17th	18th
1976-77	Division 1	19 February	Lost	2	3	11 September	Won	2	0	8th	17th
1977-78	Division 1	1 October	Won	3	0	25 February	Drew	2	2	5th	20thR
1981-82	Division 1	1 May	Won	2	0	5 December	Won	2	1	5th	9th
1982-83	Division 1	2 October	Lost	2	3	10 May	Won	3	1	10th	8th
1983-84	Division 1	7 May	Drew	3	3	10 December	Lost	1	3	6th	9th
1984-85	Division 1	2 March	Won	2	1	27 October	Lost	1	3	7th	16th
1985-86	Division 1	15 March	Won	1	0	12 October	Drew	0	0	7th	3rd
1986-87	Division 1	8 November	Drew	0	0	8 April	Lost	1	3	4th	15th
1987-88	Division 1	26 September	Won	1	0	12 April	Won	1	0	6th	16th
1988-89	Division 1	4 February	Won	2	1	1 October	Won	4	1	1st	19thR
1991-92	Division 1	2 November	Lost	0	1	14 March	Won	2	0	4th	22ndR
1993-94	Prem'ship	30 April	Lost	0	2	24 November	Drew	0	0	4th	13th
1994-95	Prem'ship	5 March	Lost	0	1	25 September	Won	2	0	12th	14th
1995-96	Prem'ship	16 September	Won	1	0	24 February	Won	1	0	5th	10th
1996-97	Prem'ship	17 August	Won	2	0	29 January	Won	2	1	3rd	14th
1997-98	Prem'ship	24 September	Won	4	0	2 March	Drew	0	0	1st	8th
1998-99	Prem'ship	26 December	Won	1	0	6 February	Won	4	0	2nd	5th

Season	League	Home Date	Result	Arsenal	WHU	Away Date	Result	Arsenal	WHU	Final Positions Arsenal	WHU
1999-00	Prem'ship	2 May	Won	**2**	**1**	3 October	Lost	**1**	**2**	2nd	9th
2000-01	Prem'ship	3 March	Won	**3**	**0**	21 October	Won	**2**	**1**	2nd	15th
2001-02	Prem'ship	24 April	Won	**2**	**0**	15 December	Drew	**1**	**1**	1st	7th
2002-03	Prem'ship	19 January	Won	**3**	**1**	24 August	Drew	**2**	**2**	2nd	18thR

FA Cup

Season	Round	Home Date	Result	Arsenal	WHU	Away Date	Result	Arsenal	WHU	Division Arsenal	WHU
1905-06	Round 1	13 January	Drew	**1**	**1**	18 January	Won	**3**	**2**	Div 1	Non L
1924-25	Round 1	21 January	Drew*	**2**	**2**	14 January	Drew	**0**	**0**	Div 1	Div 1
		26 January	Lost	**0**	**1**	Chelsea (2nd replay)					
1929-30	Q'ter Final					1 March	Won	**3**	**0**	Div 1	Div 1
1945-46	Round 3	9 January	Won	**1**	**0**	5 January	Lost	**0**	**6**	Div 1	Div 2
1974-75	Q'ter Final	8 March	Lost	**0**	**2**					Div 1	Div 1
1979-80	Final	10 May		Wembley			Lost	**0**	**1**	Div 1	Div 2
1988-89	Round 3	11 January	Lost	**0**	**1**	8 January	Drew	**2**	**2**	Div 1	Div 1
1997-98	Q'ter Final	8 March	Drew	**1**	**1**	17 March	Drew*	**1**	**1**	Prem	Prem
								won 4-3 pens			

League Cup

Season	Round	Home Date	Result	Arsenal	WHU	Away Date	Result	Arsenal	WHU	Division Arsenal	WHU
1966-67	Round 3	5 October	Lost	**1**	**3**					Div 1	Div 1
1997-98	Q'ter Final					6 January	Won	**2**	**1**	Prem	Prem

Summary	P	W	D	L	F	A	
Arsenal's home league record:	48	25	12	11	84	52	
Arsenal's away league record:	48	18	17	13	72	64	
Arsenal's cup record:	16	4	4	6	17	24	
TOTAL	**112**	**47**	**35**	**30**	**173**	**140**	(+one penalty shoot-out victory)

FACT FILE

- **Arsenal have won their last eight home games in the Premiership.**
- **Arsenal are unbeaten in their last seven matches.**
- **Arsenal won one of 12 matches between 1930 and 1962, and it was not a particularly useful win, either. As a one-off method of raising gate receipts in the aftermath of World War Two, the FA Cup of 1945-46 was played over two legs up to the quarter-finals. Arsenal won the second leg 1-0, but it was immaterial following their huge disappointment in the first leg.**
- **Arsenal have lost once in their last 16 visits to Upton Park.**
- **Between 1966 and 1974, Arsenal were undefeated in 17 league games.**

Arsenal's top scorers vs West Ham

Jimmy Brain 10
David Jack 8
Alan Ball, Ian Wright 7
Marc Overmars 6
Joe Baker 5
Dennis Bergkamp, Charlie Buchan, Thierry Henry, Brian Kidd, Jack Lambert, John Radford, Alan Skirton, Sylvain Wiltord 4

Arsenal hat-tricks vs West Ham

14 Nov 1931 David Jack
20 Mar 1976 Brian Kidd
3 Mar 2001 Sylvain Wiltord
19 Jan 2003 Thierry Henry

Played for both clubs

Dick Burgess	Arsenal 1919-22	West Ham United 1922-23
Stan Earle	Arsenal 1921-24	West Ham United 1924-32
Jimmy Marshall	Arsenal 1934-35	West Ham United 1934-37
Archie Macaulay	West Ham United 1937-47	Arsenal 1947-50
Jimmy Bloomfield	Arsenal 1954-61	West Ham United 1965-66
Jim Standen	Arsenal 1957-61	West Ham United 1962-68
Bobby Gould	Arsenal 1967-70	West Ham United 1973-76
John Radford	Arsenal 1963-77	West Ham United 1976-78
Liam Brady	Arsenal 1973-80	West Ham United 1986-90
Steve Walford	Arsenal 1977-81	West Ham United 1983-87
Lee Chapman	Arsenal 1982-84	West Ham United 1993-95
Stewart Robson	Arsenal 1981-87	West Ham United 1986-91
John Hartson	Arsenal 1994-97	West Ham United 1996-99
Ian Wright	Arsenal 1991-98	West Ham United 1998-99
Kaba Diawara	Arsenal 1998-99	West Ham United 2000-01
Nigel Winterburn	Arsenal 1987-2000	West Ham United 2000-03
Davor Suker	Arsenal 1999-2000	West Ham United 2000-01

In May 1980 Arsenal appeared in a third successive FA Cup Final but this time finished on the losing side as West Ham lifted the trophy with a rare headed goal from Trevor Brooking. Here, Liam Brady and Brian Talbot close in on Paul Allen, at 17 years and 256 days the youngest player ever to appear in an FA Cup Final.

v. Wimbledon

			Home			Away				Final Positions	
Season	League	Date	Result	Arsenal	Wimbledon	Date	Result	Arsenal	Wimbledon	Arsenal	Wimbledon
1986-87	Division 1	1 January	Won	3	1	18 April	Won	2	1	4th	6th
1987-88	Division 1	19 September	Won	3	0	28 December	Lost	1	3	6th	7th
1988-89	Division 1	17 May	Drew	2	2	27 August	Won	5	1	1st	12th
1989-90	Division 1	26 August	Drew	0	0	13 January	Lost	0	1	4th	8th
1990-91	Division 1	15 December	Drew	2	2	25 August	Won	3	0	1st	7th
1991-92	Division 1	1 January	Drew	1	1	28 March	Won	3	1	4th	13th
1992-93	Prem'ship	10 February	Lost	0	1	5 September	Lost	2	3	10th	12th
1993-94	Prem'ship	19 April	Drew	1	1	1 January	Won	3	0	4th	6th
1994-95	Prem'ship	4 May	Drew	0	0	8 October	Won	3	1	12th	9th
1995-96	Prem'ship	30 December	Lost	1	3	16 March	Won	3	0	5th	14th
1996-97	Prem'ship	23 February	Lost	0	1	2 November	Drew	2	2	3rd	8th
1997-98	Prem'ship	18 April	Won	5	0	11 March	Won	1	0	1st	15th
1998-99	Prem'ship	19 April	Won	5	1	21 November	Lost	0	1	2nd	16th
1999-00	Prem'ship	18 December	Drew	1	1	1 April	Won	3	1	2nd	18thR

Summary	P	W	D	L	F	A
Arsenal's home league record:	14	4	7	3	24	14
Arsenal's away league record:	14	9	1	4	31	15
TOTAL	**28**	**13**	**8**	**7**	**55**	**29**

FACT FILE

- **Between September 1987 and April 1998, Wimbledon were unbeaten in nine visits to Highbury, yet Arsenal won seven away matches in the same period.**
- **Arsenal scored 10 goals in two home games in 1998 and 1999.**

Arsenal's top scorers vs Wimbledon

Alan Smith, Ian Wright 7

Paul Merson 6

Dennis Bergkamp, Kevin Campbell,

Nwankwo Kanu, Ray Parlour 3

Arsenal hat-tricks vs Wimbledon

27 Aug 1988 Alan Smith

Played for both clubs

Brian Sparrow	Wimbledon 1982-83	Arsenal 1983-84
John Kay	Arsenal 1982-84	Wimbledon 1984-87
Nigel Winterburn	Wimbledon 1983-87	Arsenal 1987-2000
Martin Hayes	Arsenal 1985-90	Wimbledon 1991-92
Michael Thomas	Arsenal 1986-92	Wimbledon 2000-01
Ian Selley	Arsenal 1992-97	Wimbledon 2000-01
John Hartson	Arsenal 1994-97	Wimbledon 1998-2001

v. Wolverhampton Wanderers

		Home					Away			Final Positions	
Season	League	Date	Result	Arsenal	Wolves	Date	Result	Arsenal	Wolves	Arsenal	Wolves
1904-05	Division 1	24 September	Won	2	0	21 January	Lost	1	4	10th	14th
1905-06	Division 1	10 February	Won	2	1	7 October	Won	2	0	12th	20thR
1913-14	Division 2	3 January	Won	3	1	13 September	Won	2	1	3rd	9th
1914-15	Division 2	2 January	Won	5	1	5 September	Lost	0	1	5thP	4th
1932-33	Division 1	18 March	Lost	1	2	5 November	Won	7	1	1st	20th
1933-34	Division 1	24 March	Won	3	2	11 November	Won	1	0	1st	15th
1934-35	Division 1	1 December	Won	7	0	13 April	Drew	1	1	1st	17th
1935-36	Division 1	23 November	Won	4	0	28 March	Drew	2	2	6th	15th
1936-37	Division 1	23 January	Won	3	0	19 September	Lost	0	2	3rd	5th
1937-38	Division 1	4 September	Won	5	0	15 January	Lost	1	3	1st	2nd
1938-39	Division 1	1 February	Drew	0	0	17 September	Won	1	0	5th	2nd
1939-40	Division 1					26 August	Drew	2	2		
1946-47	Division 1	28 December	Drew	1	1	31 August	Lost	1	6	13th	3rd
1947-48	Division 1	6 March	Won	5	2	18 October	Drew	1	1	1st	5th
1948-49	Division 1	25 September	Won	3	1	19 February	Won	3	1	5th	6th
1949-50	Division 1	3 December	Drew	1	1	22 April	Lost	0	3	6th	2nd
1950-51	Division 1	24 March	Won	2	1	4 November	Won	1	0	5th	14th
1951-52	Division 1	22 December	Drew	2	2	25 August	Lost	1	2	3rd	16th
1952-53	Division 1	17 January	Won	5	3	6 September	Drew	1	1	1st	3rd
1953-54	Division 1	5 September	Lost	2	3	16 January	Won	2	0	12th	1st
1954-55	Division 1	27 November	Drew	1	1	16 April	Lost	1	3	9th	2nd
1955-56	Division 1	27 December	Drew	2	2	26 December	Drew	3	3	5th	3rd
1956-57	Division 1	23 March	Drew	0	0	10 November	Lost	2	5	5th	6th
1957-58	Division 1	7 April	Lost	0	2	8 April	Won	2	1	12th	1st
1958-59	Division 1	18 October	Drew	1	1	7 March	Lost	1	6	3rd	1st
1959-60	Division 1	2 January	Drew	4	4	29 August	Drew	3	3	13th	2nd
1960-61	Division 1	22 April	Lost	1	5	3 December	Lost	3	5	11th	3rd
1961-62	Division 1	14 April	Won	3	1	25 November	Won	3	2	10th	18th
1962-63	Division 1	27 October	Won	5	4	8 April	Lost	0	1	7th	5th
1963-64	Division 1	24 August	Lost	1	3	14 December	Drew	2	2	8th	16th
1964-65	Division 1	2 January	Won	4	1	5 September	Won	1	0	13th	21stR
1967-68	Division 1	16 March	Lost	0	2	23 October	Lost	2	3	9th	17th
1968-69	Division 1	7 April	Won	3	1	21 August	Drew	0	0	4th	16th
1969-70	Division 1	28 March	Drew	2	2	15 November	Lost	0	2	12th	13th
1970-71	Division 1	12 December	Won	2	1	2 March	Won	3	0	1st	4th
1971-72	Division 1	8 April	Won	2	1	20 November	Lost	1	5	5th	9th
1972-73	Division 1	15 August	Won	5	2	11 November	Won	3	1	2nd	5th
1973-74	Division 1	4 December	Drew	2	2	15 April	Lost	1	3	10th	12th
1974-75	Division 1	2 November	Drew	0	0	8 February	Lost	0	1	16th	12th
1975-76	Division 1	13 April	Won	2	1	30 August	Drew	0	0	17th	20thR
1977-78	Division 1	14 January	Won	3	1	27 August	Drew	1	1	5th	15th
1978-79	Division 1	24 February	Lost	0	1	14 October	Lost	0	1	7th	18th
1979-80	Division 1	29 September	Lost	2	3	16 May	Won	2	1	4th	6th
1980-81	Division 1	6 December	Drew	1	1	25 April	Won	2	1	3rd	18th

Season	League	Date	Result	Home Arsenal	Home Wolves	Date	Result	Away Arsenal	Away Wolves	Final Positions Arsenal	Final Positions Wolves
1981-82	Division 1	2 February	Won	**2**	**1**	3 April	Drew	**1**	**1**	5th	21stR
1983-84	Division 1	24 March	Won	**4**	**1**	29 August	Won	**2**	**1**	6th	22ndR
2003-04	Prem'ship	26 December	Won	**3**	**0**	7 February	Won	**3**	**1**	1st	20thR

FA Cup

Season	Round	Date	Result	Arsenal	Wolves	Date	Result	Arsenal	Wolves	Division Arsenal	Division Wolves
1925-26	Round 3	13 January	Won	**1**	**0**	9 January	Drew	**1**	**1**	Div 1	Div 2
1926-27	Q'ter Final	5 March	Won	**2**	**1**					Div 1	Div 2
1937-38	Round 4					22 January	Won	**2**	**1**	Div 1	Div 1
1954-55	Round 4					29 January	Lost	**0**	**1**	Div 1	Div 1
1963-64	Round 3	4 January	Won	**2**	**1**					Div 1	Div 1
1973-74	3rd Pl P-off	18 August	Lost	**1**	**3**					Div 1	Div 1
1975-76	Round 3					3 January	Lost	**0**	**3**	Div 1	Div 1
1977-78	Round 4	28 January	Won	**2**	**1**					Div 1	Div 1
1978-79	Semi Final	31 March		Villa Park			Won	**2**	**0**	Div 1	Div 1
1997-98	Semi Final	5 April		Villa Park			Won	**1**	**0**	Prem	Div 1
1998-99	Round 4					24 January	Won	**2**	**1**	Prem	Div 1

League Cup

Season	Round	Date	Result	Arsenal	Wolves	Date	Result	Arsenal	Wolves	Division Arsenal	Division Wolves
2003-04	Round 4					2 December	Won	**5**	**1**	Prem	Prem

Summary	P	W	D	L	F	A
Arsenal's home league record:	46	25	13	8	111	65
Arsenal's away league record:	47	17	12	18	72	84
Arsenal's cup record:	13	9	1	3	21	14
TOTAL	**106**	**51**	**26**	**29**	**204**	**163**

Billy Wright had been a great player for Wolves and England, one of the most famous names in world football after the war, but he never quite succeeded as a manager.

FACT FILE

- **Arsenal are unbeaten in the last 12 fixtures, winning the last seven.**
- **Arsenal won 11 of their first 12 home games.**
- **Arsenal went eight matches without a home win from 1953 to 1961.**
- **Wolves' longest unbeaten run in the series is eight matches (1954-58).**
- **For five years between 1970 and 1974, the losing semi-finalists in the FA Cup competed in a third place play-off. The Arsenal-Wolves fixture was held over until the start of the following season, and the idea was soon dropped.**

Arsenal's top scorers vs Wolves

Ted Drake 12
John Radford 9
Reg Lewis 8
George Graham 7
Frank Stapleton, Geoff Strong 6
Joe Baker, Cliff Bastin,
Doug Lishman, Don Roper 5

Arsenal hat-tricks vs Wolves

2 Jan 1915 Harry King (4)
5 Nov 1932 David Jack
1 Dec 1934 Ted Drake (4)
27 Oct 1962 Joe Baker
2 Jan 1965 John Radford

Played for both clubs

Joseph Cooper	Wolverhampton Wanderers 1888-91	Arsenal 1893-94
Arthur Worrall	Wolverhampton Wanderers 1889-91	Arsenal 1893-94
Charles Booth	Wolverhampton Wanderers 1889-92	Arsenal 1893-94
Billy Heath	Wolverhampton Wanderers 1891-92	Arsenal 1893-95
Adam Haywood	Arsenal 1895-99	Wolverhampton Wanderers 1901-05
Donald Cock	Arsenal 1924-26	Wolverhampton Wanderers 1927-28
Bryn Jones	Wolverhampton Wanderers 1933-38	Arsenal 1938-49
Jackie Henderson	Wolverhampton Wanderers 1957-59	Arsenal 1958-62
Eddie Clamp	Wolverhampton Wanderers 1953-62	Arsenal 1961-63
Bobby Gould	Arsenal 1967-70	Wolverhampton Wanderers 1970-72/75-77
Bob McNab	Arsenal 1966-75	Wolverhampton Wanderers 1975-76
Alan Sunderland	Wolverhampton Wanderers 1971-78	Arsenal 1977-84
Vince Bartram	Wolverhampton Wanderers 1986-91	Arsenal 1994-95
Oleg Luzhny	Arsenal 1999-2003	Wolverhampton Wanderers 2003-04

Arsenal have a curious ability to find the best of full-backs and for a decade Bob McNab served the Gunners proudly on the right side of their defence before joining Wolves in 1975.

v. Wrexham

FA Cup		Date	Result	Away Arsenal	Away Wrexham	Division Arsenal	Division Wrexham
1977-78	Q'ter Final	11 March	Won	**3**	**2**	Div 1	Div 3
1991-92	Round 3	4 January	Lost	**1**	**2**	Div 1	Div 4

Summary	P	W	D	L	F	A
Arsenal's cup record:	2	1	0	1	4	4
TOTAL	**2**	**1**	**0**	**1**	**4**	**4**

FACT FILE

- **In 1991, Arsenal finished top of Division One, while Wrexham finished bottom of Division Two, only staying in the league on a technicality. Wrexham's win eight months later, when they scored twice in the last eight minutes, was therefore one of the biggest shocks in FA Cup history.**

Played for both clubs

Tim Rogers	Wrexham 1934-35/46-47	Arsenal 1934-36
Arfon Griffiths	Wrexham 1959-61/62-79	Arsenal 1960-62
John Roberts	Arsenal 1969-73	Wrexham 1976-80
Jimmy Harvey	Arsenal 1977-79	Wrexham 1987-88

Welshman John Roberts found his way to Wrexham after leaving Arsenal in 1973.

A black day in the history of Arsenal Football Club, as Wrexham's Steve Watkins scores the winner to produce a memorable FA Cup shock at the Racecourse Ground in January 1992.

v. Yeovil Town

FA Cup

		Date	Result	Away		Division	
				Arsenal	Wrexham	Arsenal	Wrexham
1970-71	Round 3	6 January	Won	**3**	**0**	Div 1	Non L
1992-93	Round 3	2 January	Won	**3**	**1**	Prem	Non L

Summary	P	W	D	L	F	A
Arsenal's cup record:	2	2	0	0	6	1
TOTAL	**2**	**2**	**0**	**0**	**6**	**1**

FACT FILE

- **The 1993 tie was Arsenal's first FA Cup meeting with a non-league side since meeting the same side 22 years earlier. Arsenal went on to win the cup both times.**

Arsenal's top scorers vs Yeovil

Ian Wright 3

John Radford 2

Arsenal hat-tricks vs Yeovil

2 Jan 1993 Ian Wright (cup)

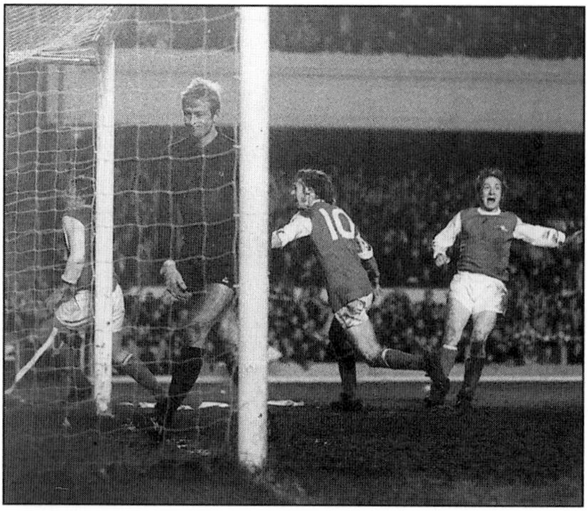

John Radford rushes past the post after scoring Arsenal's second goal in the 1970 Fairs Cup Final second leg. Charlie George (10) and George Armstrong also look quite pleased. The Gunners won 3-0, giving them a 4-3 aggregate victory and their first major trophy for 17 years. His two goals against Yeovil were to set them on their way to another trophy when they met Liverpool in the Final that year.

v. York City

FA Cup		Home Date	Home Result	Arsenal	York C	Away Date	Away Result	Arsenal	York C	Division Arsenal	Division York C
1974-75	Round 3	4 January	Drew	**1**	**1**	7 January	Won*	**3**	**1**	Div 1	Div 2
1984-85	Round 4					26 January	Lost	**0**	**1**	Div 1	Div 3

Summary	P	W	D	L	F	A
Arsenal's cup record:	3	1	1	1	4	3
TOTAL	**3**	**1**	**1**	**1**	**4**	**3**

FACT FILE

- **Another FA Cup humiliation for Arsenal in 1985 as Houchen's penalty put the third division side through.**

Arsenal's top scorers vs York

Brian Kidd 3

Arsenal hat-tricks vs York

7 Jan 1975 Brian Kidd (cup)

Played for both clubs

Reg Stockhill	York City 1929-31	Arsenal 1931-33
Colin Addison	York City 1957-61	Arsenal 1966-68
John Woodward	Arsenal 1966-67	York City 1971-78

Arsenal's Brian Kidd and Terry Mancini look on anxiously as their goalkeeper Jimmy Rimmer punches away from Liverpool's Phil Thompson. The Arsenal number seven is George Armstrong. It was ex-Manchester United player Kidd's hat-trick that saved the day in the 1975 Cup replay when the Gunners met York City.

Arsenal in Europe

Arsenal in Europe vs Austrian clubs

				Home				Away					
Year	*Competition*	*versus*	*Date*		Arsenal		*Date*		Arsenal		*Aggregate*		
1970-71	UEFA Cup R2	Sturm Graz	4 November	Won	**2**	**0**	12 October	Lost	**0**	**1**	Won	**2**	**1**
1991-92	European Cup R1	FK Austria	18 September	Won	**6**	**1**	2 October	Lost	**0**	**1**	Won	**6**	**2**

	P	*W*	*D*	*L*	*F*	*A*
TOTAL:	**4**	**2**	**0**	**2**	**8**	**3**

Arsenal in Europe vs Belgian clubs

				Home				Away					
Year	*Competition*	*versus*	*Date*		Arsenal		*Date*		Arsenal		*Aggregate*		
1963-64	UEFA Cup R2	RFC Liege	13 November	Drew	**1**	**1**	18 December	Lost	**1**	**3**	Lost	**2**	**4**
1969-70	UEFA Cup Final	Anderlecht	28 April	Won	**3**	**0**	22 April	Lost	**1**	**3**	Won	**4**	**3**
1970-71	UEFA Cup R3	SK Beveren	2 December	Won	**4**	**0**	16 December	Drew	**0**	**0**	Won	**4**	**0**
1981-82	UEFACup R2	SV Winterslag	3 November	Won	**2**	**1**	20 October	Lost	**0**	**1**	Lost away goals	**2**	**2**
1993-94	Cup-Winners R2	Standard Liege	20 October	Won	**3**	**0**	3 November	Won	**7**	**0**	Won	**10**	**0**

	P	*W*	*D*	*L*	*F*	*A*
TOTAL:	**10**	**5**	**2**	**3**	**22**	**9**

April 1970 and Anderlecht goalkeeper Trappeniers punches the ball clear during an Arsenal raid in the second leg of the European Fairs Cup Final at Highbury.

Arsenal in Europe vs Cypriot clubs

			Home				Away						
Year	Competition	versus	Date		Arsenal		Date		Arsenal		Aggregate		
1994-95	Cup-Winners R1	Omonia Nicosia	29 September	Won	3	0	15 September	Won	3	1	Won	6	1

	P	W	D	L	F	A
TOTAL:	2	2	0	0	6	1

Arsenal in Europe vs Czech clubs

			Home				Away						
Year	Competition	versus	Date		Arsenal		Date		Arsenal		Aggregate		
2000-01	European Cup GP1	Sparta Prague	25 October	Won	4	2	12 September	Won	1	0			

	P	W	D	L	F	A
TOTAL:	2	2	0	0	5	2

Arsenal in Europe vs Danish clubs

			Home				Away						
Year	Competition	versus	Date		Arsenal		Date		Arsenal		Aggregate		
1963-64	UEFA Cup R1	Staevnet Select XI	22 October	Lost	2	3	25 September	Won	7	1	Won	9	4
1993-94	Cup-Winners R1	OB Odense	29 September	Drew	1	1	15 September	Won	2	1	Won	3	2
1994-95	Cup-Winners R2	Brondby	3 November	Drew	2	2	20 October	Won	2	1	Won	4	3

	P	W	D	L	F	A
TOTAL:	6	3	2	1	16	9

Arsenal in Europe vs East German clubs

			Home				Away						
Year	Competition	versus	Date		Arsenal		Date		Arsenal		Aggregate		
1978-79	UEFA Cup R1	Lokomotiv Leipzig	13 September	Won	3	0	27 September	Won	4	1	Won	7	1
1979-80	Cup-Winners R2	FC Magdeburg	24 October	Won	2	1	7 November	Drew	2	2	Won	4	3

	P	W	D	L	F	A
TOTAL:	4	3	1	0	11	4

Arsenal in Europe vs French clubs

			Home				Away						
Year	Competition	versus	Date		Arsenal		Date		Arsenal		Aggregate		
1969-70	UEFA Cup R3	Rouen	13 January	Won	1	0	17 December	Drew	0	0	Won	1	0
1993-94	Cup-Winners SF	Paris St Germain	12 April	Won	1	0	29 March	Drew	1	1	Won	2	1
1994-95	Cup-Winners QF	Auxerre	2 March	Drew	1	1	16 March	Won	1	0	Won	2	1
1998-99	European Cup GP	Lens	25 November	Lost	0	1	16 September	Drew	1	1			
1999-00	UEFA Cup R3	Nantes	25 November	Won	3	0	9 December	Drew	3	3	Won	6	3
1999-00	UEFA Cup SF	Lens	6 April	Won	1	0	20 April	Won	2	1	Won	3	1
2000-01	European Cup GP	Lyon	21 February	Drew	1	1	13 February	Won	1	0			
2002-03	European Cup GP1	Auxerre	22 October	Lost	1	2	2 Ocvober	Won	1	0			

	P	W	D	L	F	A
TOTAL:	16	8	6	2	19	11

Arsenal in Europe vs (West) German clubs

					Home				Away				
Year	*Competition*	*versus*	*Date*		Arsenal		*Date*		Arsenal		*Aggregate*		
1970-71	UEFA Cup QF	Cologne	9 March	Won	**2**	**1**	23 March	Lost	**0**	**1**	Lost	**2**	**2**
											away goals		
1996-97	UEFA Cup R1	B'sia M'gladbach	10 September	Lost	**2**	**3**	25 September	Lost	**2**	**3**	Lost	**4**	**6**
1999-00	UEFA Cup QF	Werder Bremen	16 March	Won	**2**	**0**	23 March	Won	**4**	**2**	Won	**6**	**2**
2000-01	European Cup GP2	Bayern Munich	5 December	Drew	**2**	**2**	14 March	Lost	**0**	**1**			
2001-02	European Cup GP1	Schalke	19 September	Won	**3**	**2**	30 October	Lost	**1**	**3**			
2001-02	European Cup GP2	Bayer Leverkusen	27 February	Won	**4**	**1**	19 February	Drew	**1**	**1**			
2002-03	European Cup GP1	Borussia Dortmund	17 September	Won	**2**	**0**	30 October	Lost	**1**	**2**			

	P	*W*	*D*	*L*	*F*	*A*
TOTAL:	**14**	**6**	**2**	**6**	**26**	**22**

Arsenal in Europe vs Greek clubs

					Home				Away				
Year	*Competition*	*versus*	*Date*		Arsenal		*Date*		Arsenal		*Aggregate*		
1981-02	UEFA Cup R1	Panathinaikos	30 September	Won	**1**	**0**	16 September	Won	**2**	**0**	Won	**3**	**0**
1997-98	UEFA Cup R1	PAOK Salonica	30 September	Drew	**1**	**1**	16 September	Lost	**0**	**1**	Lost	**1**	**2**
1998-99	European Cup GP	Panathinaikos	30 September	Won	**2**	**1**	9 December	Won	**3**	**1**			
2001-02	European Cup GP1	Panathinaikos	16 October	Won	**2**	**1**	26 September	Lost	**0**	**1**			

	P	*W*	*D*	*L*	*F*	*A*
TOTAL:	**8**	**5**	**1**	**2**	**11**	**6**

Arsenal in Europe vs Dutch clubs

					Home				Away				
Year	*Competition*	*versus*	*Date*		Arsenal		*Date*		Arsenal		*Aggregate*		
1969-70	UEFA Cup SF	Ajax	8 April	Won	**3**	**0**	15 April	Lost	**0**	**1**	Won	**3**	**1**
1971-72	European Cup QF	Ajax	22 March	Lost	**0**	**1**	8 March	Lost	**1**	**2**	Lost	**1**	**3**
2002-03	European Cup GP1	PSV Eindhoven	12 November	Drew	**0**	**0**	25 September	Won	**4**	**0**			
2002-03	European Cup GP2	Ajax	18 February	Drew	**1**	**1**	26 February	Drew	**0**	**0**			

	P	*W*	*D*	*L*	*F*	*A*
TOTAL:	**8**	**2**	**3**	**3**	**9**	**5**

Arsenal in Europe vs Italian clubs

					Home				Away				
Year	*Competition*	*versus*	*Date*		Arsenal		*Date*		Arsenal		*Aggregate*		
1970-71	UEFA Cup R1	Lazio	23 September	Won	**2**	**0**	16 September	Drew	**2**	**2**	Won	**4**	**2**
1979-80	Cup-Winners SF	Juventus	9 April	Drew	**1**	**1**	23 April	Won	**1**	**0**	Won	**2**	**1**
1993-94	Cup-Winners QF	Torino	15 March	Won	**1**	**0**	2 March	Drew	**0**	**0**	Won	**1**	**0**
1993-94	Cup-Winners F	Parma	4 May	Copenhagen				Won	**1**	**0**	Won	**1**	**0**
1994-95	Cup-Winners SF	Sampdoria	6 April	Won	**3**	**2**	20 April	Lost*	**2**	**3**	Won*	**5**	**5**
											penalties (3-2)		
1999-00	European Cup GP1	Fiorentina	27 October	Lost	**0**	**1**	14 September	Drew	**0**	**0**			
2000-01	European Cup GP1	Lazio	27 September	Won	**2**	**0**	17 October	Drew	**1**	**1**			
2001-02	European Cup GP2	Juventus	4 December	Won	**3**	**1**	20 March	Lost	**0**	**1**			
2002-03	European Cup GP2	Roma	11 March	Drew	**1**	**1**	27 November	Won	**3**	**1**			
2003-04	European Cup GP	Inter Milan	17 September	Lost	**0**	**3**	25 November	Won	**5**	**1**			

	P	*W*	*D*	*L*	*F*	*A*	
TOTAL:	**19**	**9**	**6**	**4**	**28**	**18**	(+one penalty shoot-out victory)

Ian Wright scores for Arsenal against Sampdoria during the European Cup-winners' Cup semi-final second-leg game in Italy in April 1995.

Arsenal in Europe vs Northern Irish clubs

			Home				Away						
Year	*Competition*	*versus*	*Date*		Arsenal		*Date*		Arsenal		*Aggregate*		
1969-70	UEFA Cup R1	Glentoran	9 September	Won	3	0	29 September	Lost	0	1	Won	3	1

	P	*W*	*D*	*L*	*F*	*A*
TOTAL:	2	1	0	1	3	1

Arsenal in Europe vs Norwegian clubs

			Home				Away						
Year	*Competition*	*versus*	*Date*		Arsenal		*Date*		Arsenal		*Aggregate*		
1971-72	European Cup R1	IF Stromsgodset	29 September	Won	4	0	15 September	Won	3	1	Won	7	1

	P	*W*	*D*	*L*	*F*	*A*
TOTAL:	2	2	0	0	7	1

Arsenal in Europe vs Portuguese clubs

			Home				Away						
Year	*Competition*	*versus*	*Date*		Arsenal		*Date*		Arsenal		*Aggregate*		
1969-70	UEFA Cup R2	Sporting Lisbon	26 November	Won	3	0	20 October	Drew	0	0	Won	3	0
1991-92	European Cup R2	Benfica	6 November	Lost*	1	3	23 October	Drew	1	1	Lost*	2	4

	P	*W*	*D*	*L*	*F*	*A*
TOTAL:	4	1	2	1	5	4

Arsenal in Europe vs Romanian clubs

					Home				Away				
Year	*Competition*	*versus*	*Date*		Arsenal		*Date*		Arsenal		*Aggregate*		
1969-70	U EFA Cup QF	Dinamo Bacau	18 March	Won	7	1	11 Marrch	Won	2	0	Won	9	1

	P	*W*	*D*	*L*	*F*	*A*
TOTAL:	2	2	0	0	9	1

Arsenal in Europe vs Russian clubs

					Home				Away				
Year	*Competition*	*versus*	*Date*		Arsenal		*Date*		Arsenal		*Aggregate*		
1982-83	UEFA Cup R1	Spartak Moscow	29 September	Lost	2	5	14 September	Lost	2	3	Lost	4	8
2000-01	European Cup GP2	Spartak Moscow	6 March	Won	1	0	22 November	Lost	1	4			
2003-04	European Cup GP	Lok Moscow	10 December	Won	2	0	30 September	Drew	0	0			

	P	*W*	*D*	*L*	*F*	*A*
TOTAL:	6	2	1	3	8	12

Arsenal in Europe vs Spanish clubs

					Home				Away				
Year	*Competition*	*versus*	*Date*		Arsenal		*Date*		Arsenal		*Aggregate*		
1979-80	Cup-Winners F	Valencia	14 May				Brussels	Drew*	0	0	ost*	0	0
											penalties (4-5)		
1994-95	Cup-Winners F	Real Zaragoza	10 May				Paris	Lost*	1	2	Lost*	1	2
1999-00	European Cup GP1	Barcelona	19 October	Lost	2	4	29 September	Drew	1	1			
1999-00	UEFA Cup R4	Deportivo La Coruna	2 March	Won	5	1	9 March	Lost	1	2	Won	6	3
2000-01	European Cup QF	Valencia	4 April	Won	2	1	17 April	Lost	0	1	Lost	2	2
											away goals		
2001-02	European Cup GP1	Real Mallorca	24 October	Won	3	1	11 September	Lost	0	1			
2001-02	European Cup GP2	Deportivo La Coruna	12 March	Lost	0	2	21 November	Lost	0	2			
2002-03	European Cup GP2	Valencia	10 December	Drew	0	0	19 March	Lost	1	2			
2003-04	European Cup R2	Celta Vigo	10 March	Won	2	0	24 February	Won	3	2	Won	5	2

	P	*W*	*D*	*L*	*F*	*A*	
TOTAL:	16	5	3	8	21	22	(+one penalty shoot-out defeat)

Arsenal in Europe vs Swedish clubs

					Home				Away				
Year	*Competition*	*versus*	*Date*		Arsenal		*Date*		Arsenal		*Aggregate*		
1979-80	Cup-Winners QF	FK Gothenburg	5 March	Won	5	1	19 March	Drew	0	0	Won	5	1
1999-00	European Cup GP1	AIK Solna	22 September	Won	3	1	2 November	Won	3	2			

	P	*W*	*D*	*L*	*F*	*A*
TOTAL:	4	3	1	0	11	4

Arsenal in Europe vs Swiss clubs

					Home				Away				
Year	*Competition*	*versus*	*Date*		Arsenal		*Date*		Arsenal		*Aggregate*		
1971-72	European Cup R2	Grasshoppers	3 November	Won	3	0	20 October	Won	2	0	Won	5	0

	P	*W*	*D*	*L*	*F*	*A*
TOTAL:	2	2	0	0	5	0

Arsenal in Europe vs Turkish clubs

Year	Competition	versus	Home Date		Arsenal		Away Date		Arsenal		Aggregate		
1979-80	Cup-Winners R1	Fenerbahce	19 September	Won	2	0	3 October	Drew	0	0	Won	2	0
1999-00	UEFA Cup F	Galatasaray	17 May	Copenhagen				Drew*	0	0	Lost* penalties (1-4)	0	0

	P	W	D	L	F	A	
TOTAL:	3	1	2	0	2	0	(+one penalty shoot-out defeat)

Arsenal in Europe vs Ukranian clubs

Year	Competition	versus	Home Date		Arsenal		Away Date		Arsenal		Aggregate
1998-99	European Cup GP	Dinamo Kiev	21 October	Drew	1	1	4 November	Lost	1	3	
2000-01	European Cup GP1	Shakhtar Donetsk	20 September	Won	3	2	7 November	Lost	0	3	
2003-04	European Cup GP	Dinamo Kiev	5 November	Won	1	0	21 October	Lost	1	2	

	P	W	D	L	F	A
TOTAL:	6	2	1	3	7	11

Arsenal in Europe vs clubs from the former Yugoslavia

Year	Competition	versus	Home Date		Arsenal		Away Date		Arsenal		Aggregate		
1978-79	UEFA Cup R2	Hajduk Split	1 November	Won	1	0	18 October	Lost	1	2	Won away goals	2	2
1978-79	UEFA Cup R3	Red Star Belgrade	6 December	Drew	1	1	22 November	Lost	0	1	Lost	1	2

	P	W	D	L	F	A
TOTAL:	4	1	1	2	3	4

FACT FILE

- **In 1995, as European Cup-Winners Cup holders, Arsenal contested the European Super Cup against AC Milan. After a 0-0 draw at Highbury, Arsenal went down 2-0 in the San Siro. These results have not been included in the above record.**
- **No side ever successfully defended the now defunct Cup-Winners Cup, but Arsenal came closest. In 1995, they reached the final only to lose to Nayim's famous 50-yard effort in the last minute of extra-time.**
- **Possibly Arsenal's greatest European display came against Juventus in 1980. A minute from elimination on away goals, 19-year-old Paul Vaessen stunned the home crowd with the winner.**
- **Arsenal have competed in the Cup-Winners Cup on three occasions, and reached the final every time.**
- **Arsenal's most embarrassing European exit came at the hands of unheralded Belgian side SV Winterslag in 1981.**